D1395415

Education and Social Justice

EDUCATION

AND

SOCIAL JUSTICE

THE CHANGING COMPOSITION OF SCHOOLS AND ITS IMPLICATIONS

Stephen Gorard

Gift

CHESTER COLLEGE

ACC. No. 0107 3038	DEPT.
CLASS No. 370-1934 GOR	
LIBRARY	

UNIVERSITY OF WALES PRESS
CARDIFF
2000

© Stephen Gorard, 2000

British Library Cataloguing-in-Publication Data.
A catalogue record for this book is available from the British Library.

ISBN 0–7083–1619–0

All rights reserved. No part of this book may be reproduced, stored in a retrieval system, or transmitted, in any form or by any means, electronic, mechanical, photocopying, recording or otherwise, without clearance from the University of Wales Press, 6 Gwennyth Street, Cardiff, CF24 4YD. *www.wales.ac.uk/press*

The right of Stephen Gorard to be identified as author of this work has been asserted by him in accordance with the Copyright, Designs and Patents Act 1988.

Typeset at University of Wales Press
Printed in Great Britain by Dinefwr Press, Llandybïe

For Jonathan Anthony Xin Xiang

Contents

Figures and Tables

Figures

Tables

Preface

This book is based on six major datasets collected and analysed by the author over the last four years. Secondary data on all school examination results in Wales 1992–7, from Key Stage One to A level, by subject and gender were provided by the Welsh Office and the Welsh Joint Education Committee (ACCAC grant). Secondary data on student poverty, ethnicity, language and special educational need 1989–98, at school level for every school in England, were provided by the DfEE (ESRC grant R000238031). Secondary data on poverty, ethnicity, language and special educational need 1989–98 for most schools in Wales were collected from local archives by the researcher. Primary data on the process of school choice were collected from 1,300 survey respondents in south Wales, both parents and children, followed by a 5 per cent subsample of in-depth interviews (ESRC training grant). These sources have been supplemented by: primary data on lifelong patterns of participation in education collected from 1,100 survey respondents in south Wales, aged 15–65, followed by a 10 per cent subsample of in-depth interviews (ESRC Learning Society Programme grant L123251041); an analysis of trends in educational participation and qualification using the Labour Force Survey (National Assembly grant), and a number of interviews concerning technical barriers to educational participation (Spencer Foundation, USA grant SG#199900305). This information, along with publicly available data such as school examination results ('league tables'), allows the author to conduct a wide-ranging reappraisal of many previous accounts of the relationship between education and social justice. The results will be surprising to many readers.

According to many accounts, educational participation, performance and attainment in Britain have become more and more polarized in the 1990s. We are in danger of starting the twenty-first century with what is seen as an unfair and derided education system. Evidence for these failures comes from the poor performance of the home countries in international assessments of educational attainment, the marked differences in school effectiveness in the four home countries, the increasing socio-economic segregation of school intakes as a result of policies of school choice, and the consequent increase in the attainment gaps between the best and the worst schools, between students of different social backgrounds, and most notably between boys and girls. These relative failures and differences in compulsory education appear to result in an increasingly divided society, and to systematic unfairness in opportunities for lifelong participation in adult learning.

This work provides a fresh look at some of these disturbing trends in British education towards inequality of provision, and systematic differential attainment and participation. Using the central theme of the importance of proportionate analysis, the book examines in turn a series of issues relating to education and society, and shows how these trends are susceptible to an alternative and much more promising analysis. In this way, it shows that many things in education are actually getting better.

The central chapters are based on the author's own original research in the fields of school choice, school effectiveness, achievement by gender, learning targets and patterns of participation in education. In each case, changes over time in the object of study are placed in the context of other contemporary changes. When viewed in proportion, many supposed trends towards inequality disappear, and in some cases are replaced by apparent progress. For example, schools are becoming more socially mixed over time, and the gaps in attainment between many different groups of students (such as boys and girls, or state and fee-paying pupils) are actually declining. There remain several depressing trends at the end of the 1990s, but these are chiefly socio-economic and *not* educational. For example, although indicators of low family income are more evenly distributed between schools in 1998 than in 1988, there are now more families with low incomes. This is not to say that educational differences do not exist, but it is only by recognizing what the current problems in social justice are, *and* what they are not, that effective policies can be devised to deal with them in the twenty-first century.

Acknowledgements

In addition to the bodies mentioned in the preface, the author would like to acknowledge the help of Gwent, Mid Glamorgan, and West Wales TECs (as they then were), Sam Walton at the DfEE, the forty-one co-operating LEAs of England and Wales, the participating schools and all respondents. Above all, in collecting and analysing these data the author has worked with John Fitz and Gareth Rees, and this book would not have been possible without them. Ideas have also been discussed with Bob Adams, See Beng Huat, Ralph Fevre, John Furlong, Neil Selwyn, Jane Salisbury, Emma Smith and Patrick White. Thanks. However, all comments on the findings, and on the work of other researchers, are the author's own.

List of Abbreviations

ACCAC	Awdurdod Cymwysterau Cwricwlwm ac Asesu Cymru (Qualifications, Curriculum and Assessment Authority for Wales)
CBI	Confederation of British Industry
CERI	Centre for Education Research and Information
CTC	City Technology College
DES	Department of Education and Science
DfE	Department of Education
DfEE	Department for Education and Employment
EOC	Equal Opportunities Commission
ESRC	Economic and Social Research Council
ETAG	Education and Training Action Group
FSM	free school meals
GCSE	General Certificate of Secondary Education
GIS	Geographical Information Systems
GNVQ	General National Vocational Qualification
IEA	International Association for the Evaluation of Educational Achievement
KS	Key Stage
LEA	Local Education Authority
NFER	National Foundation for Educational Research
NIACE	National Institute for Adult and Continuing Education
OECD	Organisation for Economic Co-operation and Development
OFSTED	Office for Standards in Education
OHMCI	Office of Her Majesty's Chief Inspector for Schools
QCA	Qualifications, Curriculum and Assessment Authority for England
SAT	Standard Attainment Target
SEM	school effectiveness movement
SEN	special educational need
SES	socio-economic status
TEC	Training and Enterprise Council
TES	*Times Educational Supplement*
TIMSS	Third International Mathematics and Science Survey
UA	unitary authority
WJEC	Welsh Joint Education Committee

Introducing Alternative Accounts of the 'Crisis' in Education

Many commentators agree that there is a crisis in British education today and that it has been approaching for some time. The problems giving rise to this crisis relate to the apparently poor standards of attainment among British students especially when compared to other developed countries, to increasing differences between the best and the worst schools and to increasing stratification in terms of attendance and performance between different groups in society (as defined, for example, by income, ethnicity or gender). In summary, according to this account, schooling in Britain is becoming more divisive, while its standards are slipping behind those of Britain's economic competitors. Together, these related problems point to the themes of this book, which include socio-economic segregation in the school system, international comparisons of examination and test results, the differential impact of different types of schools, changes over time and growing gaps between groups of students.

'A Plague on All our Schools'

Standards in British education in 1969 were described by Cox and Dyson (1990) as lower than in 1929, indeed lower even than in 1914. This decline was attributed by them to, among other things, a philosophy of egalitarianism rather than equality of opportunity, to the comprehensivization of schools rather than selection and to the use of 'progressive' rather than traditional teaching methods. Thus, as early as 1975, a future minister of education wrote that 'British children are the most ill-mannered, undisciplined and selfish in the world' (Boyson 1975, p. 119) and by 1996 an influential writer on education believed that 'there is now a yawning gap between the standards reached by British schoolchildren and their counterparts in Europe or Japan' (Phillips 1996, p. 3). This view finds an ally in Barber (1996), who claims that there is indeed a crisis in education today as it faces the twin threats of global competition and local moral decline, manifested in a growing gap between the best and worst performing students. George Mudie (while minister for lifelong learning) recently claimed that in any other industry a performance level like that of British education 'would result in the companies concerned going out of business' (Skills and Enterprise Network 1999, p. 1). According to a personnel director of Siemens Electronics, the workforce in Britain is crucially short of key skills.

> The fact that we rate after Greece and New Zealand in world terms in literacy and numeracy was deeply worrying . . . Llew Aviss finished with an example of how far behind we were in maths from one of his former employers, Fujitsu. It was a key issue for Japanese colleagues who were sending their children to school in Britain. They would query why their children were so much further behind where they would be in Japan . . . and this was only at the primary school level. (Skills and Enterprise Network 1999, p. 5).

There is plenty of practical and academic research evidence that can be presented in support of these views. The Office for Standards in Education (OFSTED) and the National Foundation for Educational Research (NFER) have confirmed that there has been a deterioration of standards in several areas of education, while a previous chief inspector of schools believes that 'where we fail badly, in comparison with other developed countries, is with the broad range of ordinary pupils' (Bolton 1993, p. 12). The Second International Maths Study revealed not only that students in England and Wales were achieving relatively low marks in international comparisons, but also that standards in England and Wales had actually declined between 1964 and 1981 (Cresswell and Gubb 1990). By 1981, it was estimated that the mathematical attainment of English thirteen-year-old students was four years behind their peers in Japan (Prais 1990). In the Third International Maths and Science Study, the mean world-wide score for attainment in mathematics among all Year 9 students was 513, whereas for England the score was 506 and this was for children who had received, on average, an extra year of formal schooling in comparison to the sample from other countries (Beaton et al. 1996). By comparison the equivalent score in Ireland was 527, in

France 538, in Japan 605 and in Singapore a massive 643. A recent DfEE report stated that 'Britain performs badly in basic skills stakes' (Skills and Enterprise Briefing 1999), showing that of twelve countries Britain was second only to Poland and Ireland in the proportion of adults with low levels of literacy and numeracy skills. The DfEE therefore claims that the scale of the problem of literacy and numeracy in England is 'enormous' and cites an example in which 20 per cent of adults could not locate the page reference for 'plumbers' in an alphabetical index (DfEE 1999a).

Perhaps one of the reasons for this overall depressing state of affairs is the poor quality of new teachers, many of whom cannot even do joined-up writing themselves according to Philips (1996). Another reason may be that teachers now spend less time teaching than in previous generations and more time in bureaucratic tasks (Barber 1996). Porter (1990, p. 7) blames both students and teachers for the poor competitive position of British industry and refers to the educational system as 'a major barrier to . . . sustaining competitive advantage in industry': 'British children are taught by teachers less qualified than those in many nations, receive less training in maths and science, put in fewer hours and drop out more'. In an influential summary of British education at the end of the 1990s, Bentley (1998) describes the full malaise of limited literacy skills among students, large numbers of school leavers with no qualifications, an increasing performance gap between girls and boys and growing indicators for truancy and exclusion from school. Even where examination outcomes have improved over time, as evidenced by an increasing number of A grades or the introduction of the A* grade at GCSE, this can be attributed by 'crisis' commentators to a simple lowering of standards (or 'dumbing down' as it has become popularly known). For example, the mathematical ability of A-level candidates and entrants to higher education has been reported as being in decline over time, even where candidates are matched in terms of their A-level grades (in Kitchen 1999), thus showing that equivalent-sounding qualifications are now worth less than in previous years, not only in exchange-value but also in actual fact.

The media appear keen to support this pessimistic view of British education and they also describe a growing 'gulf' between students in the best and worst performing geographical areas (for example, *TES* 1999a; Russell 1999). Not only is the gap between Britain and other countries growing, then, but so are the gaps within the British educational system. State education, far from increasing social justice and providing opportunities for all, as it was intended to do by its creators, actually appears to be leading to *decreases* in social justice. In fact, according to this account, 'England's secondary school system is becoming more academically and socially divided than ever' (Budge 1999). Halsey, an author of the seminal work on the origins and destinations of school students in 1980, is quoted in the *TES* (1999a, p. 14) as saying 'the essential fact of 20th-century educational history is that egalitarian policies have failed'. The introduction of free secondary schooling in 1944 and the later comprehensive revolution in schooling led to the hope that 'poverty would no longer disbar working-class children . . . but here we are at the glowing fag end of the century and, in some respects, little has changed'. A recent large-scale study shows that from 1994 to 1998 successful schools are 'becoming more socially advantaged than lower-ranked schools and it's a vicious spiral' (Mooney 1999, p. 2). Chris Woodhead, the chief inspector for schools in England, was also quoted recently as saying that 'a staggering 55 per cent of boys have not learnt to write properly . . . These are the 11-year-olds who will grow into the 16-year-olds who leave schools unemployed and . . . unemployable' (Woodhead 1999). A recent MORI poll on family life in Britain found that the public perception of Britain's education system was poor compared with elsewhere in the European Union and a majority believed that standards in schools are falling (Petre 1999). The same report by Petre also stated that universities are now giving degree students lessons in literacy and that the demand for such courses is increasing. This is seen by critics as evidence that schools are failing to teach basic skills even to the most talented individuals in society.

There is presumably no need to continue this catalogue of the woes of the British educational system. All readers will have been aware of it and many may even subscribe to at least part of it. In addition, the main strands in this crisis story are described in considerably more detail in the chapters of this book, where they are subjected to a more thorough critical analysis. The increasing social, economic and academic polarization of schools is discussed in Chapter 2. The achievement gaps between British and overseas students, and the regional variations within Britain, are discussed in Chapter 4. The increasing gap in social and academic terms between sectors of education, such as state-funded and fee-paying schools, is discussed in Chapter 6. The increasing gap in academic outcomes between groups of students, such as boys and girls, is discussed in Chapter 8. For each of these claims there is substantial evidence presented by well-informed and often well-meaning commentators. The topics have all been chosen because they are important and because they relate to a common theme of increasing inequality in education.

Suggested solutions to these problems have been many. Some have taken the form of large-scale and national programmes, including allowing families the 'freedom' to use a wider range of schools, rigorous inspection schedules, using the findings from school effectiveness research to 'improve' schools, performance-related pay for teachers and promoting participation in lifelong education and training. Other solutions have been suggested which are more local or small-scale, including summer schools, homework clubs, school–parent pacts, educational action zones and specific plans for the seating of students within classroom settings. All such policies generally deal with the two issues of social justice and school effectiveness as though they are closely related and they claim that increasing social justice in education will help improve standards while helping (or eliminating) 'failing' schools will improve equity in the system.

An Alternative Account

On the other hand, although substantial evidence can be cited in support of the 'crisis' narrative in British education, a closer examination of the relevant data can also reveal a very different story. Britain may be suffering from what Hamilton (1997) calls 'a pathological view of public education in the later twentieth century . . . a plague on all our schools' (p. 126) and what Slee (1998) calls 'a pathological discourse of derision of poor teachers and failing schools' (p. 261). The central premise of this book is that the loose alliance of policy-makers, media commentators and academic researchers who push their various components of the crisis story may have made very simple errors in their respective analyses: most frequently the error of not looking at changes over time as proportions. When these simple errors are corrected, the current picture of the relationship between educational performance and social justice changes dramatically. In fact, it is then not at all clear that the two phenomena are closely related, or that the one necessarily impacts on the other in the way that has been presented so far.

The book examines in turn the evidence for each of these major criticisms of education and social justice in Britain today – the claims that schools are becoming more socially segregated over time, that Britain compares badly in international assessments of education and that there are growing gaps in attainment between sectors of schooling and groups of students. In each part the book outlines the general evidence for the crisis narrative in that area of study and then shows how it is open to an alternative interpretation. Specific evidence is selected as an example for presentation not simply because it can be shown to be wrong, but because it is both respected and believed and thus has real practical implications for policy and practice. Each section of the book continues with a detailed discussion of the same issue using a case study relating to the general theme, explaining the methods used in a large-scale reanalysis of publicly available evidence and outlining the resultant findings. In this way, it is argued in successive sections that, far from becoming more stratified, schools are actually becoming more mixed in social terms over time, that educational standards in Britain are not slipping in international terms and that the gaps between types of schools and groups of students may be decreasing rather than growing. This is not to say that the book documents a kind of 'Whig history' of linear progress towards an ideal state in education. The author has already published arguments elsewhere that in some respects lifelong education in Britain may have been in a healthier state in the recent past than it is now (e.g. Rees et al. 1997; Gorard et al. 1999a). However, it is important for many reasons to distinguish between the general malaise proposed by the simple crisis account and the genuine, but more complex, problems that face British education today. One purpose of this book is to help distinguish between these two versions.

Many of the problems discussed here should and will remain high on the social justice agenda. However, it is only by a more realistic appraisal than hitherto of the precise nature of those problems that practical and sensible solutions can be constructed. This book argues that greater precision is the best path for progress towards increasing social justice both in and via education. There are clear implications for programmes of action to ameliorate the purported problems of education and social justice, which lead to important questions about the role education can be seriously expected to play in terms of creating greater justice through social 'engineering'. There are also implications for the field of educational research more generally and the book therefore addresses some current concerns about the quality and relevance of publicly funded educational research. There are implications for the conduct of educational research and the relationship between research, policy-making and practice. All of these issues are discussed briefly in the final chapter.

The Politician's Error and Changes Over Time

The purpose of this section is to set the scene for the reanalyses of publicly available datasets that appear in the following chapters. The first chapter in each of the next four parts of the book presents an account of British schooling which entails increasing social injustice as a result of educational processes. Chapter 2 suggests that schools are becoming increasingly polarized in terms of the socio-economic status of their intakes, Chapter 4 suggests that schools in Britain are underperforming and being increasingly left behind in international comparisons, Chapter 6 describes an apparently growing gulf in the achievements of different sectors of schools, while Chapter 8 suggests widening gaps between students of different social backgrounds. The evidence on which these accounts are based is public and valid (and is therefore to be distinguished from accounts which are neither transparent in their method nor publicly replicable) and is used by respected and influential figures to back up their specific part of the account of the overall worsening crisis in education. Now, the reader may imagine that by presenting such 'evidence' even-handedly this book also accepts the conclusions that are usually drawn from it by the crisis narrators. This is *not* so. In each of the examples above, the crisis narrative is at least overstated and possibly totally incorrect. This section begins to explain why, and how, this might be so.

In essence, the general problem with the crisis narrative is a lack of proportionate analyses, in which the figures presented are considered both in proportion to each other and to other factors to which they are clearly related. It is possible to distinguish three main elements in the importance of proportionate analysis for comparisons of figures over time (and space). It is chiefly these three elements that give the results described in this book their originality and it is these three which are most frequently overlooked by commentators on the state of education today.

The first of these elements is a recognition of the distinction between percentages and percentage points, ignorance of which has led to what the author has termed the 'politician's error' (see Gorard 1999a). It has actually become quite commonplace for writers, media commentators and researchers, as well as politicians, to refer to percentage points as though they were percentages. For example, if unemployment decreases from 8 per cent to 7 per cent it may be reported on the TV news as a decrease of 1 per cent, whereas it actually represents a decrease of one percentage point, or 12.5 per cent of the original. Since this usage has become commonplace, and if the two figures being compared are stated at the same time, such a method of reporting may be acceptable and lead to no great confusion for its audience. This style has become almost accepted practice. However, the lack of differentiation between percentages and percentage points can lead to serious misinterpretation in other circumstances, such as when at least two such sets of figures are involved. For example, one region may have had unemployment running at 10 per cent last year and another region had unemployment of 5 per cent. If the unemployment rates this year drop to 9 per cent and 4 per cent respectively, then a commentator may say that both regions have experienced a 1 per cent drop in unemployment. This is not true. Both regions have experienced a drop of one point, but the drop in the first region is 10 per cent (1/10) while in the second it is 20 per cent (1/5). Another way (of many possible alternatives) of looking at the same situation involves the ratio of the two figures. In the first region unemployment is now nine-tenths of its original figure and in the second region it is now eight-tenths of its original. Therefore progress in the second region has been greater. The politician's error lies in ignoring this difference and calling both changes 1 per cent, rather than 1 percentage point from a differing base figure in each case. To put it simply, percentages are by their very nature already proportionate (to one hundred), whereas percentage point changes are not.

Table 1.1. Example of proportionate changes over time

Gender	1992 (%)	1997 (%)	Points change	Ratio
Girls	79	83	4	1.05
Boys	70	77	7	1.10
Achievement gap	6	4		

One of the problems leading to this very frequent error may be that commentators are not working from the 'raw' data. Using the actual numbers rather than starting from data already converted to percentages can make the distinction clearer. Suppose there are two groups of schools whose performance in terms of examination results is being compared over a period of time. Group A has a constant 2,000 students of whom 200 met a particular target in year one, while group B has 10,000 students of whom 2,000 met the target in year one. If, in year two, 300 of group A and 3,000 of group B meet the target then the 'gap' between the groups has not changed. Group A has increased its proportion meeting the target by 50 per cent and so has group B, so that the proportion of 'success' in group A (10 per cent initially rising to 15 per cent) is exactly half that of group B (20 per cent initially rising to 30 per cent). The politician's error consists of ignoring these proportions and insisting that since the gap between groups A and B was 10 percentage points in year one but 15 percentage points in year two, the gap must be getting larger over time.

This book uses a standard way of presenting differences between two or more groups over time (see Table 1.1). In this table, representing a change in the GCSE pass rates for boys and girls in Wales, the change in percentage points is shown alongside the ratio of the second figure to the first. In 1992, 79 per cent of girls gained five or more GCSEs graded G or higher, while 70 per cent of boys achieved the same. In 1997, 83 per cent of girls gained five or more GCSEs graded G or higher, while 77 per cent of boys achieved the same. From 1992 to 1997, the improvement for boys was therefore twice that for girls since 77/70 equals 1.10 whereas 83/79 equals 1.05. In effect, the benchmark for boys improved by 10 per cent and that for girls by 5 per cent. Where only two groups are being compared (as in this example), it is also possible to calculate an achievement gap between them. As with the improvement ratio, this gap is calculated as a proportion of the figures in which it appears (for further details see Chapter 9). In Table 1.1 the gap between boys and girls in 1992, assuming equal numbers of each gender in the cohort, is 9/(70+79) or 6 per cent. By 1997 the gap has reduced to 6/(83+77) or 4 per cent. The results are rounded and multiplied by 100 in each case for ease of presentation.

The second element commonly ignored in analyses supporting the crisis account is that of an appropriate second comparator. It is surprising how often commentators have a 'missing comparator' when describing changes over time. In some cases this lack is obvious and a case in point is described in Chapter 8 where the claim is made that there is a growing gap in the school performance of boys and girls. This claim is backed up by the benchmark percentages for boys and girls separately but for only one year. However, figures from one year can only be used in this context to establish the existence of a gap (or not). They cannot tell us anything about growth over time. A similar example appears in a media report by Ghouri (1999a, p. 9) as: 'Ministers are alarmed by a *growing* literacy gender gap. In last year's key stage 2 tests, almost two thirds of boys failed to reach the required standard in reading compared with 20 per cent of girls [*my italics*].' Nowhere in the piece is there any justification given for the use of the word 'growing'. The reader is given only the figures for one year. Perhaps in the same way that low achievement is now commonly referred to as 'underachievement' by politicians (e.g. ETAG 1998), a large gap in achievement has now become indistinguishable from a *growing* gap for some commentators, almost by definition. Journalists may be allowed by their editors to blur these important distinctions. Professional educators and social scientists, on the other hand, need to be rather more precise.

A more common, and complex, version of the same problem arises when figures from two or more years *are* used, but in a way that suggests that the figures are directly comparable over time. For example, a school manager might note that the number of children with dyslexia in the school has increased in the last five years. The manager might correctly calculate this number as a proportion of the school roll over five years, which is necessary since the school may also have changed in size. If the number of students with dyslexia has increased as a percentage of those in the school, the manager may believe that this calculation *proves* that the school is taking an increasing share of dyslexics compared with other schools. Such a conclusion should, of course, actually involve a consideration of the picture in those other schools, or at least a consideration of changes in the frequency of dyslexia in the population. It is possible that the manager is totally in error and that the school is actually taking a *decreasing* share of the dyslexics from the population since the growth of dyslexia in the population may be out-stripping the growth in that school (examples of such a conclusion appear in Chapter 2). To put it simply, when examining changes over time it is important to recall that all of the numbers involved are liable to change. For the purposes of this book, such a problem would be resolved by the use of 'double proportions' or proportions of proportions. The question for the school manager interested in student share is not whether the percentage of dyslexics in the school has grown, but whether it has grown faster than the percentage in the population from which the school derives its students. Put in arithmetic terms, the index for any year would be: $(d/n)/(D/N)$ where d is the number of dyslexics in the school, D is the number in the population, while n is the number of all students in the school and N is the number in the population. If this index grows over time, then the manager can justly 'complain' of increasing share, but it should be noted that the index could decrease even where d/n increases (and vice versa). This is one of the main reasons why small-scale studies of changes over time may be of little worth.

The third element of a genuine proportionate analysis involves the use of contextual factors. Typically this involves trying to make 'fair' comparisons of the examination performances of differing groups of students, although the use of context is equally important in many other comparisons as well. This is what is done in 'value-added' analyses and in attempts to uncover 'school effects' for example. However, despite the apparently wide acceptance of the principle (although analysts may debate the specific methods used), many of the proponents of the crisis account of British education still make comparisons on the basis of raw scores (examples of this appear in Chapters 4 and 6). League tables of GCSE results are still published as though they were performance indicators for schools and the examination outcomes of significantly different groups of students are compared to make

points about the relative success and failure of particular schools
and methods of teaching. As is shown in Chapter 4, perhaps the
most convincing research finding of the school effectiveness
movement is that only a small part of the differences in
examination outcomes is attributable to the influence of teachers,
schools or even entire education systems. For the most part,
examination results are predictable at an aggregate level from the
social and economic background of the students taking them. Since
this is so, it is essential to take account of any socio-economic
differences between students before attempting to judge the
efficacy of the schools they attend.

When all three of these elements are appropriately present in an
analysis, as I hope they are in the new analyses presented in this
book, then the crisis account of British education is transformed. It
is important to emphasize at this stage that this does not mean that
significant social justice has already been attained, or even that it is
attainable. The socio-economic divisions within Britain remain
deep, while some indicators of poverty are increasing at a
surprising rate and this should be seen as a fundamental failing for
our society. What a proportionate analysis of education does show
is that we may need to be more careful in our initial research into
the nature of the relationship between education and social justice.
This is the foundation on which further research in this area should
be based. The problem appears to lie partly in a current lack of a
simple arithmetic tradition in British educational research: a
tradition that was exemplified in the past by the political arithmetic
of Halsey et al. (1980) perhaps. What we have now is an apparently
increasing dichotomy in methodological terms between statisticians concerned with the complex models available to them via
computer and those who apparently eschew *any* form of rigorous,
public or replicable analysis.

The latter group may be disproportionately powerful in the field
of education and social justice, where their justified concerns for
justice may lead them to take sides *before* collecting the necessary
empirical evidence, as actually advocated by some 'researchers'
(e.g. Griffiths 1998). I reject absolutely Griffiths's principles for
researching social justice in education. The researcher cannot
afford to 'take sides' with anything but the truth (examples of the
dangers of politically motivated research may be seen in Vance
Randall et al. 1999). One potential outcome of this dichotomous

methodological trend within British educational research is shown in the story of a researcher on racism in schools who did not require evidence in his research, since he believed himself to be 'not that kind of researcher' (in Fitz-Gibbon 1996). As a further example, in 1996 one of the most influential sociologists of education in Britain stated in reply to a conference question that he was not overly concerned with the truth of his claims, since they were made primarily to get a point across and perhaps shock listeners out of their complacency. The danger is that both of these 'researchers' may be using the rhetorical appeal of the word 'research', which stems at least in part from the more labour-intensive evidence-based work of others, to write pretty much what they like and then have it listened to with respect by policy-makers, journalists and even other academics.

It may be precisely the prior expectations, desires and political commitments of such researchers that appear to have produced the one-sided accounts involving the politician's error in all its manifestations. We need to sort out first and foremost what is happening in our schools and our society. Only then can we form policy and suggest remedies, if remedies are needed. For these reasons, however well-meaning, the kind of 'qualitative' research proposed by Griffiths (1998) is sometimes no better than the flawed 'quantitative' reasoning illustrated in this book. In fact, the very distinction between the two supposed paradigms of research is perhaps overused and seemingly an excuse for some to evade the limitations of generalization, transparency, replicability and so on that are the hallmark of convincing and cumulating social science. In the same way that one would not refuse to engage in conversation because one was once lied to verbally, one cannot lose trust in numbers simply because of some questionable uses of statistics. If this book has an alternative theme then it is a plea for a middle way in educational research: balanced, rational and *numerate*.

A Worked Example of Reanalysis

This introductory chapter concludes with an example from a well-known piece of research which has already begun permeating through the research literature and into a national debate on the desirable nature of schools. This example contains many of the problems with proportionate analyses described in this chapter. Therefore, although apparently convincing to many readers, since the example is evidence-based with a clear method of analysis and set within a report of otherwise excellent and substantial research, once a genuinely proportionate analysis is carried out, the conclusions drawn are actually the *exact opposite* of those published.

On pp. 40–3 of their Equal Opportunities Commission book, *Educational Reform and Gender Equality in Schools*, Arnot et al. (1996) argue that 'gender segregation has a substantial influence on gender performance' (p. 42) and that 'girls in single-sex schools might be at a substantial advantage' (p. 43). They back their claims up with the GCSE benchmark figures for 1994 from seven types of school, each divided into mixed, boys' and girls' schools. They discover that 'all-girls schools obtain higher ratings than all-boys schools in all seven categories' (p. 42). Such a finding would not surprise most readers of their book since the first part of the same chapter is devoted to the gender gap in favour of girls in most subjects at GCSE. Thus, if girls are doing better than boys in all schools, one would expect schools containing a high proportion of girls, such as girls' schools, to attain a higher benchmark figure than schools of the same type containing a high proportion of boys. The question is: is the difference between the results at girls' schools and mixed (or boys') schools greater than the difference one would naturally expect? The answer on the data for 1994 would seem to be 'no'.

In 1994, the published DfEE figures for the attainment of five GCSEs at grade C or above in local education authority (LEA) controlled comprehensives are 35.9 per cent for boys and 45.1 per cent for girls. These give a realistic estimate of the predicted performance of girls in girls-only schools and boys in boys-only schools, assuming that the children in single-sex schools are no different in any other relevant way from the majority of children in mixed comprehensives. Of course, if the type of children attending single-sex schools differs, for example in occupational class backgrounds or eligibility for free school meals, then a raw-score comparison of the type made by Arnot et al. would be inappropriate anyway. Under the assumption of no difference between intakes except by gender one would expect girls in girls-only schools to have an average benchmark of 45.1 per cent. In fact, according to Arnot et al. they achieve 41.1 per cent, which is less than the national average for girls in all LEA comprehensives. Thus, if the two sets of figures are comparable, there is an indication that girls in single-sex schools are underachieving in comparison to girls in mixed schools. This is the exact opposite of the conclusion drawn by Arnot et al., which has had relatively wide publicity and influence.

Although it represents only a tiny part of the main argument about social justice in this book, the example above serves as a useful introduction to the lack of an arithmetic tradition in British educational research (and its potentially important consequences). Where datasets and methods of analysis are not clearly presented in published work, it is not possible for readers to check the veracity of the conclusions. Where data and methods *are* clear, as they are in this example, it is somewhat disconcerting to discover how often the conclusions and the data do not match (and this discovery can suggest alarming implications for our default opinion of the reported research that does *not* give us direct access to the evidence). There has been much talk recently of evidence-based policy-making in Britain, particularly in the light of regional devolution, and this book is intended to be a contribution to the discussion on what precisely constitutes the evidence base for educational policy in Britain. Genuinely proportionate analyses of issues to do with attainment and social justice in education suggest that the current crisis in education is markedly different from that in the standard account used by politicians. It cannot be right that some commentators simply use numbers as rhetorical devices for their own ends (see above), while others ignore all numerical analyses just because they have encountered such abuses in the past. As Winston Smith says in *Nineteen Eighty-Four*, freedom is the freedom to say that 2+2=4. From that all else follows.

2

The Social Composition of Schools

It has been well established by correlational studies and confirmed by the recent growth in studies of school effectiveness, as well as by the creation of value-added analyses, that school outcomes are strongly linked to the social and economic composition of their intake. Put simply, schools with a high proportion of children from poor families will not generally have high raw-score public examination results (see Chapter 4). Similar conclusions have been drawn about schools with a high proportion of children from certain ethnic minorities, those with a first language other than English and those with a statement of special educational need. Therefore, a preliminary consideration of the patterns of enrolment in British schools is an essential precursor, by providing the context, to any attempt to analyse patterns of attainment. This chapter examines changes over time in the distribution of several indicators of the socio-economic composition of school intakes in Britain. Since it is clear that school outcomes in the form of examination scores are closely linked to school intakes in the form of student characteristics, some observers have attempted to argue back from an observation of an increasing polarization of the results between schools to the implied existence of an increasing polarization of intakes. Such arguments are considered in Chapter 6. This chapter concentrates on the actual composition of schools.

Evidence for Increasing Segregation

For a variety of theoretical reasons, backed up by apparently strong empirical support, it has become almost an article of faith among British researchers that schools are becoming more segregated in social terms over time. What commentators generally mean by this is that students from wealthy families are becoming increasingly concentrated in some schools, while students from poor families are more concentrated in others. All other indicators that are linked to relative wealth and poverty are, therefore, increasingly segregated between schools as well. Such indicators include parental occupation, parental education, ethnicity, first language, special educational need and student attainment. According to this account, therefore, student experiences of school in Britain are increasingly determined by their family background and increasingly polarized.

Explanations of the spirals of decline in some schools, and circles of advantage (as they have been termed) in others, have been chiefly based on criticisms of the programme of increased parental choice introduced in the 1980s, on inner-city decline, poor public transport and sociological theories of class advantage derived from writers such as Bourdieu. According to these explanations, while middle-class families have always enjoyed privilege in education, the recent reforms have made the situation worse, thereby decreasing social justice and increasing social divisions. In summary, recent changes in the simple act of allocating students to schools have actually been reinforcing social injustice rather than combating it.

Recent reforms in Britain, Australia, New Zealand, the USA and several nations in continental Europe and Scandinavia have attempted to alter the organization of the allocation of public services. One repeated feature of this process has been the encouragement of competition between and within public-sector institutions, the advocacy of choice for newly constituted consumers of public services and the consequent manufacturing of client–provider relationships in the pursuit of efficiency gains in public-service provision (e.g. Osborne and Gaebler 1993). These themes are clear for education in the interlocking policy initiatives culminating in the 1988 Education Reform Act in Britain aimed at forcing competition between schools and increasing parental choice. The creation of markets in education, increasing explicit parental choice, advancing the autonomy of educational institutions and the implementation of a per capita funding regime all exemplify the features of the so-called 'new public management'. The institutional policy instruments employed in market creation have been discussed fully elsewhere (e.g. in Fitz et al. 1993; Whitty et al. 1998). In England and Wales this limited market in schools was created and advanced by legislation such as the Assisted Places Scheme 1981, the Education Reform Act 1988 and subsequent legislation in 1992 and 1996. An intrinsically monopolistic state provision has supposedly been replaced by choice and diversity. A decade on, what has the application of new public management techniques and values, in particular, marketization, yielded in education? What changes have been wrought on schools and their composition and to what extent has the market forced distinctions between what are perceived as good and bad schools?

The academic response to these questions has been an outpouring of research examining the operation of the limited market in schools from a number of perspectives (see Gorard 1997a, 1999b). Some writers have been primarily concerned to theorize the nature of a system of parental choice of schools (e.g. Le Grand and Bartlett 1993), others have wished to describe and analyse the micro-political process of choosing a new school (e.g. Gewirtz et al. 1995). Some have been concerned to find out which members of the family are involved in the process of choosing (e.g. David et al. 1994), while others have considered the implications for schools (e.g. James and Phillips 1995). Some writers have been avowedly in favour of the strengthening of market forces in the system of educational planning (e.g. Tooley 1994), but perhaps the majority of British research has emphasized the negative consequences of the policy (e.g. Glatter et al. 1997), with many observers simply taking the results for granted (e.g. Hatcher 1998a). Some of the outcomes of this work are that the nature of limited markets is better understood, the difficulties of choosing schools for some sections of the community have been emphasized and the criteria used to make choices have been well-rehearsed.

In Britain, advocates of increased choice and diversity in education have tended to concentrate on the purported beneficial effects of programmes of choice on the standard of schools. Their principal argument can be summarized as a suggestion that most families are able to make wise educational choices. Therefore, 'good' schools will prosper and 'bad' schools will either have to improve or close through lack of students. Although advocates of choice in the USA and elsewhere have suggested that there may be social justice benefits as well (that is, fairer access to good schools), not much has been made of this argument in Britain. In fact, the reverse has happened. It is the opponents of market forces in education who have followed the social justice agenda, while tending to ignore the potential impact of choice on educational standards. Such writers generally suggest that allowing parents to choose schools will privilege those who are already privileged, since making a good choice, and perhaps making any choice at all, requires families to have resources which are unequally distributed in society. Such resources might include literacy, confidence, taste, knowledge of legislation, leisure time and private transport. Their argument can be very simply summarized as suggesting that poor families will not be able to 'play' the market successfully and will not, therefore, make 'wise' educational choices. Thus, choice will further advantage those families who are already well off. Reay (1998, p.1), for example, claims that the 'market system of education provides the middle-classes with a competitive edge, of which they will increasingly take advantage'. Theoretical models have generally predicted a growth in social stratification between schools as a result of increased market forces in school placements (Bourdieu and Passeron 1992; Bowe et al. 1994).

Small-scale empirical studies of school choice in urban areas of England have reported finding evidence that supports these predictions (Blair 1994; Gewirtz et al. 1995) and the results from studies of school choice in England, Scotland, Israel and New Zealand have provided apparent confirmation (Willms and Echols 1992; Goldring 1995; Ambler 1997; Glatter et al. 1997; Waslander and Thrupp 1997; Woods et al. 1997; Lauder et al. 1999; also see Gorard 1999b for fuller discussion of this issue). Levačić and Hardman (1998) suggest that, within a system of choice, schools with high levels of students from poor families tend to lose student numbers, and therefore budget share, over time. Bagley and Woods (1998) report that families in their study were avoiding schools on the basis of current student intake characteristics such as race, religion and ability, suggesting that socio-economic segregation is linked to segregation in terms of other indicators as well. Hook (1999) describes how schools with low pass rates in examinations gain poor local reputations, which then have a strong deterrent effect on many residents. These so-called sink schools also have a high proportion of transient students, who may be both partly the cause and partly a symptom of the problem (Berki 1999). Families in these areas who have high aspirations therefore tend to move away (or use alternative schools), leading to a cycle of decline in inner cities and an ever-increasing gap between the schools servicing the rich and those used by the poor. Worpole (1999, p. 17) observes that the average length of trips to and from schools has increased from 2.1 to 2.7 miles over the last decade and that the increasing use of family cars further exacerbates the educational divide between haves and have-nots: 'Schools which are left behind can get trapped into a vicious circle of decline.' In effect, social segregation between schools is increasing, leading some disadvant-aged schools into a 'spiral of decline' and creating a clear system of winners and losers.

Media stories of high-profile government ministers, and even radical left-wing politicians, seeking to avoid their local comprehensive and using more distant grant-maintained (GM) schools can be seen as illustrations of this much larger trend. The policy of allowing grant-maintained schools (as they then were) to opt out of LEA control has supposedly increased polarization between institutions (*TES* 1999b), simply because they exist or because they 'covertly select pupils by ability' according to Levačić and Hardman (1999). Much academic writing is, therefore, based on the social science 'fact' that markets in education have an increasingly stratifying impact on the make-up of schools (Conway 1997). Waslander and Thrupp state that 'those endowed with material and cultural capital will simply add to their existing advantages through choice policies' (1995, p. 21). Similarly, Gipps (1993, p. 35) states that 'the concept of market choice allows the articulate middle and educated classes to exert their privilege, whilst not appearing to'. Commenting on experiments from the USA (where 'choice' has generally involved schemes providing free places at private schools for poor students), Powers and Cookson (1999, p. 109) suggest that 'perhaps the most consistent effect of market-driven choice programs across the studies . . . is that choice programs tend to have the effect of increasing stratification to one degree or another within school districts'. According to a study from Exeter University, 'within local markets, the evidence is clear that high-performing schools both improve their GCSE perform-ance fastest and draw to themselves the most socially-advantaged pupils' (Budge 1999, p. 3).

The first major component of the crisis account of British education therefore seems solid enough. Children are segregated in socio-economic terms by the schools they attend and the situation is apparently getting worse over time. In fact, the near-consensus from research on the process of school choice in the UK appears to be that the limited market is a class strategy used to extend the privilege of the already privileged (see also Ball et al. 1996; Whitty et al. 1998).

Another View of School Allocation

What the crisis account suggests is that schools today are less mixed in socio-economic terms than when allocation of places was by residential catchment and before that by universal selection at 11+. On reflection, does this seem likely? In the USA, where 'quantitative' research is more common and where programmes of choice have been limited in application, the consensus about the segregating effect of school choice is not so clear (Coons and Sugarman 1978; Bauch 1989; Zhou et al. 1998). In another light, markets can be seen as extending to wider participation a privilege that some members of society already have (Witte 1990). Social stratification routinely takes place in schools based on a catchment system (Maynard 1975; Spring 1982) and previous compulsory state education schemes have up to now appeared powerless to do anything about it (Cookson 1994). Choice programmes in the USA are, therefore, especially popular with the disadvantaged sections of many communities, such as immigrant, minority and one-parent families, who have been deserting some large inner-city schools (Levin 1992; Wells 1996). Witte (1998) reports that a voucher scheme in Milwaukee attracted primarily families with considerably below-average incomes for local public schools (even below the average of those eligible for free lunches). These families were mainly Black or Hispanic in origin and often had only one parent, suggesting that some choice programmes properly designed could actually lead to desegregation by income and ethnicity over time. Low-income and minority families may see themselves as trapped in poor schools, and the evidence is that they view choice more favourably as a result (Elmore and Fuller 1996). In fact the overwhelming majority in the USA support school choice (as do the majority in Britain according to MORI polls), and the policy has become a 'sacred pillar of federal anti-poverty programs' backed by the political left (Fuller et al. 1996, p. 3).

However, even in the USA, the cumulated conclusions about choice and equity are confusing (see Lee et al. 1994). There have been many small policy experiments, but the resulting information is very limited and the outcomes in terms of equity (as well as standards) are still in dispute (Archbald 1996). Powers and Cookson (1999) agree that the results of school-choice research are not clear cut. Although the Milwaukee review shows that choice has disproportionately benefited families on welfare and low income, including ethnic minorities and single-parent families, the mothers of these families tended to be better educated than the control population. Witte (1998) found that the poorer families attracted to the voucher scheme had mothers with higher than average educational backgrounds (somewhat similar to the concept of the 'artificially poor' in England, in Edwards et al. 1989). This 'controversy exists for a reason' (Witte 1998, p. 248) because different studies have produced different answers to what is apparently the same research question. Sometimes the reasons for these differences could be the nature of the choice programme being studied and sometimes the nature of the methods used, the sample selected or the timing. A voucher scheme is not the same as a policy of open enrolment, while a few hundred interviews cannot encapsulate socio-economic movements within a national school system, and a change of policy can produce markedly different effects in the early and more established stages of implementation, for example. The methods used and the timing of research into the impact of markets are, therefore, crucial.

Mainstream educational research in Britain has been primarily 'qualitative' in nature, focusing on the process of choice and, as in the USA, methodological debates have developed over the validity of some of the most prominent results (e.g. Gewirtz et al. 1995; Ball and Gewirtz 1997; Gorard 1997b; Tooley 1997; Waslander and Thrupp 1997; Gorard and Fitz 1998a). The difficulties for these small-scale studies in assessing socio-economic segregation between schools have arisen partly due to changes in the number of schools in many authorities since 1988, coupled with changes in the characteristics of families in each area. For example, a headteacher may have witnessed a significant rise in the number of children eligible for free school meals, or with a statement of special need, in one school. Even if this growth takes into account changes in the number on roll, bearing in mind that many schools have grown in size due to closures, a local rise in indicators of disadvantage is not evidence of increasing segregation. Even if the school is now taking

a larger share of disadvantaged children compared with its neighbouring schools than it used to, this is still not evidence of greater
segregation. For example, the school in question may have started
the period with less than its 'fair share' of poor students and be
simply catching up with its more disadvantaged neighbours, so
leading to less segregation in fact. It is likely that all headteachers
have witnessed a rise in indicators of disadvantage over the last ten
years (see Chapter 3), so increasing segregation can only be said to
take place when all of the changes in the number of students and
their indicators are calculated relative to other schools in the region
of analysis.

At least by implication, post-1988 markets in education have
been compared in this body of British work with the status *ante* of
rigid catchment areas allocating students to their nearest schools,
which has been variously referred to as 'state monopoly schooling'
(Chubb and Moe 1990) or 'selection by mortgage' (Hirsch 1997).
However, there has been no direct comparison of the extent to
which social stratification, which also undoubtedly occurred under
the catchment-area system, has been transformed by the post-1988
market-led principle of educational provision. In principle, it is
possible for markets to have a clearly stratifying effect and for
them still to lead to less segregation between schools than a pure
catchment-area system. What have been missing until now in
British research have been larger-scale studies of the American
kind which sought to examine the impact of market forces across a
large number of schools, although more recently some studies have
emerged that begin to address directly one or more of the
theoretical justifications advanced for markets in education (e.g.
Levačić et al. 1998). There may be a variety of reasons for this gap.
First, there have been difficulties of access to the sensitive school-
level data held locally and nationally. Second, writers in the school
effectiveness tradition, who have developed powerful techniques
for large-scale data analysis, have not generally been concerned
with the operation of the market. Third, it may also be the case that
many observers believe enough evidence of diverse kinds has
already been collected. The next chapter introduces recent British
research which addresses some of the lacunae, most notably in the
scale of the research thus far undertaken, in the absence of longitudinal studies and in the perceived difficulties of the construction
of reliable comparators. The remainder of this chapter involves a

reassessment of the evidence presented thus far for the increasing segregation of schooling in Britain (whether related to market forces or not).

Some of the evidence cited above which suggests increasing polarization between schools has serious technical deficiencies, among which four general patterns appear (see Gorard 1999c). Commentators do not generally have an agreed definition of what segregation (or stratification or polarization) actually is, making it hard to recognize in practice. It is sometimes incorrectly assumed that the socio-economic characteristics of a population remain constant and that therefore the only change is in their distribution between schools (see the discussion of Lauder et al. 1999 below). The growth of postcode information systems has encouraged some researchers to ignore actual school populations and actual student characteristics and to rely instead on proxy indicators from the 1991 census arranged into artificial school 'catchment' areas (e.g. Parsons 1998). Such data are insufficient for the detailed calculations necessary to identify the necessarily tiny annual changes in segregation. In addition, such Geographical Information Systems (GIS) studies make a similar mistake to Lauder et al. and many others in assuming that the 1991 indicators have not changed much over time.

Some of these deficiencies are minor but significant. As described above, Worpole (1999) correctly points out that journeys to school have lengthened over the last decade, but before this can be used as evidence of an increasing educational divide the calculation would need to factor in the concurrent decrease in the number of schools. In the last decade many schools have been closed as a way of cutting excess places in the system in an attempt to save money. On average, then, one would expect the distance from home to school to increase and, undesirable as this increased travel may be, it may have nothing to do with school choice or privilege and no impact on segregation.

Some of the deficiencies in the work cited above are more serious. Ambler (1997), for example, claims to present evidence of segregation due to the programme of parental choice in Britain. He actually does no such thing. He uses data from Halsey et al. (1980) which only apply to men and are from the 1960s, a period long before the Education Reform Act 1988. Ambler also uses figures from a study by Edwards et al. (1989) which was actually concerned with choice of schools in a small part of the small private sector in Britain. Like all of the evidence cited by Ambler, this dated from before the Education Reform Act 1988.

Perhaps the most common problem in the interpretation of the remaining evidence stems not from technical deficiencies but from the fact that the researchers concerned did not set out to assess changes in segregation over time. This does not apparently stop advocates of the crisis account from using such studies as seren-dipitous evidence. For example, Willms and Echols (1992) used a relatively compact sample and used data only from the first two years after the relevant legislation became 'operational' (which may be considered too few to display a trend). They showed that parents not using designated local schools in Scotland were, in general, better educated and of more elevated social class. What they did *not* show, nor even attempt to measure, was increasing segregation between schools. Their work only predicts that this would happen, and as a side issue to their main and undisputed findings about the process of choice, in the same way as Bowe et al. (1994) for instance.

The Smithfield Study in New Zealand

Before looking in detail at what has actually happened to the composition of schools in England and Wales since 1988 (in Chapter 3), it is interesting to consider one of the largest and most influential studies in this area so far. The Smithfield study in New Zealand, previously one of the largest and most direct accounts of the impact of markets in schools, suggests that the dezoning of schools has led to increased social segregation between them. This study is not chosen to be considered in detail here because of its clear weaknesses, but because of its importance and influence. It was a large-scale piece of work combining various sources of longitudinal data for a number of schools. It has been accepted, thus far, as a definitive body of evidence on the markets and segregation thesis. The rest of this chapter therefore considers the findings from the quantitative elements of the Smithfield study as exemplified by Waslander and Thrupp (1995), Hughes et al. (1996a) and Lauder et al. (1999).

The study involved eleven of the schools in one New Zealand city, over a period of at least four years. The purpose of the study was to examine the impacts of the dezoning of schools in 1991, to consider whether the policy had further advantaged those already advantaged or whether it had freed at least some of those less privileged families 'trapped in the iron cage of zoning' (Waslander and Thrupp 1995, p. 3) and to decide whether schools became more or less socially segregated as a result. Dezoning as a policy of allocating school places allowed all families to select non-adjacent schools for the first time. In 1991, where places were over-subscribed (or contested) the allocation was done by drawing random lots.

A key assumption underlying the study was 'that changes in school composition did not result from substantive demographic shifts' (Waslander and Thrupp 1997, p. 442). The measures of social composition used are parental unemployment, mean socio-economic status (SES) and ethnic group. The authors describe the annual changes in SES in their sample as 'fluctuating marginally' and parental unemployment as being 'almost constant', and it is on this basis that they claim 'the general picture then is one of stability from year to year which makes it most likely that any com-positional changes experienced by schools were primarily the result of between-school processes rather than underlying demographic shifts' (Waslander and Thrupp 1995, p. 5).

Even if these claims of relative stability in terms of social composition were true, which is questionable on the figures published, the study does not explain why the changes that *did* take place should not be factored in to calculations so that between-school processes can be assessed more accurately. It should be axiomatic to include even minor changes in the composition of the potential intake to schools in the calculation of segregation. In fact, the Smithfield data shows that parental unemployment varies from 7 to 5 per cent and back again over the four years (increasing proportionately by 40 per cent from 1991 to 1992, for example), SES moves from 3.12 to 3.66 and 'up' again (an increase of 17 per cent from 1990 to 1991, for example), while the proportion of Maori families declines by 14 per cent (from 14 per cent in 1992 to 12 per cent in 1993). These changes in the overall composition of the sample from year to year are proportionately much larger than the between-school changes later reported to be the *significant* outcomes of dezoning. This means that, as the key assumption of the study is incorrect, the findings are not trustworthy.

Table 2.1. Percentage of students by ethnicity and locality of school

Ethnicity/locality	1990	1991	1992	1993
MAORI				
Local	82	71	75	69
Adjacent	12	24	21	25
Distant	6	5	4	6
PACIFIC ISLAND				
Local	87	72	65	67
Adjacent	10	22	32	28
Distant	3	6	4	5
PAKEHA				
Local	75	69	71	72
Adjacent	12	17	18	16
Distant	13	14	11	12

Source: Waslander and Thrupp 1995, table 3.

Waslander and Thrupp (1995) then state that their approach is to identify which families are now using schools which they would not have been entitled to use before 1991. This shows whether the parents who have gained through choice are those previously 'trapped in the iron cage of zoning' (p. 3). They present a summary in their table 3, showing that the increase among users of non-local schools since 1991 has been most obvious in ethnic-minority families (see Table 2.1). On the basis of their own figures, then, it is the Maori and Pacific Islander families rather than the majority white Pakeha who have gained most from the abolition of dezoning and the scale of the gain is remarkable. The proportion of Maori families not using their local school doubled from 12 per cent to 24 per cent from 1990 to 1991 and the proportion of Pacific Islanders more than doubled from 10 to 22 per cent. However, rather than conclude that it was, therefore, primarily these families who had been in the 'iron cage', which is what they said they would do at the start of the paper, the authors actually state the opposite conclusion. Having obtained the data and completed the necessary analysis the authors claim that their figures are not to be trusted (perhaps because they show the opposite of what was expected).

The authors conclude from their table 4 that there has been an increase in the mean SES of those using schools for which they would have been ineligible before 1991, and, therefore, that dezoning leads to the reinforcement of privilege. According to this account, even if some ethnic minorities gain from dezoning it is the more privileged among them. There are three points against this conclusion. First, there is no attempt to look for the interaction between ethnicity and SES, so there is no reason to assume that the ethnic-minority families in their table 3 and the high-SES families in table 4 are the same ones. There could be two groups of gainers from dezoning. Second, table 3 has shown that the growth of 'active' choosers among ethnic minorities is proportionately greater than among the majority Pakeha, whatever their social status. Third and most importantly, their data simply does *not* show what the authors claim (see Table 2.2). In fact, the mean SES of those using 'adjacent' schools declined by 11 per cent during 1990 to 1993, while the mean SES of those using distant schools increased by 5 per cent. Given that more families use adjacent schools than distant ones, these figures make it clear that the mean SES of those released from the 'iron cage' is lower than the average for the school population as a whole, which suggests that school composition will become less segregated after 1990 (which is what they eventually found, as shown below). The peculiarity is, therefore, that the tables say one thing and the authors conclude the opposite. Subsequent commentators on this work appear to have read only the text and not considered the actual evidence presented in support. Perhaps this confusion stems from the fact that a 'high' SES has a low number (e.g. 1) attached to it and a 'low' SES has a high number (e.g. 5) attached.

In their original paper, the authors now move further away from answering the simple question of who has taken advantage of dezoning by bringing into play the SES of the neighbourhood in which the school was placed. In other words, having neglected to use the SES of the school population as a framework for assessing changes in social segregation, they now use the SES of the local residents instead, whether they are school users or not (despite having the SES scores of all actual school users which they decide *not* to use). It is almost as though the authors are willing to try anything to find a mode of analysis that supports their 'conclusions'. The SES of school users is thus converted to a score relative to the SES of their 'neighbourhood' and it is found that those who are less well off than the average potential users of their

Table 2.2. Mean SES of students by locality of school

Locality	1990	1991	1992	1993
Local	3.20	3.22	3.26	3.19
Adjacent	3.02	3.27	3.40	3.36
Distant	2.70	2.59	2.51	2.56

Source: Waslander and Thrupp 1995, table 4.

local school are now more likely to use their local school (Waslander and Thrupp 1995, p. 8). Again, although this finding is presented by the authors as evidence of the potentially segregating effects of choice, it is not clear why. They have shown that, after dezoning, poorer families are *more* likely than they were before to use local schools if they live in areas with a higher mean SES. This is the opposite of segregation. Segregation, on these calculations, would involve poorer families being progressively excluded from schools in richer areas.

The argument is carried further in another publication from the same project. It is shown that active choice, in the form of families not using their local schools, has increased significantly in New Zealand since 1990 – from 24 to 35 per cent in 1995 (Hughes et al. 1996a). These changes are largely the result of movement by students of ethnic-minority or low-SES background. This is a slightly different picture but it leads to the same conclusion. The authors state that 'it appears that de-zoning increased the number of lower SES students attending an adjacent school', but then interpret the implications of this by concluding, 'however, these figures ignore the fact that students living close to schools with good reputations have no reason to bypass them and, of course, these schools tend to be in higher socio-economic areas' (Hughes et al. 1996a, p. 15). Of course: this is precisely what writers such as Coons and Sugarman (1978) would have predicted and what observers concerned with social justice would have wanted. Those in lower socio-economic groups appear to have evaded the stratifying effects of selection by residence.

Questions concerning changes in segregation since 1990 in New Zealand can be answered much more simply by comparing the proportion of each category of student (by ethnic group or SES) in

Table 2.3. Dissimilarity indices for socio-economic segregation

Indicator	1990	1991	1992	1993
SES	58.3	48.1	49.3	53.4
Unemployed	58.2	51.6	52.6	55.2

Source: Waslander and Thrupp 1995, table 8.

each school with the proportion of each category of student in all schools. This is what has been done in table 8 of Waslander and Thrupp (1995), where segregation between schools in terms of the dissimilarity indices for parental unemployment and mean SES is shown to have declined since 1990. Again the authors attempt to evade this conclusion by claiming that, whereas their table 7 shows that segregation by ethnic group has risen since 1990 (which on these figures it has), their table 8 using the same method does not show that segregation by parental background has declined (see Table 2.3). They argue that the apparent socio-economic deseg-regation is not correct, partly because 'findings at this level of aggregation are misleading' and partly because the '1992 and 1993 figures are tending to rise . . . so that in the next year . . . segregation may be greater' (p. 11). There is, therefore, some incon-sistency in their analysis here. The figures for segregation by ethnicity are at the same level of aggregation as for SES and un-employment and the dissimilarity index for Pakeha/Pacific Islanders is less in 1993 than 1992. To be consistent the authors should treat the apparent rise in ethnic segregation with the same suspicion as the apparent decline in economic segregation. How-ever, all evidence of increasing segregation in this paper is reported without question and all statements about the figures showing progressive desegregation are muted (or simply false). It would be good news if segregation between schools were declining and understandable if it were not, but both results are beyond the power of the empiricist to make it so.

What is not clear is how the data presented can lead to the conclusion that 'our study has found that the concerns of market critics are justified' (Waslander and Thrupp 1997, p. 455). The abstract to the 1995 paper states that 'by enlarging the . . . group of higher socio-economic students bypassing their local schools, choice intensified socio-economic segregation between schools'. Yet their table 8 shows quite clearly that the peak of segregation was in 1990, *before* the reforms and the lowest segregation was in 1991 when allocation to school was by ballot. If it is true that observers are writing of the 'negative effects of choice, before clear evidence of them is at hand' (Hargreaves 1996, p. 138), there are indications here that they will continue to do so even after evidence of the opposite is at hand (see Appendix A for further discussion of this issue).

Conclusion

Although a considerable number of studies and writers have reported evidence of increasing segregation between schools in Britain and elsewhere, on closer inspection some of this evidence may be of dubious value or limited relevance. For most studies this is simply because describing patterns of segregation between schools was not the primary purpose of that research, and it has been other commentators who have since invested it with a significance that it did not originally claim. In each of these cases, these concluding comments have no bearing on the relevance and value of the cited studies for other research questions (for which they have, in many cases, been excellent). Clear examples of this phenomenon are provided by studies providing valuable accounts of the process and micro-politics of choice, which also suggested as a subsidiary finding that segregation was increasing but made no attempt actually to measure it. Until recently, there has been no direct comparison of the extent to which social stratification which undoubtedly occurred under the prior catchment area system has been transformed by the post-1988 impact of market-led principles of educational provision. In practice, it would be possible for markets to have a clearly stratifying effect but for them still to lead to less stratification than a pure catchment-area system (compare also the rapid desegregation by ethnicity following the replacement of apartheid with more liberal market policies in the universities of South Africa, MacGregor 1999). It is to the settlement of such questions that I now turn.

3

Investigating Segregation between Schools, 1988–1998

This chapter outlines the findings of a recent large-scale study of changes over time in the social composition of schools. The study is probably the largest of its kind ever undertaken. The methods have been described in several previous publications, and are touched on in the previous chapter. Nevertheless, since the implications of this analysis underpin much of the remainder of this book, it is important that at least the basic concept is described here. Readers are referred to Gorard and Fitz (1998b, 2000a) for further discussion of the development of these methods of investigating changes over time.

Methods Used to Investigate Segregation

Dataset
The data used for the analysis described in this chapter come chiefly from two large datasets provided by the archived returns from schools to the DfEE annual Form7 and the Welsh Office STATS1 form respectively. For England the dataset runs from 1989 to 1998, and contains the returns for every state-funded school (primary and secondary, LEA-controlled, grant-maintained and voluntary-aided). For Wales the dataset is similar, but contains data relating only to secondary schools, and is incomplete both in terms of a few LEAs and for some years from 1989 to 1991. The figures include the number of students on roll, the numbers eligible for and taking free school meals, the number in each ethnic group, the number for whom English is a second language and the number of students with a statement of special educational need. Each record also contains the school type, size, age range and LEA.

Further data used in this study come from the following sources:

• Population census 1991: LEA-level data on population density and characteristics, via NOMIS;

- The *Education Authorities Directory and Annual* (1998): school names and types, details of local government reorganization;
- DES (1990, 1991, 1992), DfE (1993, 1994, 1995a), DfEE (1996, 1997, 1998a, 1998b) and Welsh Office (1998): LEA-level data on number and types of schools, figures for independent schools and CTCs, ethnicity, exclusions and SENs.

In total, this study uses records relating to around 8 million students, in around 23,000 schools. Complete data from 123 LEAs for 1989 to 1998 are used in the analysis below, including all LEAs in England (although the City of London has only one school for primary age students). Where possible, schools have been traced through as though they were always within the smaller authority in which they ended up (for example, the Welsh schools are analysed by their reorganized 1996 unitary authority).

Free school meals (FSM) are a widely used and easily understood indicator of poverty which has the added advantages of being an administrative measure (the most appropriate and convenient measure of disadvantage according to Rutter and Madge 1976) whose definition has not changed during the period of study (Smith and Noble 1995), and whose collection in Wales via the STATS1 forms has been consistent over the same time. FSM, which denotes the proportion of children eligible for meals without charge at school, is therefore the chief comparator between schools employed in this book. FSM is used because (a) it is a widely accepted and understood instrument to measure the proportion of relatively socially disadvantaged children in a school or local education authority; (b) longitudinal datasets are available; (c) it is a flexible instrument which, when used in combination with other indicators of socio-economic context and with educational outputs (such as performance in public examinations), can be used to explore the relative effectiveness of a variety of educational institutions and agencies (see Gorard 1998a, 1998b).

During the period of this study (1988–99) the only criterion for FSMs was Income Support (the successor to Supplementary Benefit). The Social Security Act 1986 (in force 1988) abolished the discretion of LEAs to allow FSMs for other deserving cases, and deleted Family Credit (the successor to Family Income Supplement) as a criterion for eligibility. This may not have been fair, but it has the advantage for research of leading to an unambiguous and consistently applied rule. FSM is the indicator of social and educational need most usually used by LEAs in allocating scarce resources (Smith and Noble 1995). FSM remain a powerful indicator of school performance (e.g. Kelly 1996; Thomas et al. 1997; ESIS 1998; OFSTED 1998) as well as a useful proxy for family poverty. It is interesting in this regard that the FSM segregation index, unique to this study, has been shown to be significantly better as a predictor of performance than either raw figures of eligibility or percentage eligible per school, each of which are in turn clearly better than measures based on take-up alone. For example, 88 per cent of school-level variance was explained by the FSM index in Gorard (1998b), compared to 46 per cent explained by FSM percentages in Gibson and Asthana (1998a). FSM is the most consistently collected and powerful indicator of the social make-up of schools that is now available retrospectively to 1988.

The segregation index employed here (see below) overcomes any major methodological problems in using free school meals as an indicator of poverty. Some of these lie at the level of the compilation of official statistics. For example, in Wales, the Welsh Office STATS1 forms have asked schools for the number of students eligible for FSM every year, while the DfEE Form7 asked schools about FSM take-up on a particular day until 1993, and since then has asked for eligibility as well. Figures are not available on the proportion of families potentially eligible for FSM who do not register for Income Support, and some LEAs suspect that there are such individuals outside the system (Smith and Noble 1995). Nevertheless, it is clear that eligibility is a much safer measure than take-up, which could be affected by systematic regional variation such as special Asian dietary requirements. However, the change in record-keeping in 1993 makes regional comparisons and year-on-year comparisons more complex. Abrupt changes in the number of FSMs may be due to policy changes or changes in methods of collecting the statistics, as well as being produced by external 'social effects' such as the local economy or changes in patterns of school choice. Happily, the method of calculating the proportion of two proportions, used here, ameliorates most of these problems. By converting the number of students eligible for (or taking) FSM in each school to a measure of how far that number is away from what would be the school's fair share of such students, the resulting index has the same metric and the same theoretical distribution whichever measure of social background or educational disadvantage is used. This makes cross-year and cross-border comparisons feasible. It is also true that, despite the reservations above, the correlation between eligibility for FSM and take-up in any school is above +0.98 for the data collected so far (Pearson's r coefficient).

There are other measures that can add to the FSM picture and give alternative estimates of any social movement. Among these are student gender, parental occupation, statements of special needs, ethnicity, stages of English and performance at Key Stages 1 and 2 (and all of these are discussed in this book). Unfortunately no LEA has yet been able to provide a complete history back to 1988 of most of these indicators in the way that they can for FSM. The figures for most other indicators, such as statements of special educational need (SEN), are less complete, not being required in the annual returns from schools until 1994 (1995 for Wales). It should also be borne in mind that the figures such as those for SEN are likely to be less accurate than those for FSM. Although there will clearly be random errors in FSM records as well, there are several indications of more serious discrepancies in the completion of Form7 and STATS1 by schools. Thus, significant annual changes may be produced by a simple change in the procedure of recording. In Bristol LEA, for example, the number of cases of SEN recorded on the Form7 in the first year that the question was introduced was of a different order of magnitude to those in any subsequent years, possibly due to a confusion over the distinction between the numbers to be used in columns A and B of the form.

In addition, while prior attainment in Key Stage assessments may be a good baseline for assessing the later progress of individuals (Plewis and Goldstein 1997), it may not be suitable as an estimate of composition at the school level since it 'designs out' the continuing impact of local social background. As a proxy for any missing school-level data, 1991 census data is used, disaggregated at ward/catchment area level. Unfortunately these local data suffer several defects for the purposes of this study, most notably their age and consequent inability to chart the continuous small changes in population characteristics. Nevertheless, the analysis of all these additional figures is important because it triangulates with the other findings, producing a very similar picture to the other indicators.

Method of analysis

In each case, the raw figures of 'disadvantage' per school (such as number of SENs) are converted into a segregation index and a segregation ratio for each year 1989–98. The index is defined as the proportion of students who would have to change schools for there to be an even spread of disadvantage between schools within the area of analysis (nationally, regionally, by LEA, and by school). More precisely the segregation index is the sum of

$$(|dps - (dpa * tps/tpa)|) / 2*dpa$$

where dps is the number of disadvantaged pupils in a school, dpa is the number of disadvantaged pupils in the area, tps is the total number of pupils in a school, tpa is the total number of pupils in the area.

This gives an accurate measure of how many children with that characteristic of disadvantage would need to be added to or subtracted from the school in order for all schools in the district to have an even spread of disadvantage. The sum is multiplied by 100 for convenience (and to make it easy to distinguish from the ratio figures). The sum of the residuals for each school divided by the number of disadvantaged children in the district produces a scaled index of stratification (the segregation index) that can be used to compare different districts, different years and different measures of disadvantage and social background. Once this calculation has been understood it can be seen to be precisely what is meant in general usage by the term 'segregation' of a social characteristic (other very similar indices used by previous researchers are compared in Appendix B). It can be used to decide whether schools are becoming more or less mixed in terms of parental poverty, or any other indicator such as ethnicity, stages of English or special needs (which can be substituted for eligibility for free school meals). The index would be 0 if there was no segregation.

The segregation ratio is defined as the proportion of disadvantaged students within a school over or below its 'fair share'. More precisely it equals: (dps/dps)/(tps/tpa). This is used to trace the 'trajectory' of segregation for individual schools, and would have the value 1 for all schools if there was no segregation in a particular year. A figure less than 1 shows that a school is taking less than its fair share of disadvantaged students within the area used for analysis, and a figure more than 1 shows a school is taking more than its fair share. In this way, it is possible to see whether any individual school is in a spiral of decline, for example, taking a successively greater and greater proportion of disadvantaged students.

Both the ratio and the index measures are closely related to, and can be derived from, the Hoover coefficient used to assess inequality of income in a society. In a comparison of several indices of inequality, Kluge (1998, p. 45) suggests its use

> if you need to know, either which ratio of the total wealth or which ratio of the population has to be redistributed in order to reach complete equality. The Hoover coefficient is the normalized mean deviation from proportionality. It strictly indicates plain disproportionality only. Thus, it is the least disputable coefficient among the other coefficients described here.

It is worth repeating that the method of calculating a segregation index overcomes many problems caused by differences in the actual numbers taking and eligible for free school meals, in a way that simply presenting percentages per year does not. When calculated for both measures in those years for which both figures are available, the results are mostly in reasonably close agreement (see Table 3.1). Sometimes the index for take-up is larger, and sometimes smaller, than for eligibility. It is interesting that the largest consistent difference is between the two figures for Hammersmith and Fulham LEA (and this could be significant in the light of the results for that LEA, see below). In fact, the change in recording FSM from take-up to eligibility, if anything, is likely to have increased the apparent segregation between schools, making the overall downward trend, to be described below, even more convincing. Perhaps the most important evidence that either measure is equally useful at this level of aggregation lies in the similarity between the overall results for Wales (where only eligibility is used) and England (where take-up is used until 1993).

The analysis of changes over time is notoriously problematic, but the same method of measuring relative change in a variable whose 'raw' values are also changing is used here as in previous work in other fields by the same author (e.g. Gorard et al. 1999b). The change in segregation within an LEA between two years is defined

Table 3.1. Comparison of eligibility for FSM (and take-up)

LEA	1993	1994	1995	1996	1997	1998
Camden	18 (17)	15 (16)	16 (18)	17 (15)	17 (14)	–
Hammersmith and Fulham	20 (19)	21 (19)	23 (20)	24 (22)	27 (21)	–
Haringey	15 (15)	17 (17)	16 (16)	18 (20)	17 (16)	19 (18)
Hounslow	17 (20)	17 (18)	18 (19)	20 (21)	18 (18)	18 (20)
Islington	10 (10)	9 (9)	6 (9)	7 (11)	5 (9)	–

as the difference between the two years divided by the total for the two years (multiplied by 100 for convenience). For each area the change in segregation from 1989 to 1997 is defined as:

$$(Index97 - Index89)*100 / (Index97 + Index89)$$

Relationships between pairs of variables are calculated using Pearson's r correlations (and only results significant at the 1 per cent level are cited). The change in segregation indices over time is also used as the dependent variable in a multiple linear regression analysis (Berry and Feldman 1985), using potential explanatory variables such as appeals against placement, local diversity of schools and school closures.

Segregation between Schools since 1988

Using the proportionate methods of analysis described above, this section examines the changes in the socio-economic composition of schools over time. It concludes that, contrary to the expectations of many observers, indicators of social and educational disadvantage are now more evenly spread among schools than they were in 1988. In general, where patterns of enrolment have changed over time, the trend is towards greater social justice. Note that this is the complete opposite of what had been predicted by theorists, and what has apparently been observed by many of the researchers described in Chapter 2. Not only has segregation between schools *not* increased, it has actually decreased.

The national picture

When the analysis is applied to all secondary (11–18) schools in England using the most reliable and complete indicator of disadvantage (free school meals), segregation between schools has declined from a high of 36 per cent to around 30 per cent (Figure 3.1). The values in Figure 3.1 are calculated as the total for each school in relation to the relevant national figures for families in poverty. Segregation is higher in England (around 30 per cent) than in Wales (where it has declined from around 24 to 22 per cent). It is worth noting that the most important drops come in 1991/2 and 1992/3, *before* the change in recording from take-up to eligibility for free school meals (to which they cannot therefore be related). The graph also shows a slight temporary increase in segregation for 1990, which was also observed in Wales, and tentatively explained in terms of a policy-related 'starting-gun' effect (see below).

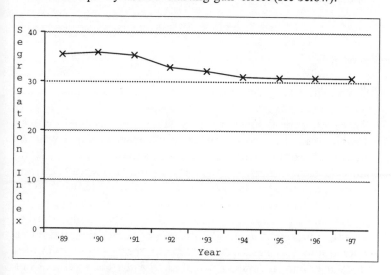

Figure 3.1. Change in FSM segregation over time in England

The changes in figures for all primary schools are almost identical to those for the secondary sector, as are the more limited figures for families from ethnic-minority backgrounds, or with a first language other than English, and students with special educational needs (see Tables 3.2, 3.3). While it is difficult to claim much about a 'trend' over as few as three years, and there are interesting variations in the actual level of segregation for each indicator, it is significant that all indicators show a decline in segregation over time. There is certainly no evidence of increasing segregation between schools on any of these indicators at a national level.

Table 3.2. Alternative indicators in all English secondary schools

Indicator	1996 Index (%)	1997 Index (%)	1998 Index (%)
SEN statement	29	28	27
English second lang.	68	67	66
Ethnicity non-white	–	15	13

Table 3.3. Alternative indicators in all English primary schools

Indicator	1996 Index (%)	1997 Index (%)	1998 Index (%)
SEN statement	39	38	36
English second lang.	70	68	68
Ethnicity non-white	–	16	15

In effect, poor families are now more evenly spread between schools than they were before 1988 when local education authorities used simply to allocate students to their neighbourhood school. In retrospect, perhaps this should not have been surprising because neighbourhoods vary so much in social terms that the previous system was often derided as 'selection by mortgage'. Families could only use a high-status school if they could afford to live in its catchment area. The process of choice may indeed be unfair to some families, but in retrospect it seems to be working out *more fairly* than the system it replaced. When the results of this study were first published (Gorard and Fitz 1998b), an attempt was made by some academics to marginalize their significance. After all, it was claimed, they were *only* about Wales, and might have no relevance to more developed and diverse 'markets' in England for example (Gorard 1998c). However, as shown above, the same method of analysis applied to all schools in England and Wales, using several indicators, reveals an interesting phenomenon. Social segregation between schools has actually decreased faster in

England than in Wales over the last ten years (Gorard and Fitz 2000b). This is not to suggest that markets are an appropriate system for public education, but that maybe the opponents of markets are wrong in one major respect. Maybe, despite a generation of sociological opposition to the notion, poor families *can* make 'wise' educational choices.

On the basis of these new findings, one interpretation is that, whatever the stratifying effects of market forces and competition may be, the effects of catchment areas and 'selection by mortgage' may have been a good deal worse. What some commentators appear to assume is that the situation was somehow *less* stratified before 1988 in England and Wales. One would only expect the introduction of schemes of choice to lead to segregation if they started from a relatively well-integrated system. They did not (Hirsch 1997). As far back as 1974 it was clear that there were wide discrepancies in students' experiences of school and the opportunities presented (Kelsall and Kelsall 1974). Explanations at that time focused more on the impact of selection, streaming and the 'elaborated code' used in all educational settings but only by some families, rather than looking at housing, transport and school choice as reasons for segregation. The picture presented in Figure 3.1 indicates a considerable degree of social segregation both before and after the impact of policies of parental choice. In other words, prior to 1988 in England and Wales, local patterns of use and preference already led to clear segregation by income and social class. When policies of choice and competition were super-imposed on this pattern of use, there was often a noticeable, but temporary, increase in the segregation index for a year or two. The figures for Lambeth and Wandsworth in London are used here as a typical example (Figure 3.2) and it should be noted how similar this graph is to those for Swansea and Rhondda Cynon Taff in Wales (Gorard and Fitz 1998b). Segregation then declines and settles at a lower level than before, as the market becomes 'established'. If some sections of society are more aware of changes in policy and more attuned to their new rights as 'consumers', one might expect that these 'alert clients' would produce a shift towards stratification in the immediate aftermath of choice reforms whatever the long-term outcomes. This is what is termed here the 'starting-gun effect'.

Although more privileged families may, at the outset, be more alert to their new rights under choice legislation, and more capable

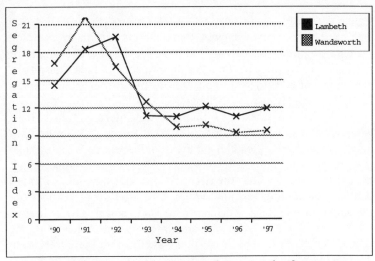

Figure 3.2. Changes in segregation between schools over time (London)

of making a choice in the short term, in the longer term choice may become more popular (Echols et al. 1990), with the poorer sections of any community eventually participating fully (Cookson 1994). In Britain this participation could involve selecting a school in a catchment area where the individual in question would be unable to afford to live, or sending a child to a fee-paying school via the now defunct Assisted Places Scheme. However well, or poorly, these schemes worked out in practice, they do at least extend to other groups rights in principle that have always been, and continue to be, available to the socio-economically privileged. It is also the case that choice policies may undermine the prevailing source of social stratification in education, namely the catchment-area system of allocating schools. That this is so is evidenced by DfEE data on the growth of appeals (see Figure 3.3). Given this growth in four years from 3.5 per cent to 6 per cent of families prepared to appeal, and the indication that this growth is set to continue, and taking into consideration the fact that appeals are only relevant to those not obtaining their first choice of school, it can be deduced that the proportion of alert clients has grown significantly since 1988. Studies made immediately after the introduction of policies to increase school choice, such as the Education Reform Act 1988,

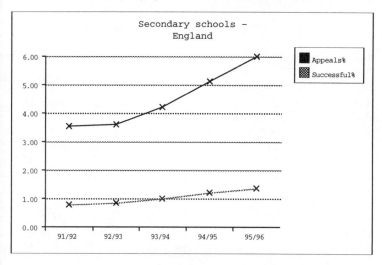

Figure 3.3. The growth of appeals over time

may, therefore, quite validly produce quite different findings from those of studies made some time later.

The regional picture

The overall pattern of reduced segregation between schools also appears in every region in England and for the increasingly separate principality of Wales. The values in Table 3.4 are calculated as the total for each secondary school in relation to the relevant regional figures for families in poverty (again the figures for the primary sector, and for other indicators, show similar declines). The greatest proportionate decreases are in Inner London, Outer London, the South East and the South West. Of these, the first three are the most densely populated regions and, therefore, perhaps the most likely to show change in a market-like situation. It would be expected that choice of school, or any other change in the policy of allocating school places, would have less impact on patterns of enrolment in rural areas with fewer candidate schools within a reasonable travelling distance of most families.

Another observation from Table 3.4 is that the absolute level of segregation is generally lower in regions like Inner London, where

Table 3.4. Regional change in FSM segregation over time

Region	1989	1990	1991	1992	1993	1994	1995	1996	1997
North East	24	24	25	23	24	23	23	22	22
North West	31	32	33	32	31	30	29	29	29
Yorkshire/ Humberside	32	33	34	32	30	30	29	29	–
East Midlands	31	32	32	30	29	28	28	28	29
West Midlands	34	35	35	34	32	31	31	32	31
Eastern	30	31	32	29	27	26	27	27	–
Inner London	–	18	19	19	16	16	16	15	15
Outer London	–	30	30	28	27	25	25	25	25
South East	34	34	34	33	32	30	30	30	30
South West	27	28	27	25	23	23	22	24	23
Wales	–	–	24	24	23	22	22	22	22

poverty is greatest, and in the North East and Wales, where the population itself is less variable in terms of class structure, income and other socio-economic indicators (Gorard 1998c). Perhaps this is a clue that segregation depends on the local variability of potential school users as much as their allocation to schools. If so, it may be important that, although the total school population of the secondary schools featured in this paper grew from 2,958,268 students in 1989 to 3,216,135 in 1997, the number of students eligible for free school meals grew from 506,066 in 1993 (the first year in which eligibility was returned by all schools) to 590,379 in 1997. At least part of the desegregation could, therefore, be due to this increase from 17 to 18 per cent of students eligible for free school meals, which represents a considerable increase in the official assessment of children from families in poverty – a form of equality of poverty perhaps. A similar relationship has been observed between inequality of income and periods of recession. Kacapyr (1996, p. 3) reported that

> the Gini coefficient for the US has been rising steadily since 1970, but it did decline slightly in 1973, 1974, 1980, 1990, and 1991 – all recession years. This is not surprising. Unequal income growth is part and parcel of economic growth. A recession means negative economic growth, so we might expect to see backpedalling in the way of less income inequality.

This could turn out to be the single most important finding of this study, forcing commentators to begin to worry less about increasing divisions between schools, and concentrate instead on the steadily increasing problem of relative poverty in society. Unfortunately, despite the most ardent claims of human capital theorists, this is not something that education by itself can do very much about (see Chapter 10).

The local picture
The overall pattern of reduced segregation between schools at both national and regional levels also appears in eighty-four of the 122 local education authorities (LEAs) in England and Wales (Tables 3.5–8). A further nine LEAs show no overall change in segregation from 1989 to 1997, and the remaining twenty-nine LEAs show some *increase* in segregation. The figures are calculated as the total for each secondary school in relation to the relevant local figures for families in poverty. Although the first forty-four LEAs showing a considerable decline in segregation contain a variety of urban and rural, English and Welsh, and large and small areas, none of the very small or sparsely populated areas appears in this list, nor do the predominantly rural counties with very large numbers of schools (such as Essex, Gloucestershire). There is an overall impression of middle-sized urban areas with relatively high population density (Table 3.5).

These LEAs are perhaps precisely the kind to contain local markets comprising a relatively large number of schools within easy reach of each family that market theorists predicted would show declining segregation in a system of choice. However, it is also the case that several of these LEAs have reduced the number of their schools as part of a reorganization to cut out spare places, and some are faced with significant numbers of families who use schools in adjacent LEAs. Both of these phenomena might reduce segregation, the first by forcing the redistribution of under-privileged students among schools, and the second by reducing variation among the families using local schools. These can only be partial explanations, since substantial reorganization for most LEAs has been a one-off event, and anyway segregation in the whole of England and Wales has declined, and this could not be due to families shuffling between LEAs since all cases are involved in the analysis and any such decrease in one area would show up as

Table 3.5. LEAs showing marked decline in segregation, 1989 to 1997

LEA	1989	1990	1991	1992	1993	1994	1995	1996	1997	Gain %
Islington	10	15	11	11	10	9	6	7	5	−33
Southwark	14	13	12	13	9	10	7	7	7	−33
Wandsworth	18	17	22	16	13	10	10	9	9	−33
Knowsley	12	10	11	14	8	8	6	6	6	−32
Stockport	30	32	32	28	25	23	19	18	16	−30
Brent	29	27	26	26	19	17	16	15	16	−29
Waltham Forest	26	27	29	29	17	15	15	16	16	−24
Westminster	22	17	21	21	17	15	14	13	14	−22
East Sussex	27	26	23	23	21	16	18	18	18	−20
Manchester	15	16	17	17	14	11	11	9	10	−20
Wiltshire	27	27	26	22	19	19	20	19	18	−19
Cornwall	17	18	18	17	13	12	12	12	12	−18
Isle of Wight	18	17	17	16	12	11	12	13	13	−18
Rotherham	24	24	24	21	21	18	19	16	17	−18
Trafford	35	28	29	26	27	26	26	26	25	−17
Harrow	17	16	14	16	15	15	16	14	12	−16
Rochdale	24	25	20	23	20	20	18	18	18	−15
Tower Hamlets	15	17	19	18	12	12	9	9	11	−15
Swansea	35	35	33	31	30	28	26	27	26	−14
Camden	22	17	16	18	18	15	16	17	17	−13
Doncaster	24	23	25	21	18	18	18	18	18	−13
Oxfordshire	38	36	35	32	31	30	31	29	29	−13
Wrexham	14	14	14	14	14	14	14	10	11	−13
Bexley	30	28	31	27	21	21	22	22	24	−12
Cambridge	34	35	34	31	28	27	26	27	27	−12
Bedfordshire	37	38	38	35	29	28	29	29	30	−11
Hampshire	33	33	32	29	27	25	26	26	27	−11
Lambeth	15	14	18	20	11	11	10	11	12	−11
North Tyneside	25	26	30	27	21	17	18	18	20	−11
Wakefield	28	29	30	29	24	21	21	22	22	−11
Warwickshire	28	30	29	27	25	25	25	23	23	−11
Leeds	34	35	37	34	31	30	31	29	28	−10
Leicestershire	37	38	37	33	31	30	31	30	30	−10
Newham	11	12	12	13	12	11	12	10	9	−10
Northamptonshire	33	31	30	31	27	27	25	27	27	−10
Avon	29	28	27	23	23	23	24	24	24	−9
Bradford	31	31	32	31	28	26	25	26	26	−9
Richmond	19	19	18	18	20	16	17	15	16	−9
Bridgend	21	21	21	21	19	18	16	19	18	−8
Calderdale	29	30	31	31	27	30	27	27	25	−8
Croydon	27	29	28	24	27	23	24	23	23	−8
Merton	23	26	24	25	19	19	19	18	19	−8
Solihull	43	43	43	40	43	39	38	36	37	−8
West Sussex	23	23	29	26	23	21	22	20	20	−8

an equivalent increase in another. Similarly these changes could not be due to an increase in the use of fee-paying schools or schools in Scotland, since numbers of these have not increased and are anyway very small as a proportion of the school population, especially in Wales (see Gorard 1996).

The next forty LEAs also showed declines in overall segregation. Although the proportionate desegregation is less in each of these areas, there is no threshold of significance between Table 3.5 and 3.6 and in most of these authorities there are again signs of powerful social movements over time. Again, despite the variety, there is an overall similarity in this list. Most areas are suburban or relatively densely populated rural counties (Table 3.6).

There are nine LEAs showing no change in segregation after ten years. It should be noted that several of these show years in which segregation has changed from its base figure in 1989 (Table 3.7). In some cases their overall lack of change may be to do with lack of alternative schools (the Scilly Isles, with only one school, being the most extreme case) or low population density (Dyfed being the most extreme case, with an average 0.2 persons per hectare and no towns greater than 5,000 inhabitants). In other cases the reason for the lack of change is harder to find. Perhaps a reason should not be needed. Rather, a reason should be sought for why inner-city areas such as Islington or Hammersmith and Fulham (see below) have such markedly different changes in the measured segregation between their schools. One possible explanation lies in the LEA procedure for allocating contested secondary school places. In Cardiff, for example (and in many other LEAs), secondary schools have until recently operated matched 'feeder' primary schools whose leavers are guaranteed a place. The primary schools run a catchment-area system in which places at each school are allocated fairly strictly by area of residence. Therefore, the secondary schools fed by those primary schools effectively run a catchment-area system as well, thus restricting the impact of the choice policy at both primary and secondary level. Although it is clear that similar systems operate in other areas as well, further information needs to be collected about the detailed procedures in each case before a general conclusion about the impact of this hidden catchment procedure can be drawn.

Similar considerations apply to LEAs which are only prepared to fund free travel to the closest school to home, thereby reducing

Table 3.6. LEAs showing decline in segregation, 1989 to 1997

LEA	1989	1990	1991	1992	1993	1994	1995	1996	1997	Gain %
Hereford Worcester	27	25	27	30	27	25	24	24	24	−7
Lewisham	11	11	10	10	12	11	9	9	10	−7
Sefton	32	29	30	33	31	30	28	27	28	−7
St Helens	27	23	23	25	25	22	23	23	23	−7
Tameside	19	19	20	23	20	17	16	18	16	−7
Cleveland	25	26	25	24	25	22	22	22	22	−6
Lancashire	30	31	33	28	28	26	26	26	26	−6
Northumberland	30	31	29	30	30	26	27	28	27	−6
Nottinghamshire	30	29	29	28	27	26	26	25	26	−6
Redbridge	24	26	28	24	22	25	23	22	21	−6
Somerset	20	21	22	23	17	15	16	16	18	−6
Surrey	28	27	29	28	27	23	24	25	24	−6
Gloucestershire	33	33	33	32	28	28	26	28	29	−5
Hackney	11	13	13	11	8	8	10	10	10	−5
Hertfordshire	32	30	31	29	30	28	29	29	29	−5
Salford	25	25	27	27	29	24	22	22	22	−5
Sandwell	18	23	24	23	20	17	14	15	16	−5
South Tyneside	15	14	15	15	13	13	13	11	13	−5
Wigan	24	23	23	23	24	19	21	21	21	−5
Cheshire	34	34	34	33	33	31	31	30	31	−4
Coventry	20	21	21	19	20	20	20	19	19	−4
Essex	28	30	31	29	27	26	26	26	26	−4
Greenwich	13	16	14	11	10	10	10	11	12	−4
Humberside	31	30	30	29	29	29	29	28	28	−4
Birmingham	25	27	27	25	24	24	23	23	24	−3
Camarthenshire	19	19	19	19	19	19	21	20	17	−3
Norfolk	20	20	22	19	21	19	19	19	19	−3
Devon	24	26	23	23	22	22	23	23	23	−2
Hillingdon	27	23	19	22	25	25	25	26	26	−2
Liverpool	19	18	20	19	18	17	17	18	18	−2
Rhondda Cynon Taff	18	18	18	18	18	19	17	17	17	−2
Barnet	25	28	24	26	25	25	22	25	25	−1
Cardiff	35	35	35	34	36	34	34	35	34	−1
Derbyshire	26	28	29	28	26	26	26	25	25	−1
Gateshead	25	26	28	25	24	23	25	24	24	−1
Kent	30	31	32	30	30	29	29	28	30	−1
Kingston	24	23	28	26	23	23	26	24	23	−1
Merthyr Tydfil	13	13	13	15	13	12	13	13	13	−1
North Yorkshire	28	29	28	28	29	28	28	28	28	−1
Shropshire	26	27	26	28	28	27	26	26	25	−1

the possibility of choice for poorer families. In effect, these LEAs are saying to poor families, the government claims you can choose any school you like but if you choose a non-adjacent one you are left to pay for the travel. This would make it especially difficult for poor families, less able to afford travel, to escape from their local school which is, therefore, likely to over-represent students from poor families just as it would have done in the old catchment-area system before choice. Another factor inhibiting change in some areas could be the guidelines used to allocate contested places. For example, a rule that siblings of those already in school take priority, while understandable, must lead to a slight inhibition in the year-on-year socio-economic variation within a school.

Table 3.7. LEAs showing little change in segregation, 1989 to 1997

LEA	1989	1990	1991	1992	1993	1994	1995	1996	1997	Gain %
Berkshire	35	34	33	36	32	33	33	35	35	0
Clwyd	16	16	16	16	16	16	16	16	16	0
Dorset	24	25	24	24	23	23	23	23	24	0
Dyfed	15	15	15	15	15	15	16	15	15	0
Kirklees	30	33	32	30	30	28	29	28	30	0
Scilly Isles	0	0	0	0	0	0	0	0	0	0
Suffolk	24	28	27	26	22	20	22	24	23	0
Sunderland	13	14	19	15	17	16	16	16	13	0
Walsall	26	26	28	26	25	24	24	25	25	0

Of the twenty-nine LEAs showing an increase in segregation over time, many show years in which segregation declined below the 1989 figure (Table 3.8). These segregating LEAs include all types – urban and rural, English and Welsh, large and small – just like the desegregating LEAs. However, six showed very significant increases: Barking, Ealing, Hounslow, Caerphilly, Haringey, and Hammersmith and Fulham – only the last of which showed a regular year-on-year increase. It was clear from Table 3.1 that at least part of the remarkable change in Hammersmith and Fulham may be due to the change in recording of data in 1993. These six 'segregating' LEAs share some similarities to each other as 'suburban' areas of a capital city (i.e. London or Cardiff). Some LEAs, such as Bromley and Buckinghamshire, run an overtly

Table 3.8. LEAs showing increase in segregation, 1989 to 1997

LEA	1989	1990	1991	1992	1993	1994	1995	1996	1997	Gain %
Dudley	24	24	29	26	27	24	25	25	25	1
Lincolnshire	30	32	31	30	31	29	29	30	30	1
Staffordshire	25	26	26	26	26	25	24	25	25	1
Sutton	36	37	41	37	34	34	35	35	37	1
Buckinghamshire	41	41	39	41	44	41	41	42	43	3
Bury	20	23	25	27	27	21	22	24	21	4
Enfield	22	23	25	25	27	27	25	24	24	4
Newcastle upon Tyne	21	23	23	23	23	22	22	21	23	4
Pembroke	13	18	15	15	15	15	15	16	14	4
Sheffield	24	23	24	25	24	25	26	27	26	4
Wirral	24	23	25	28	26	26	25	27	26	4
Wolverhampton	17	22	18	20	17	19	17	17	18	4
Bromley	29	37	37	33	30	31	31	32	32	5
Neath Port Talbot	12	12	15	14	12	14	15	12	13	5
Barnsley	17	20	20	19	18	19	21	18	19	6
Oldham	28	31	32	35	31	29	30	30	31	6
Flintshire	17	17	17	17	17	18	18	19	19	7
Havering	26	30	30	32	31	30	33	31	30	7
Cumbria	24	28	27	29	30	30	29	27	28	8
Durham	17	18	19	18	19	19	20	19	20	8
Bolton	27	28	30	26	28	29	29	30	32	9
Conwy	14	14	14	14	14	14	14	16	16	9
Barking	9	19	12	8	11	9	8	8	12	11
Ealing	14	13	12	11	11	11	12	13	17	12
Kensington	15	18	20	25	25	16	18	17	19	12
Hounslow	14	18	16	19	17	17	18	20	18	13
Caerphilly	9	8	8	9	10	9	10	10	12	14
Haringey	13	9	15	20	15	17	16	18	17	15
Hammersmith	13	16	17	19	20	21	23	24	27	35

selective system of grammar schools, while others, such as Haringey, are deeply affected by the policy of GM schools. These factors may explain part of their difference from the majority of the 122 LEAs in this analysis.

In fact, further analysis reveals an interesting relationship between policies of selection and changes in segregation. Figure 3.4 shows this pattern for the secondary schools in LEAs in England, comparing the change in segregation from 1989 to 1998 with the percentage of selective schools in each LEA in 1991. Very similar

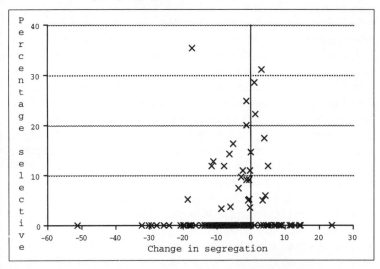

Figure 3.4. Change in segregation by percentage selective schools in 1991

patterns emerge when segregation is plotted against the proportion of grant-maintained and fee-paying schools as well, and for the cumulated proportion of all non-comprehensive schools. In general, areas with a large number of grammar schools show little change in segregation, and areas with large changes have no grammar schools. It may be that the element of selection inherent in a system with more diversity is inhibiting changes in the distribution of intakes that are occurring in other areas. If so, this finding suggests a lack of relationship between desegregation and markets, as they are usually envisaged by their advocates with essential elements of both choice *and* diversity. Market theorists may have expected areas with a greater diversity of schools to show the greatest changes in patterns of enrolment. This is clearly not so. In fact, it is the areas primarily populated by notionally equivalent LEA-controlled comprehensives that have shown the greatest changes (in either direction).

The large variations between LEAs reinforce the importance of considering regional differences in the sociology of education (Rees et al. 1997), and highlights the danger of attempting to generalize from a small-scale study using only one or two LEAs (as has been attempted many times, see Chapter 2). An analyst working in only one LEA, for example, may select one of the London or Metropolitan boroughs from Table 3.8 and, despite including the necessary caveats in his or her reporting, may lead readers to believe that a national picture can, therefore, be deduced.

In the original six LEAs used for the study in Wales (Gorard and Fitz 1998b), it was possible to use detailed local knowledge to group the schools into districts within LEAs. Analysed at the district level, the same picture of overall desegregation with minor variations was obtained. It is, therefore, worth noting here that this is further evidence that the specific level of aggregation used in any analysis does not obscure variations at any other level. For example, it would be impossible for desegregation at LEA level to be due solely to cross-border movements between adjacent LEAs in London, since this would show up at the regional level. It would, for the same reason, be impossible for segregation to increase at a sub-LEA level and not show up at a higher level of aggregation unless balanced by a superior and opposite process of desegregation elsewhere. Therefore, suggestions, such as those of Gibson and Asthana (1999), that segregation is actually increasing at one level of analysis while decreasing at another, are necessarily incomplete until they can explain how such an apparent paradox can be resolved.

There is no intention here to dispute the notion that schools operating in a performance-led market may indeed feel compelled to 'privilege the academic', thereby marginalizing the interests of students with special educational needs (SEN) and their parents (Bagley and Woods 1998). Nevertheless, the fact remains that, where the appropriate figures have been analysed at a local level, they show, like those for FSM, that the spread of SEN is becoming more even across schools. Indeed, unlike other measures of educational disadvantage such as family poverty, this decrease in stratification is not apparently related to any overall increase in the number of statemented children in secondary schools. For example, although in Bolton LEA statements of special educational need increased from a total of 213 in 1994 to 473 in 1997, in Cornwall they declined from 2,515 to 1,497, while in Wrexham they remained steady, increasing only from 365 to 368. Despite these differences all three exemplar LEAs experienced desegregation over time (see Table 3.9).

A very similar pattern emerges from the limited analyses available at a local level using primary schools. Segregation

Table 3.9. *SEN segregation index (secondary), 1994–1997*

LEA	1994	1995	1996	1997
Bolton	25	25	20	20
Cornwall	22	22	11	12
Wrexham	–	17	16	14

Table 3.10. *FSM segregation index (primary schools), 1994–1997*

LEA	1994	1995	1996	1997
Hounslow	19	16	17	15

between schools in terms of families in poverty is decreasing over time (see for example Table 3.10).

The school-level picture

In trying to decide what is producing the overall desegregation and its local variations, perhaps the first step should be to look at the history of individual schools. Do some LEAs display 'polarization' whereby most schools are moving towards a more equal share of FSM students, while one or two schools are becoming 'sink' institutions, taking the surplus students from a disadvantaged background? In fact, this possibility is already catered for by the method. The figures are calculated as the total for each secondary school in relation to the relevant local figures for families in poverty. The number of schools moving away from the 'ideal' of a proportionate share of children from poor families and the size of that movement are directly related to the segregation index for their LEA. For example, Haringey has nine schools which collectively show an increase in segregation from 13 to 19 per cent. It should, therefore, be no surprise to discover that seven of these schools are further from an equal share of FSM, while only two are closer (Table 3.11). However, it is also clear, as it was in the detailed analysis of six LEAs from Wales, that no school has become anything like a 'sink' school in a spiral of decline over the ten years. In fact, the most disadvantaged school in 1989 (school

B), which was the closest to a sink school in 1989, is the school showing the largest shift towards an even share of FSM students. Similarly, the school showing the next largest shift towards desegregation (school A) was initially the second most segregated.

Table 3.11. Changes in segregation ratio for each school in Haringey

Haringey	A	B	C	D	E	F	G	H	I
1989	1.42	2.18	0.41	0.93	1.01	1.01	0.90	0.85	0.88
1997	1.37	1.47	0.27	0.71	0.73	1.46	1.25	0.84	1.32

In Islington, on the other hand, with the same number of schools as Haringey but an overall drop in segregation from 15 to 5 per cent, only one school (I) moves away from an equal share of FSM (and this is a voluntary-aided school moving towards a decreasing share of disadvantage). The other eight all move closer to parity in terms of segregation (Table 3.12). As in Haringey, the most disadvantaged school in 1990 (F) shows the largest shift towards an even share of FSM students, matched by an equal and opposite shift by the most advantaged school (C), which starts with nearly half of its fair share of FSM students and now takes slightly more than its fair share. In every LEA that has been examined in detail so far a similar picture emerges. As with England and Wales over all, and the regions and LEAs within them, the schools themselves are generally moving towards an even spread of FSM students, and there are few absolute 'losers' in this process. As already stated, if polarization between schools had occurred it *would* be picked up by this form of analysis at the school level.

Table 3.12. Changes in segregation ratio for each school in Islington

Islington	A	B	C	D	E	F	G	H	I
1990	0.80	0.69	0.56	0.93	0.81	1.72	1.49	1.17	1.13
1997	0.94	1.12	1.08	0.96	1.10	1.10	0.96	0.98	0.76

The Implications of a Proportionate Analysis

Once accepted, the implications of the foregoing analysis are significant. The segregation indices at national, regional, local district or school level can be used as very valuable information about the context of performance in education. It is only by understanding the socio-economic characteristics of schools and their intakes that one can begin to measure school performance in any meaningful way, or to make comparisons between schools (see Chapter 7). The measures of segregation used here have already proved more powerful in predicting school outcomes than some standard measures of context used in school effectiveness research.

What is Driving this Process?

One key potential explanation for the socio-economic desegregation of schools since 1988 could be the concurrent increase in parental choice. It may be that programmes of choice, by ending 'selection by mortgage', have allowed poor families greater access to desirable schools. It has been suggested earlier that the 'starting-gun' effect could be caused by slowly increasing awareness of consumer rights among poorer families, resulting in an enormous increase in appeals against allocation of a non-choice secondary school. A recent DfEE report suggested that appeals related to secondary-school places in England were increasing by 15 per cent per year (Dean and Rafferty 1999). One might expect the pattern of changes in segregation in any area to be related to the proportion of parents prepared to appeal. Appeals are being used here as an indicator of competitiveness in the local market in which they occur, and of the proportion of 'alert' families willing and able to appeal (Willms and Echols 1992). If the changes noted above are related to market forces, then the changes should perhaps be greater in areas where a higher proportion of parents go to appeal. In fact, this is not so (see Figure 3.5). There is no significant relationship between appeals per LEA in 1994/5 and desegregation, and no clear pattern in the graph. One of the LEAs with the largest decline in segregation had zero appeals (Knowsley), while the LEA with the largest proportion of appeals had an increase in segregation close to zero (Enfield). All of this suggests that there is

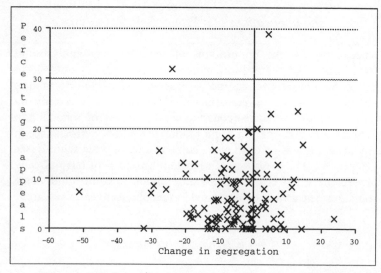

Figure 3.5. Relationship between appeals and desegregation

no positive relationship between the observed changes in segregation and the level of competition for places in schools. Coupled
with the findings described earlier about the relationship between
diversity of school provision and changes in segregation, this must
cast considerable doubt on whether the powerful social movements
described here have anything to do with the action of markets. It
also suggests that, despite prevailing opinion in educational
research, at least some poor families *can* make 'wise' educational
choices.

Although the method of analysis used in this chapter overcomes
differences in the raw figures for FSM in each region, it may be
that the changes in segregation are linked to differences in socio-
economic structure between areas and over time. This is backed up
by the strong link between the level of segregation, its change over
ten years, and the initial percentage FSM figure for each LEA.
Areas with a higher proportion of pupils taking FSM tend to have
lower levels of segregation (-0.54), and to show a greater
proportionate drop in segregation over time (-0.27). This is
interesting because it is contrary to the initial misconception that
segregation would be worse in areas with high levels of poverty. It
is also noteworthy that, despite the overall lack of relationship

between appeals and desegregation, appeals are slightly more common in areas with higher proportions of FSM (+0.25). This is also contrary to preconceptions which would assume that areas with higher levels of poverty would have fewer families prepared to appeal. Another way of reading the same data would be that areas with highly polarized family incomes are generating more appeals in a system of choice based on league-table indicators.

Simpson's Paradox

The possibility that students are becoming more polarized within institutions, even though the schools themselves are becoming more mixed, is discussed in Chapter 9. The possibility raised here is that the indicators used are not sensitive enough to distinguish the segregation that must surely be taking place between schools (according to the crisis account). Having been surprised that schools are becoming less segregated by poverty, class, ethnicity, first language and special need, some crisis commentators now posit a set of differences that lie beneath the surface of these grosser indicators. Elmore and Fuller (1996), like Willms and Echols (1992) before them, present evidence that choosers (those who do not accept allocation to their nearest school) differ systematically from non-choosers. A common observation is that single mothers from poor families in voucher schemes in the USA or the (defunct) Assisted Places Scheme in Britain were more frequently better educated than mothers in equivalently poor families not using the schemes. A potential explanation is that they are part of a growing 'artificially poor' (Edwards et al. 1989), who have become single through death or divorce. Even if this were true, and it may well be, this does not have to lead to segregation (unless it is a more stratifying process than that of school allocation by residence). In support of their notion of segregation by stealth, both Elmore and Fuller (1996) and Witte (1998) cite secondary evidence from Wells (1996). This claim has had a large impact and has spread through the research literature as a social science fact. It is, therefore, of some interest to consider the nature of this evidence.

Wells refers to the results of an apparently large study by Lissitz, but this study is unpublished and is, therefore, not open to scrutiny. Her own primary evidence is based on thirty-seven children (and the parents of some of these), and she compared the characteristics for families of Black students choosing to stay in a local city school, transfer to a school in the suburbs, or transfer but then either return to the city school or drop out. She concludes, for example, that 'city students who stay behind in the urban schools . . . tend to be more disadvantaged in terms of parental education and employment than the transfer students'. Her evidence for this statement in respect of parental employment is reproduced below (Table 3.13). The first noticeable thing is that by ignoring the drop-out and returnees, Wells now has only twenty-four cases on which to base her findings. The main figures in the table are those observed, while the figures in brackets are the expected values for each cell using the standard method for a cross-tabulation (see Siegel 1956). For example, if the proportion of families in employment and the proportions using each type of school are held constant as observed, she would expect 9.5 parents of those in city schools to be employed. She actually observed eight. The difference is not significant, either statistically or in any other sense of the word. Yet this is the primary data on which the notion of sub-indicator polarization rests.

Table 3.13. Parents of city and transfer students

	City	Transfer
Parents unemployed	4 (2.5)	1 (2.5)
Parents employed	8 (9.5)	11 (9.5)

Source: Wells 1996, p. 87.

Conclusions

If it has been true until recently that 'the debate over school choice is rich in rhetoric but dismally poor when it comes to hard evidence' (Fuller et al. 1996, p. 11), then it is true no longer. Having considered changes over ten years in all of the state-funded schools in England and Wales, in terms of their student intake as assessed by four different measures of socio-economic disadvantage at five different levels of aggregation, it is clear that segregation between schools has not increased as a result of marketization. In fact, the intake to schools is now significantly more socially mixed than in 1989, in the sense that each school is now generally a better reflection of the society from which it recruits (except in regions with a high proportion of selective schools). The changes in school enrolment observed in previous small-scale studies would seem to be partly explicable in terms of changes in society rather than changes in school admissions, and the chief problem for previous studies has generally been the lack of a proportionate analysis. School choice led to a small temporary increase in segregation, which soon disappeared. There is little evidence here that this ongoing desegregation by poverty, language, need and ethnicity is otherwise related to the introduction of the limited market for schools. In time, markets may be found to have much less impact on education systems than is popularly believed (see Levin and Riffel 1997). The success or failure of a market policy may depend not so much on the nature of the policy itself as on the nature and scale of socio-economic segregation in the system that it replaces. In Britain the advent of choice may be truly both less beneficial than some advocates suggest and less harmful than some critics fear.

In themselves, market forces in education do not appear either to segregate or to desegregate, although it should be stressed that the evidence presented here focuses on changes in the distribution of the least advantaged sections of society (and it remains possible that different processes are at work among wealthier or more privileged families). Despite the relative lack of solid research concerning the impact of markets in education, there is general agreement that the specific nature of any choice programme is part of what determines its results (Weiss 1996). Their actual impact may also depend significantly on the status ante. In an education system which is totally segregated, as happened in South Africa in terms of ethnicity under the apartheid regime (MacGregor 1999), opening the possibility of choice can lead to rapid desegregation. In an education system committed to desegregation, as happened with the US busing policy in some states, the change to a system of choice can lead to rapid segregation (compare also the 'white flight' in the Netherlands). Britain in the 1980s, on the other hand, had a comprehensive system of schooling but one in which places at school were allocated strictly by area of residence. The student intake at comprehensive schools reflected the nature of the local housing, and there were consequently wide variations between schools. In a society of the form envisaged on a small scale at Poundbury in Dorset, in which different types and costs of houses are mixed in small communities, then a policy of residential allocation to school *could* lead to mixed intakes in socio-economic terms. Britain is not such a society, and the relatively stratified nature of its schooling is at least partly a consequence of the relatively stratified nature of its housing. It is, therefore, likely that socio-economic changes are more significant in producing changes in segregation than educational processes are. This theme is returned to in Chapter 10.

An intriguing possibility is that one of the actual determinants of residential segregation has actually been its implications for school-based segregation. Although the intake to schools is clearly linked to the nature of nearby residences, the desirability of residences is partly measured by the nature of the intake to the nearby school. Any estate agent in Britain would attest to this. If this catchment area link has been weakened, even slightly, by a programme of choice, then perhaps residential segregation will also decline over time, creating a circle of integrating forces. This is what Taeuber et al. (1981) describe as the 'Belfast' model. Using a proportionate index of dissimilarity equivalent to the segregation index used here, Taeuber et al. found some evidence that residential segregation by ethnicity declined in Kentucky following the increasing integration of schools.

4

School Effects and International Comparisons

Schools and students in Britain have been compared unfavourably with those elsewhere for many years now. International comparisons of school effectiveness and outcomes suggest that British schools are underperforming, and consequently that British students are underachieving. This has led to repeated calls by researchers and politicians for policy-borrowing from countries with more 'successful' educational systems. In the same way, the growth of 'home international' comparisons has suggested marked differences between the increasingly devolved regions within Britain. Examinations results in regions such as Wales are generally poorer than in England, for example, and so schools in Wales are seen as 'failing'. This view of the relative ineffectiveness of schools in Wales has permeated official publications and regional attainment targets in the 1990s. The next two chapters consider some of the findings and problems in studies involving international comparisons, and conclude that, viewed proportionately and in the light of background factors, there is little evidence of either failing or falling standards in England or Wales.

Failing and Falling Standards in England and Wales?

The view that schools in England and Wales are underperforming was introduced in Chapter 1. Despite ever-increasing government expenditure on education, longer and longer initial schooling, and lower pupil–teacher ratios, standards of literacy among school leavers have not improved, and may even have fallen, since 1944 according to some influential observers (e.g. Boyson 1975). Stories about poor educational performance in Britain with its long tail of underachievement are not new, and the evidence has often been presented before (e.g. Postlethwaite 1985; IEA 1988). Reading standards among seven- and eight-year-olds were found to have dropped in the 1980s, just as the number skills among eleven- to fifteen-year-olds deteriorated (National Commission on Education 1993). However, the crisis appears to have peaked in the 1990s. In a speech at the Lord Mayor's banquet at the Guildhall in London in 1993, the then Prime Minister, John Major, said 'Let me give you just one example. In arithmetic, 13-year-olds were asked to multiply 9.2 by 2.5. In Korea and Taiwan 70% got it right, in Western Europe 55%, in England 13%.' According to the director general of the CBI, the UK was ranked twenty-second out of twenty-two in an international comparison on the ability of its education system to meet the needs of international competition in the 1990s (Corbett 1993).

A survey of 500 headteachers found that standards of literacy (among primary-school leavers) were still falling in 1991 (Phillips 1996, p. 4), while

> a core of about 20% of 7-year-olds have failed to reach the standard for their age since the first of these tests . . . was held in 1991 . . . [and] the first tests for 11-year-olds held in 1995 revealed that more than half were not up to scratch.

Among school leavers, 'the UK . . . lags behind many of its European and international competitors' (ETAG 1998, p. 11). For example, at age sixteen the percentage gaining a GCSE grade C+ (or equivalent) in mathematics, a science and the national language was 27 per cent in England in 1991. In Japan the corresponding figure was 50 per cent, in Germany 62 per cent and in France 66 per cent (Phillips 1996). By the age of eighteen a comparable qualification was attained by 29 per cent in England, 48 per cent in France, 68 per cent in Germany and 80 per cent in Japan (National Commission on Education 1993). In the population as a whole, only 45 per cent of those in the UK have attained the equivalent of National Vocational Qualification (NVQ) level 2, whereas in France the figure is 65 per cent and in Germany 70 per cent (ETAG 1998).

A series of international comparisons over twenty years, some based on examination outcomes and some on purpose-designed tests, have confirmed these relatively poor figures from British (primarily English) students. The comparisons tend to concentrate on the subjects of mathematics and science in which it is seen as

Table 4.1. *Performance of the top twenty-three countries in TIMSS*

Country	Mathematics score
Singapore	643
Korea	607
Japan	605
Hong Kong	588
Belgium	565
Czechoslovakia	564
Slovenia	547
Switzerland	545
France	538
Hungary	537
Russia	535
Ireland	527
Canada	527
Sweden	519
New Zealand	508
England	506
Norway	503
USA	500
Latvia	493
Spain	487
Iceland	487
Lithuania	477
Cyprus	474

easier to overcome the difficulties of 'common currencies', since of all school subjects they have the fewest cultural influences, according to Reynolds and Farrell (1996) and others. In a review of these international comparisons, Reynolds and Farrell claim that the use of standardized attainment tests in all participating countries solves the 'common currency' problem. Of course, any differences could have non-educational reasons and the difficulty for any research in this area lies chiefly in separating out the impact of educational and socio-economic determinants of academic performance (see below). Nevertheless, Reynolds and Farrell claim that, as there are no *known* non-educational causes of differential attainment in mathematics and science, 'it is clear, then, that the educational systems of different societies are key factors in determining their educational attainment' (1996, p. 52). It is therefore noteworthy that, in all the studies reviewed, the attainment of students from England (and Wales in some studies) was poor over all. In addition this attainment has been getting worse relative to other countries since the 1960s. Student performance in England is generally of greater variability than in most countries, with a few very good scores and a lot of very poor ones. This is despite a longer experience of compulsory school than average, and a low response rate from England which is liable to lead commentators to over-estimate the scores. 'It would in our view need rather more than the above list of caveats to persuade one that the English performance is anything other than poor' (Reynolds and Farrell 1996, p. 53). It is on the basis of this conclusion that the report continues to examine potential reasons for this poor national performance, and to suggest models for improvement based on the classroom practice of more 'successful' countries from the Pacific Rim as evidenced by the Third International Maths and Science Survey (TIMSS) (see Table 4.1). The report gained wide publicity and media attention, and has led to significant changes of policy and practice, especially for trainee teachers.

Failure in Wales?

Given the above evidence, schools and students in Wales are in the unenviable position of facing unfavourable comparisons even with England. Although education in England is seen by many commentators as poor and possibly getting worse over time, the situation in Wales is clearly even worse than that. On almost any indicator of educational attainment or participation, the students of Wales lag behind those of England (and even within England there are reports of a 'growing gulf' between the achievements of different regions: *TES* 1999c; Russell 1999).

In a seminal piece of work for schools in Wales, Bellin et al. reviewed the indicators of school 'performance' and examined the practice of schools in Wales, to conclude that the system in Wales is 'both ineffective, as indicated by its high failure rates, and very traditional in its ethos' (1994, p. 6). Whereas, for example, students in Wales then gained an average fourteen A-level points per candidate, in England the figure is sixteen points. In their study,

Bellin et al. compare five schools in the Forest of Dean in Gloucestershire with five schools from similarly deprived catchment areas in south Wales. The English schools gained 42, 38, 36, 34 and 32 per cent GCSE benchmark scores (proportion of students gaining 5+ GCSEs A*–C). The five Welsh schools gained 27, 26, 24, 22 and 19 per cent respectively. Clearly the schools in Wales have scores a long way below 'equivalent' schools in England, which is why the authors concluded that children in Wales are 'schooled for failure' (a phrase originally used in the *TES* in 1981). They go on to suggest that 'it is difficult to avoid the conclusion that things are done to develop the attainment of pupils in the English schools that are not done in schools in Wales' (Bellin et al. 1994, p. 7). Therefore, the findings have not only fed into the creation of ambitious targets for school improvement in Wales, but they have also been used to justify the proposed policies for achieving that improvement. In a sense, a common strand to this chapter and Chapter 6 is presented by the work of Reynolds, who took part in the international comparisons used to justify policy-borrowing for England from the Pacific Rim, the work used to justify policy-borrowing for Wales from schools in England and the comparison between types of schools within Wales used to justify policy-borrowing for LEA comprehensives from Welsh-speaking schools. In a sense, the majority of schools in Wales (local comprehensives) are, therefore, at the bottom of a very long pecking order of borrowing from their 'superior' performing neighbours.

It has been shown elsewhere how the notion that schools in England are outperforming those in Wales is a seductive one (Gorard 1998d). As early as 1974, reports suggested that schools, or students, in Wales were underperforming to some extent. A national survey of non-attendance at school found the situation in Wales much worse than in England, even in areas with similar socio-economic disadvantages (Reynolds 1995), but particularly in urban areas like Merthyr Tydfil and Cardiff in the 1980s (Reynolds 1990a). The 1981 Loosemore report found that Welsh schools seemed overly concerned with the most able children, and that consequently too many of the others were leaving school with no qualifications at all. In 1977/8, 28 per cent of students left school in Wales without any qualification (Jones 1990). This 'failure' rate has always been higher than in England. Even by 1989, when only 9.5 per cent of children in England left school with no qualifications, and this figure was decreasing every year, the figure for Wales was 17 per cent, twice the size (Reynolds 1995). The introduction of league tables of GCSE examination results since 1993 has shown a similar picture, with Welsh schools producing significantly lower scores than English ones (*TES* 1993, 1994, 1995, 1996). The proportion of children leaving schools with no qualifications is higher in Wales than in England, while the proportion of children with 5+ GCSEs at grades A–C is lower (see Table 4.2).

Table 4.2. School leavers in Wales and UK by highest exam results, 1991/2

Indicator	UK %	Wales %
2+ A level	24.9	21.3
5+ GCSE	15.2	13.6
No graded passes	6.3	12.4

Source: Istance and Rees 1994.

Fewer gain the qualifications, two or more A levels, that will allow them direct continuation to academic higher education (Istance and Rees 1994). According to Her Majesty's Inspectorate the relative lack of achievement in Welsh schools is not only manifested in examination results, but also in the quality of day-to-day lessons (OHMCI 1993). The same report concludes that 'in Wales overall . . . much under-achievement remains' (OHMCI 1993, p. 2) and Reynolds (1990a) decided that Welsh children are, in some respects, 'schooled to fail'.

The Wales effect is generally based upon raw-score comparisons (Jones 1996), or raw-score comparisons with some attempt to argue a match between the comparison groups (Reynolds 1990). For example, as an indication that local prosperity plays little part in outcomes, it was argued that, while South Glamorgan LEA had the second highest rate of students leaving with no qualifications in Wales (18.6 per cent), it was an area of relative affluence. This prevailing view is reinforced by the relatively low level of qualification among the working population in Wales (Eurostat 1995), which is reflected in the Welsh performance in terms of

National Training and Education Targets (Delamont and Rees 1997). One suggested reason for the high 'failure' rate in Wales is that the examinations taken are of a higher standard, so that the WJEC papers are not comparable to those of the English examination groups. However, Reynolds (1990a) also found that Welsh secondary pupils performed worse than their peers in England on standardized tests given by the Assessment and Performance Unit. On almost any score of educational achievement that can be devised, it seems that the results in Wales are inferior to those in England (see Tables 4.3 and 4.4, for example), and these comparisons have had real implications for local educational policies.

Table 4.3. Relative progress towards Foundation Target 1

% 5+ GCSEs A*–C	Spring 1991 %	Autumn 1995 %
England	53.5	67.4
Wales	51.2	62.2

Source: Istance and Rees 1994.

Table 4.4. Percentage of working-age population in job-related training, 1992

South East England	10.8
North England	9.9
Scotland	9.3
Wales	8.6

Source: Istance and Rees 1994.

The Wales 'effect' has been used by school-effectiveness researchers to demonstrate the importance of what happens in schools in determining results (Reynolds 1995), and by politicians as a spur for regional school improvement (Welsh Office 1995a). This negative view of the effectiveness of schools in Wales as identified by academics was taken up by policy-makers in the previous government who made it the cornerstone of their improvement strategy and targets (Welsh Office 1995a, 1995b,

1996a, 1997a). When alternative evidence contradicting the consensus was presented to them, the Conservatives continued to defend the usefulness of their raw-score comparisons (*Western Mail* 1997a). Interestingly, the then Labour education spokesman for Wales claimed that he never had and never would make such 'unfavourable' comparisons with England. However, in the new administration of which he is a part, raw-score comparisons with England remain the 'research' basis for government policy-making in Wales. They underlie the important message of the White Paper put before Parliament called *Building Excellent Schools Together*, which states that 'standards of achievement are still far too low, progress in raising them far too slow' (Welsh Office 1997b, p. 2). This is justified by statements such as 'results at GCSE A*–C lag behind those in England . . . 11% of pupils leave school without GCSEs, where 8% do so in England' (p. 3). Underachievement in Wales continues to be the basis for educational policy for the National Assembly, backed up by findings such that 'Wales lags behind the rest of the UK in terms of the level of qualifications in the workforce' (ETAG 1998, p. 11). The new government is supported in this position by the same media who had declared in April 1997 that the 'England–Wales gap does not exist', saying in December that the gap (presumably rediscovered) is now 'closing' (*Western Mail* 1997a, 1997b; see also *TES* 1997a).

In summary there can be little doubt that, despite shifts and changes from year to year, almost any educational indicator shows schools in Wales in a weaker position than those in England. School attendance figures, assessments from Key Stage 1 to A level and GNVQ, progress towards Lifetime Targets and rates of participation in post-compulsory education and training all tend to show Wales in a worse light. So clear are these differences that all political parties for the past twenty years have adopted policies based on the premise that Wales faces a problem of 'underachievement', in just the same way that they have read international comparisons to show that British education leads to chronic underachievement.

Falling Standards?

The issue of judging standards over time is a difficult one to investigate without having a close definition of the term 'standard'.

As an illustration of how elastic the term can be, consider the very real situation in which an educational attainment indicator such as an A level becomes more common over a period of ten years. One group of politicians may claim that standards have therefore improved demonstrably, as more students now attain the A-level standard. Their opponents may claim that standards have fallen, since the A level is now demonstrably easier to obtain and also worth less in exchange. A similar example was outlined above where the mathematical ability of university students, who had achieved the same grade at A level, was seen to have declined (Kitchen 1999). However, on closer inspection the changes could be interpreted as related to concurrent changes in the policy of university recruitment, and changes in the relative popularity of courses.

The point to be made here is that knowledge is not a static commodity, and comparisons of changes over time in school attainment have to try and take these changes into account. One analogy for the complaint by the National Commission on Education (1993) that number skills have deteriorated for eleven- to fifteen-year-olds would be the clear drop over the last millennium in archery standards among the general population. Nuttall used the example of the word 'mannequin' to make the same point. If the number of children knowing the meaning of this word drops from 1950s to the 1970s, is this evidence of some kind of decline in schooling? Perhaps it is simply evidence that words and number skills have changed in their everyday relevance. On the other hand, if the items in any test are changed to reflect these changes in society, then how do we know that the test is of the same level of difficulty as its predecessor? In public examinations, by and large, we have until now relied on norm-referencing. That is, two tests are declared equivalent in difficulty if the same proportion of matched candidates obtain each graded result on both tests. The assumption is made that actual standards of each annual cohort are equivalent, and it is these that are used to benchmark the assessment. How then can we measure changes in standards over time? But, if the test is not norm-referenced, how can we tell that apparent changes over time are not simply evidence of differentially demanding tests? This apparently insuperable problem has, to my mind, not been adequately addressed by crisis commentators.

It has been claimed that the level of attainment required to gain level 4 at Key Stage 2 has fallen over time. The evidence for this is that, whereas students needed 52 per cent to gain level 4 English in 1997, the corresponding figures for 1998 and 1999 were 51 and 47 per cent (Cassidy 1999a). The response from the Qualifications and Curriculum Authority is that percentages are bound to change over time, as the difficulty of the tests vary year on year, but that these differences are not educationally significant. A counter-response has been that the QCA deliberately reduced the threshold because David Blunkett (Secretary of State for Education) had staked his career on 80 per cent of eleven-year-olds gaining level 4 by 2002. Since in 1998 only 65 per cent of the population gained level 4, it is claimed that, while the target has been retained, the passmark has been conveniently lowered. An independent inquiry was ordered, the results of which have mainly supported the QCA position. This debate encapsulates the problems of discussing changes in assessments over time (also see below).

When serious attempts have been made to compare standards of attainment over time, and taking into account all of the above caveats, the results are generally that standards are *not* falling. In some cases there is no firm evidence of change, and in others there are improvements over time. For example, an analysis of successive GCSE cohorts from 1994 to 1996 found a significant improvement in performance over time (Schagen and Morrison 1998). It is possible to question the reality of this improvement in strict criterion-referenced terms, but there is at any rate no evidence of any decline, and some suggestion that things are getting better.

Problems of Assessment

This brief section indicates a few of the common problems faced by researchers when judging the reliability and validity of formal school assessments. Since the majority of publicly available (rather than anecdotal) evidence cited for the crisis account of British schooling is of this form, it is important at least to glance behind the façade of objective rigorous testing procedures and thus consider for the remainder of this book the possibility that any sets of figures will be based at least in part on subjective judgements, or error components, or worse. For the purpose of the present chapter, the following question has to be asked: if assessments are not totally reliable, then how can one attribute the differences between countries to real educational differences? Put simply, the size of the differences between countries would have to be larger than the variation in the results for each country which is attributable to these errors for them to be even considered as potential evidence of real educational differences.

Britain may be unique among the countries in Table 4.1 in using different regional authorities (local examination boards) to examine what are meant to be national assessments at 16+ and 18+ (Noah and Eckstein 1992). This raises an issue of whether the same qualification is equivalent between these boards in terms of difficulty. It is already clear that even qualifications with the same name (e.g. GCSE history) are not equivalent in terms of subject content as each board sets its own syllabus. Nor are they equivalent in the form of assessment, or the weighting between components such as coursework and multiple-choice. Nor is there any evidence that the different subjects added together to form aggregate benchmarks are equivalent in difficulty to each other, yet the standard GCSE benchmark of percentage gaining five good GCSE passes gives the same value to an A* in music, a B in physics, and a C grade in sociology. Nor is there evidence that qualifications with the same name are equally difficult from year to year. In fact, comparability can be considered between boards in any subject, the years in a subject/board combination, the subjects in one board and the alternative syllabuses in any board and subject. All of these are very difficult to determine, especially as exams are neither accurate nor particularly reliable in what they measure (Nuttall 1979). Pencil-and-paper tests have little generalizable validity, and their link to other measures such as occupational competence is also generally very small (Nuttall 1987).

The supposedly national system of statutory assessment is producing a flood of complaints about irregularities and inconsistencies. I have come across examples from local schools in the last set of tests where class teachers, and sometimes even head teachers, reveal the tests beforehand to their students. In one school two classes took a SAT test simultaneously. One assessment took place in one and a half hours of strict silence. The other assessment took all morning, and the teacher was heard to give clues by standing over a child and saying 'you may need to get your rubber out for that one'. How can the ensuing results be considered comparable even though they are from the same school?

Some heads condemned the marking system for national tests after it was claimed that scripts had been lost and test scores added up incorrectly. One school checked the results after return to them and found nine errors in adding up the marks in sixty Key Stage 3 mathematics scripts (Cassidy 1999b). According to some English teachers, students taking 1999's tests in English for thirteen- to fourteen-year-olds would have needed a reading age of sixteen (Cassidy 1999c). Of course, claims such as these have not been substantiated by the kind of rigorous data analysis advocated in this book (and used by Nuttall above), but the fact that they are even possibilities does help to lift some of the façade of rigorous reliability of examination processes. The fact is that even the narrow version of propositional knowledge tested by examinations is very difficult to assess. There is general confusion between the uses of examinations for formative, summative and target purposes (Holt 1981; Daugherty 1995). In a letter to *The Times* in 1976, Nuttall says 'The message is clear: examination standards do not necessarily tell us anything about educational standards.'

The Difficulties of International Comparisons

This section begins to examine some of the more specific methodological difficulties in carrying out international comparisons of educational systems and their outcomes, and concludes that, even for the different regions of Britain, such comparisons are fraught with problems. In this way, the scene is set for the next chapter which presents an entirely different interpretation of existing comparative data.

Much of the so-called evidence which has been used to show that standards in Britain are falling, or that they are poor in international terms, can be dealt with very quickly. Much is hearsay, misinterpretation or 'academic Chinese whispers' (from Tooley and Darby 1998). For example, when describing the early results of the SATs at Key Stages 1 and 2, Phillips (1996) deplores the fact that many children failed to reach the standard in assessment that was expected for their age (see above). There have, of course, been disputes about the precise meaning of SAT results, but the reader can consider two possibilities to see how absurd Phillips's complaints could be. If the 'standard for their age' is the minimum level that seven- (or eleven-) year-olds should reach, and in the first years of testing too many children did not reach that level, then who is to blame? The children or the target-setters? How is it possible to define a minimum standard for an age group without consideration of the *actual* standard of the age group? On what basis was the test calibrated? On the other hand, if the 'standard for their age' is an average figure, then a large number of children might be expected to achieve a lower grade, and an equal and opposite number might be expected to achieve a higher grade. The complaint is similar to those described by Huff (1991), where anxious parents worry that their child is not talking by the time of the average age for starting to talk. As Huff points out, around half of all parents should expect to be in this situation. It is what average means in this context.

There are also examples of what Huff calls the 'missing comparator'. Both the *TES* and Russell (1999), when describing the 'growing gulf' between the best and worst performing parts of Britain (see above), actually present the figures for only one year. It is, of course, not possible for a snapshot year to give rise to reports of a *growing* gulf. The authors, therefore, must either have extra data which they do not reveal or even refer to, or they are mistaken. Whether, on the one set of figures they do have, the differences between regions can be called a 'gulf' is the subject of the next chapter. However, it should be noted at this point that even when the comparisons are 'home internationals' involving the supposedly similar educational systems of Scotland, England, Wales and Northern Ireland, the considerable difficulties of making fair comparisons have been emphasized in a recent project represented by Raffe et al. (1997).

This neglect of the quality of evidence (or in some cases lack of logic) has been seen by some as endemic in the debate. Black (1992, p. 5), for example, says

> Sweeping claims are made and repeated so often that the public come to accept them as self-evident truths. The outstanding example is the claim that standards have fallen. Such a claim cannot be supported by any review of the extensive evidence that such a sweeping generalisation must embrace.

An astounding example is recalled by Gipps (1993). In 1991, when the first Key Stage 1 SATs were held, the Secretary of State for

Education announced to the press before the results were publicly available that nearly a third of all children aged seven were unable to recognize even three letters of the alphabet. If true, this would indeed have been newsworthy. It was not true, and the actual figure revealed a few days later was 2.5 per cent of all children aged seven being unable to recognize three letters of the alphabet. The original story was, of course, the headline in all media reports on the day. No public retraction or correction was ever made. Presumably, many of the public still believe the original story to be true.

The findings from formal international studies of student performance are often more substantial, and worthy of greater attention. This is generally so for two main reasons. The researchers involved are academics (not politicians), and they generally face up to rather than ignore the difficult challenges of making systems comparable. Nevertheless, we must not underestimate these challenges simply because the findings are often presented by other commentators as more definite, or more simplistically unfavourable to Britain. The problems faced by researchers in this field include the comparability of different assessments, the comparability of the same assessments over time, using examinations or tests as indicators of performance at all, the different curricula in different countries, the different standards of record-keeping in different countries and the competitiveness (especially) of developing countries (see O'Malley 1998). Yet what international comparisons seek to do is solve not one but *all* of these problems at once. An observer who claims that, on the basis of a standard test, one country has performed better than another, is also saying that the test involved similar children (it would not be fair to compare boys in one country with girls in another), who had followed a similar curriculum (it would not be fair to test people in a subject they had not studied), that the test was a useful indicator of educational progress and that it was administered in the same way in both countries. To use an extreme example to make the point, one would expect sixteen-year-old boys in Wales to have a better knowledge of the laws of the game of Rugby than eleven-year-old girls in Japan. Such a result would not make a useful international comparison.

Yet, in fact, most studies reported make precisely these types of 'unfair' comparison, although in less extreme (or perhaps more disguised) forms. One of the first such studies looked at the results in Switzerland and compared them to those of Barking and Dagenham in Essex (in Brown 1998a). There are no prizes for guessing which 'country' came out on top. Students in Norway may look poor in assessments of their basic skills (see below), but then Scandinavia generally does not 'revel' in assessments as some countries do (OECD 1996). The Norwegian EMIL project leads to a curriculum covering as broad a range of content as possible, and this breadth is what is assessed by them. As the OECD (1996, p. 17) succinctly states 'you get the school you test for'. This may be partly why students in Singapore appear to do well in international comparisons of mathematics and science, since their assessment system favours progress in these areas in a 'lopsided' way, at least according to O'Malley (1998). When tests are not used, but the comparison is made between local qualification systems, it is almost impossible to decide on fair equivalencies for GCSE in Britain, the baccalaureate in France and the abitur in Germany, for example (Rafferty 1995). There is, therefore, considerable potential for the 'fiddling' of figures by governments concerned to present a well-trained workforce to their potential overseas investors.

In Britain, at least, there is some balance in the use of fiddled figures. Although some sections of the government wish to argue that five GCSEs is equivalent to a baccalaureate and so elevate Britain's international ranking, there are other sections who ally with the media to present the more standard picture of education in crisis. Good news, such as that in the 1988 International Assessment of Educational Progress study in six countries, is, therefore, simply not reported. This study suggested that students in England and Wales excel in logic and problem-solving, beating even South Korea which excelled in almost everything else (Brown 1998a). A British review of several international studies by Reynolds and Farrell (1996) was used to press for the re-introduction of whole-class teaching on a Taiwanese model, since results were consistently better in Taiwan. However, the *Panorama* programme used to push this argument did not report that even in Taiwan there was the same 'long tail of achievement' as in England. The *Independent* on 11 June 1997 reported that 'English came bottom of class in Maths' in the Third International Maths and Science Study (TIMSS), although reading the piece in full revealed that England actually came tenth out of seventeen countries mentioned. The same study reported that results from

England were 'excellent' and improving in science and geometry (in Brown 1998a).

The apparently poor performance of schools in Wales is the subject of the next chapter, and is therefore discussed only briefly here. There are some dissenters from the 'schooled to fail' in Wales thesis, and Thomson (1998), for example, suggests that south Wales valley schools are actually doing better than *equivalent* schools in England. The word 'equivalent' is the key. When Bellin et al. (1994) compared five schools in south Wales with five in Gloucestershire (see above), they claimed that the schools were all matched in terms of relative deprivation in their catchment areas (see above). Yet the Gloucestershire schools had an average intake that included 10 per cent of students eligible for free school meals (FSM – a standard indicator of parental poverty), while the schools in Wales averaged nearly 30 per cent. The schools' intake was, therefore, not matched at all in this respect. There is a clear link between FSM as a measure of poverty and attainment. The highest percentage of students with FSM (31 per cent) was at Cathays and Cynffig schools with the lowest GCSE indicators of the ten schools in the study; Cwrt Sart with 29 per cent FSM had the next lowest, and so on up the scale. So Bellin et al. actually provide no clear evidence from equivalent schools, but simply confirm the already well-known and clear inverse relationship between poverty and school achievement (see below).

One serious outcome of these comparisons is that real policies affecting the education of real children are thereby justified. For example, the apparent evidence of the poor performance of primary-school students in Wales at mathematics has led to a proposal for banning the use of calculators (Costley 1999). Now, such a change may be good, or it may be bad. The point here is that it *cannot* be justified by the research cited in evidence. Poor educational research can, therefore, lead to ill-thought-out changes in schools based on misunderstanding and misinformation (see also Chapters 5 and 10).

Third International Mathematics and Science Study

This section is devoted to consideration of perhaps the most convincing evidence for the relative failure of schools in England

Table 4.5. Performance and mean age of the top twenty-three countries in TIMSS

Country	Mathematics score	Mean age
Singapore	643	14.5
Korea	607	14.2
Japan	605	14.4
Hong Kong	588	14.2
Belgium	565	14.1
Czechoslovakia	564	14.4
Slovenia	547	14.3
Switzerland	545	14.2
France	538	14.3
Hungary	537	14.3
Russia	535	14.0
Ireland	527	14.4
Canada	527	14.1
Sweden	519	13.9
New Zealand	508	14.0
England	506	14.0
Norway	503	13.9
USA	500	14.2
Latvia	493	14.3
Spain	487	14.3
Iceland	487	13.6
Lithuania	477	14.3
Cyprus	474	13.7

and Wales, the results of the Third International Mathematics and Science Study (TIMSS). The results for mathematics are repeated in Table 4.5. Sixteenth place for England is far from impressive, but better than several countries including USA, Norway and Spain. Many of the sixteen other countries taking part but not in Table 4.5 also scored lower, but were omitted by the researchers from analysis as they did not meet the sampling requirements for the study. Of these sixteen, six did not meet the required participation rates, four did not meet the age-limit requirements, three were judged to have poor sampling methods, and another three had more than one of these sampling problems. In this study of the attainment of fourteen-year-olds, one South American country

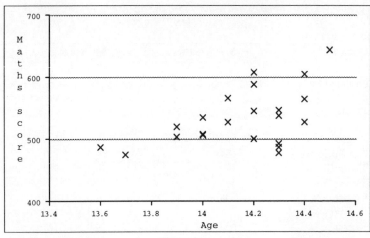

Figure 4.1. Scatterplot of TIMSS maths score and mean age

submitted scores for a cohort averaging sixteen years of age (Brown 1998a).

Despite the necessary restrictions to samples imposed by the researchers, it is clear that Table 4.5 contains significant variation in the age of respondents. The oldest average age is for Singapore, at the top of the table in terms of score, and the youngest is for Iceland, near the bottom. The reasons for some differences are quite clear. Some countries (such as England) allocate students to school years strictly by age while other countries have yearly assessments and 'retake' years leading to very different distributions of age per teaching class. In some comparisons, the entire grade or year cohort is used in order to minimize disruption on the day of the test, so there have been reports of children aged sixteen in Germany taking part in tests meant for thirteen-year-olds (Brown 1998a). The linear correlation between age and score in Table 4.5 is +0.53 (Pearson's r, significant at the 1 per cent level). Figure 4.1 shows this relationship graphically. This means that one would expect countries with older children in the test to have higher scores, and that nearly 30 per cent of the variance in outcomes is explicable by differences in mean age alone (for interest, the expected score per age can be calculated from the linear regression function: score = −925+age*103). Using figures for the other sixteen countries that did not meet participation rates makes the relationship between age and score even stronger.

There may be further problems with the sampling, unchecked by the guidelines used by the researchers. Some countries have special schools for those with special educational needs, who would not therefore take part, while others have a policy of integration. Many countries, including Singapore, do not have compulsory schooling for all, so that in Thailand, for example, only around 32 per cent of the relevant age group go to school. Attendance rates matter, since only those students in school took part, and there is no reason to assume that those not attending school would have performed at the same level. In England some LEAs refused to participate in TIMSS from the start. Of the 300 schools that were asked to participate, 162 agreed, and for some parts of the study the response rate from these 162 schools was as low as 87 per cent (Keys et al. 1996a). The implication is that, for England, the overall response rate was below 50 per cent. One can only imagine what the equivalent participation data would be for many other countries. It is partly for these reasons that Brown (1998a) concludes that the information in international league tables is generally too flawed to be of any use at all.

Even if the samples used were good random samples of each country, which they clearly were not, the results would still have a standard sampling error. On this very generous assumption, the sampling error would mean that any population statistic, such as a mean score, is 95 per cent likely to lie within two standard deviations of the corresponding sample statistic (Keys et al. 1996a, p. 47). Using this as a guide shows that only the Russian Federation and Sweden (of the countries meeting the sample criteria) had an equivalent or younger mean age than students in England, *and* a higher mathematics score without 95 per cent confidence intervals overlapping with those of England. Singapore, for example, has an average age of 14.5 versus 14.0 for England. New Zealand had the same mean age as England, but although its score is 2 points (0.4 per cent) higher than England, this score has a standard deviation of more than twice that difference (Keys et al. 1996b, table 1.1). Therefore, the probability is quite high that at least some of the scores appearing to be greater than those from England are taken from a population whose mean level is actually lower than England (and vice versa of course).

One reason that mathematics and science are used in comparisons is that they are felt to be more culture-free than other school subjects (such as English language). Even so, on close examination, the variation in what had been taught to children in each country by the age of fourteen was considerable. The curriculum in England had only covered an estimated 57 per cent of the content of the TIMSS test by age fourteen, leading to the situation of children being tested on material they had not learnt. They had, instead, covered other topics in mathematics which were not in the test. Children from the USA had the best match between curriculum and test material, perhaps because the USA were the primary funders of the study and therefore created the test. It is interesting to note that children in England still scored higher than those in the USA (Brown 1998a).

At least part of the reason for this apparently poor showing by the USA may be due to motivational factors. American students were reportedly held back from a games lesson to take part, and told that the test did not count towards their grades. In South Korea, on the other hand, the children were urged to do well for the sake of the country, and marched in to the sound of school bands. If generally true, these systematic differences are sufficient in themselves to negate the generally small differences between many scores, which are obscured by the use of ranks in reporting the outcomes. In the same way, the use of means alone as scores hides the variation within each country. This within-country variation is usually similar, except that many of the more 'successful' Pacific Rim countries have a higher standard deviation than England, signifying more varied outcomes and a longer 'tail' below the mean.

What Difference does a School Make?

Much recent educational research stems from the influence of the school effectiveness movement. This field of study has attempted to describe the characteristics of a successful school in a way that could form the basis of a blueprint for school improvement. Ironically, the major undisputed outcome of all of this work has been the reinforcement of the importance of non-school context. National systems, school sectors, schools, departments and teachers combined have been found to explain approximately zero to 20 per cent of the total variance in school outcomes (depending upon the study). The remainder of the variance in outcomes is explained by student background, prior attainment and error components. Despite this, most educational policies are based upon comparisons between schools that do not take these incontrovertible findings into account. Such policies include league tables of results, programmes of inspection and national and regional targets, all of which have presented attainments in raw-score forms. Models can be designed to test what a difference a school actually makes to these raw scores, and these models underpin much of the rest of this book.

The very large-scale studies by Coleman et al. (1966) and Jencks et al. (1972) showed that, once individual student characteristics had been taken into account, very little of the variance in school examination outcomes was left to be explained by a 'school effect'. In essence, what these studies showed is that specific schools as institutions, and schooling as a process, may have very little impact on the results attained by students. To put it simply, any individual would be expected to attain pretty much the same results whichever school they attended. The variability in student outcomes can be almost entirely explained by student 'context' factors such as family background. More recently, the school effectiveness movement (SEM) claims to have uncovered systematic variation between schools as institutions, and has attributed these large differences (in their terms) to school effects. Put simply, they are saying, in contradiction to the earlier studies, that it does matter which school a student attends, and that there are, therefore, good schools and bad schools.

To some extent the differences between these two groups of researchers can be seen as rhetorical rather than real. For the SEM group, Reynolds (1990b, p. 154) states that up to 8 per cent of the variance in school results is due to school effects rather than individual characteristics, and he calls these 'large school effects'. The OECD (1995) on the other hand says that most of the variation in schools results can be explained by school input factors (such as student socio-economic indicators or scores of prior attainment). According to their review, the residual that could be explained by schools is *only* 12 per cent. Rather like the story of the full/empty beer glass, 8 per cent is a large amount to one school effectiveness researcher, but 12 per cent is only 12 per cent to another. Harker and Nash (1996) claim that the school effect on outcomes in New Zealand is 'small', but then show that only between two-thirds and three-quarters of variance in the School Certificate is due to the ability and social mix of each school. From the USA, the evidence since the first studies has been largely pessimistic about school effects. In all studies the effect is very small, and the larger the sample used the weaker is the evidence of any school effect at all (Shipman 1997). The social background of the children is still apparently all-important.

The actual proportion that is, or could be, explained by school-level processes (the difference a school actually makes) is fairly well agreed within limits. Daly (1991) estimates between 8 and 10 per cent, Creemers (1994) attributes 12 to 18 per cent of the variance to schools once the background of students is taken into account, while Stoll and Fink (1996) put the figures at 8 to 14 per cent. Reynolds (1990b) suggests a maximum of 10 per cent. In a review of effectiveness studies, Gray and Wilcox (1995) attribute from 2 to 10 per cent of the variance to school effects. Lauder et al. (1999) demonstrate that 80 to 99 per cent of the variance in school outcomes is attributable to measures from the individual student (actual figure depending on the specific outcome measure). If these individual-level variables (such as SES, ethnicity, gender and prior attainment) are aggregated to a school level there may also be a 'school-mix' effect (see Thrupp 1997). The individual student characteristics, the mix, and related non-academic items like school size and the stability of the number on roll, leave very little variance to be explained by both school educational processes and error components combined. The specific figures vary from study to study, but the overall pattern is clear. Much recent work shows that the adjusted differences between schools are very small, so it is difficult to distinguish schools from each other (Ouston 1998), especially as 'outlier' scores such as those from children with special needs are routinely eliminated before analysis (Hamilton 1998). The main difference between researchers, therefore, lies in their reactions to these significant findings.

For some, school effectiveness has become a kind of cult and, therefore, difficult to argue against. Several of its most devoted adherents have become government advisers, and so the movement itself is becoming more and more part of the official discourse, mixed with an economic vocabulary about targets for lifelong learning, and market-driven performance indicators. One of these advisers is Barber who concludes from a review of the evidence that

> the research into school effectiveness over the last two decades has made an immense contribution to our understanding of school performance. Whereas in the 1960s and early 1970s the prevailing view of education and social researchers was that the effect of school on a pupil's performance was negligible in comparison to the impact of social class and upbringing, it is now demonstrable that schools make a significant difference to how well children do. (Barber 1996, p. 127)

When researchers have attempted to relate this small school effect to school characteristics and processes, so producing a blueprint for school improvement, the results have generally been negligible. The factors making up a 'good' school are frequently rather nebulous or blindingly obvious and tautological (Ouston 1998), consisting of items like an academic emphasis or high-quality leadership or good discipline. Reviews of the SEM exceed empirical studies, and the results of all studies are so far correlational rather than experimental in nature. The dangers of taking correlates as though they are the factors underlying school effects was recently illustrated in a spoof article presenting evidence that schools should be built on higher ground (Gorard et al. 1998a). SEM researchers are generally aware of this danger, but some have been found to move, almost unwittingly, from using factors as descriptors of successful schools to referring to them as potential determinants of school improvement (Hamilton 1997). It is also the case that the long lists of correlated factors produced by SEM research sometimes contain apparently contradictory items. For example, one such list contains both 'strong firm leadership' and 'reciprocity'. Another list moves from effective leadership as exemplified by collegiality to the rigorous selection of teachers.

One unintended impact of SEM studies has been the apparent marginalization of the role of important context factors. 'Adjusting for social factors has led some to a delusion that social factors don't matter' (Ouston 1998, p. 7). The irony is that when school effectiveness models based on explaining the residual variance are used to push for small-scale policy changes like homework clubs or compulsory uniforms, their findings are often seized upon by ministers. When identical methods are used to point out the importance of value-added analyses, and the almost overriding role of socio-economic context in school outcomes, then politicians are less happy. Tim Eggar (then an education minister) stated 'we must not cover up underachievement with fiddled figures', while Michael Fallon claimed 'we will not be dressing up the facts, obscuring the real level of performance by altering outcomes to take account of spurious measures of disadvantage or deprivation' (in Gipps 1993). Despite these assertions, every study in this field has come to the conclusion that the role of context is paramount (e.g. Nuttall et al. 1988). But there is no real sign that the government wishes to tackle the social inequality that lies at the heart of educational inequality, relying instead on school improvement (Hatcher 1998b).

> The problem of underperformance has been largely . . . conceived of as a failure of schools and of teachers . . . What School Effectiveness Research has failed to provide . . . is to develop an understanding of the processes which have led to the remarkably strong and surprisingly consistent relationship between socio-economic context and school performance. (Gibson and Asthana 1998b, p. 207)

Another, unintended, impact of these SEM studies may have been an exaggeration of the importance of examination results. While the researchers themselves have often been scrupulous in pointing out that results measure only some of the activities of a school, the fact that examinations appear easy to measure and monitor means that more complex school outcomes have been neglected. A good school has come to mean one with good exam results (Ouston 1998), even though this is only a small part of what families look for when they choose a new school (Gorard 1997a).

> If schools are to be judged by examination results, there will be great pressure on schools to reflect this bias in their teaching. And the fact is that although . . . results are generally esteemed by parents and employers, they measure only a small part of what teachers would regard as desirable educational outcomes. They place a premium on propositional knowledge . . . so evidently does the public at large, to judge by the popularity of games of the 'mastermind' type. But what is more important is to use this knowledge procedurally . . . [and] . . . there

still remains the whole area of a pupil's personal and social development which parents and employers rightly expect a school to foster. (Holt 1981, p. 18)

School effectiveness cannot be seen as a unitary trait applying to all subjects, departments, ages and abilities, and to both genders (Nuttall et al. 1988), and schools may have both academic and non-academic effects. Schools that promote the first do not necessarily enhance personal and social development, for example (Smyth 1998). While there is some indication that school effects may be consistent over time, they are not necessarily consistent over different outcomes or for different groups of students (Sammons et al. 1996). They may have very limited and short-term impacts outside schools, not carrying over with the individual into university performance for example (Hughes et al. 1996b).

International Indicators

Of the twenty-three countries in an OECD comparison in 1992, only Germany, Norway, Switzerland and the USA had a very much higher proportion of their population than the UK educated to upper secondary level (Table 4.6); the situation remained the same in 1996 and is predicted to remain so until at least 2015 (CERI 1997). It was at tertiary level that the UK fell markedly behind many OECD 'competitors' (OECD 1993). By 1996 this deficit had been corrected according to the figures, and the net entry rate for university-level education was 41 per cent in the UK, the fourth highest of eighteen countries in the study (CERI 1998). In 1996 the UK had one of the largest number of 'expected' years of education, and the third highest ratio of university-level graduates to population, along with perhaps the most balanced figures for participation by gender at all levels of initial education.

Although there are systematic inequalities in participation and qualification in the UK, these are generally smaller than in other OECD countries and diminishing over time (Eurostat 1998).While all of these figures need to be treated with the same caution applied to other sources in this chapter, and indeed OECD stresses the difficulties and compromises involved in making international comparisons of this sort, there is no evidence from successive

Table 4.6. *Highest education level of those aged 25–64 in 1992*

	Upper secondary	Tertiary (university and HE)
USA	84.1	30.2
Germany	81.9	21.4
Switzerland	80.7	20.9
Norway	78.9	25.2
Canada	71.3	41.1
Sweden	69.9	24.1
UK	68.0	18.4
Austria	67.9	6.9
Finland	62.1	19.2
Denmark	58.9	19.2
Netherlands	57.8	20.9
New Zealand	56.4	23.6
Australia	52.8	22.4
France	52.2	15.9
Belgium	45.2	20.2
Ireland	42.2	16.9
Italy	28.5	6.4
Spain	22.9	13.0
Portugal	14.2	6.7
Turkey	13.7	4.8

OECD and EU figures since 1985 that initial education in the UK is either poor or inequitable in international terms.

Conclusion

The thrust of this chapter has been to suggest that a consideration of the effectiveness of a school system is not a simple matter of counting and comparison. Even where simplifying assumptions are made about the outcomes from schools, such as a concentration on statutory assessment and test results, philosophical and methodological difficulties persist. In light of these difficulties, there is certainly no evidence here of falling educational standards over time in Britain, and no convincing evidence of under-performance relative to the educational systems of other developed nations. In fact, it is sometimes difficult to discover what difference schools actually make to attainment in these terms. The next chapter considers further the claims about differential school effectiveness within Britain, through a detailed study of school examination results in England and Wales.

5

Investigating the Performance of National School Systems

The discussion in Chapter 4 drew attention to several discrepancies in the standard descriptions of British schools as performing poorly in comparison to their international 'rivals'. In most of the examples cited, there is only limited evidence that British schools are producing worse results than other systems of education in terms of raw-score indicators. However, raw-score comparisons do show up clear differences, such as the apparently poor performance of schools in Wales compared to those in England. The purpose of this chapter is to examine this 'home international' more carefully in light of the clear socio-economic differences between England and Wales.

The chapter examines a widespread and long-held belief about the quality of education in Wales compared to other parts of Britain, especially England. It has become commonplace to observe that, on almost any indicator of educational attainment, progress or participation, the people of Wales lag behind those in England (see Chapter 4). This observation has led to an official view expressed in successive government documents that schools in Wales are underperforming, and that students in Wales are underachieving. The official view thus affects the regional policy of school improvement, the use of English schools as a model of better practice and the nature of the targets set for schools, and has been adopted as the provisional basis of educational policy by the new National Assembly for Wales. The evidence for this view is in two parts. First, there are the official indicators of education in England and Wales. Second, there is the similarity of the educational systems in England and Wales. The argument for the official view therefore runs as follows. Education in Wales is worse than in England *despite* the similarities of the educational processes in the two regions, and so Wales must be underachieving. One researcher who has been instrumental in propagating and confirming this official view has explained that children in Wales are in fact 'schooled to fail'.

The evidence for this view is re-examined here by considering both parts of the argument in turn. A detailed reanalysis of the data is used here to illustrate the difficulties of drawing firm conclusions about underachievement from a simple comparison of raw figures in different regions. Given these difficulties, it can be imagined how much harder such comparisons must be when the regions are truly international, with totally different educational systems, curricula and forms of assessment. The substantive purpose of this chapter is to argue that all such comparisons can be rhetorically misleading and to show that, under closer analysis, the differences and effect-sizes claimed by the advocates of these positions of the relative performance of Britain in international terms, and Wales in home-international terms, are less significant than initially supposed.

Wales and England

One assumption underlying the comparison between England and Wales is that both areas, unlike Scotland, are using the same educational and assessment system based on the same 'National' Curriculum. This, it could be argued, is what makes direct comparison of their results fair. Since this assumption is not actually true, the comparison begins to suffer the same defects as the more truly international comparisons described in Chapter 4. Despite earlier attitudes stemming from a 'for Wales see England' mentality, the education system in Wales is now markedly different from that in England, more so than simple regional variations within England, and the differences are increasing (e.g. Raffe et al. 1997). Initial education in Wales is administered by the National Assembly office (formerly the Welsh Office), not the Department for Education and Employment. The majority of public examinations are taken using papers from the Welsh Joint Education Committee. There are several differences between the National Curriculum for Wales and that for England, with subjects such as history, geography, art and music having separate orders. These differences are in perspective as well as content, since according to legislation all pupils in Wales have the right to learn about Welsh language, culture and history. There is, or should be, a 'general Welshness pervading pupil's learning experiences' (Jones and Lewis 1995, p. 24). The National Curriculum for Wales also specifies that Welsh-language teaching is compulsory in all state-funded schools.

The uniformity of schools in Wales is remarkable. Among the 2,048 schools of all types in Wales, there are no city technology colleges, or similarly specialist schools for drama, sport or languages (Welsh Office 1995c). At peak there were only twelve grant-maintained (GM, as they then were) schools altogether. In fact, fewer than 1 per cent of schools in Wales opted out of LEA control, compared with more than 4 per cent in England (Halpin et al. 1997). Of the 484,322 full-time pupil equivalents in Wales in 1994, only 5 per cent of the school population were in GM, independent, and special schools combined (Welsh Office 1995c). Most parents in Wales do not have a realistic option of using local fee-paying schools, since there are so few such schools, none in mid-Wales, and only eight which until recently were able to offer Assisted Places (Gorard 1996). On the other hand, Wales has one type of school unknown in England, the *ysgolion Cymraeg* or Welsh-medium schools (see Chapter 7).

Wales is clearly different from England in terms of population. Until 1995 Wales had eight local education authorities (LEAs), while England had 109, any two of which (for example, Hampshire and Essex) might have a population in excess of the whole of Wales. As an analogy, comparing examination performance in Wales with England is like comparing the rest of England with a region made up solely of Barnsley, Doncaster, Rotherham, Sheffield, Bradford, Calderdale and Kirklees. Even though Wales is also much smaller in area than England, its population density is minimal by comparison. The least densely populated LEA in England is Northumberland and even that is three times as densely populated as Powys in Wales. The most densely populated LEA in England, Kensington, is over twelve times as dense as South Glamorgan. The remoteness of parts of Wales mean that notions of choice and diversity in schooling simply cannot work (Gorard 1997a). Schools are often either smaller than in England, with fewer facilities and more limited curricula, or children have to travel further there and back each day.

Wales has traditionally lacked a large middle class, and even today the occupational class profile is clearly different from many parts of England, being generally flatter in structure. Wales has an older and ageing population, with a high proportion of retired, early retired and long-term sick, while registered unemployment in some parts is still high. Given these problems of remoteness, relative poverty and economic inactivity, it is perhaps not surprising that many observers have been less than impressed by the levels of attainment in schools in Wales. The relative problems may be sufficient by themselves to explain the lower levels of attainment in schools in Wales compared to England. This chapter describes the methods used to test this proposition, the results obtained and their implications for policy and the crisis account more widely.

Welsh underperformance at school is chiefly supported by the kind of figures that would never be accepted in a comparison between schools, where the demand for value-added models has long been documented (e.g. Gray and Jones 1986; Mortimore and Mortimore 1986; Reynolds et al. 1994; Sammons et al. 1994), but which are deemed sufficient for the creation of international league tables. It is simply not sensible to compare the performance of the whole of England with Wales, and the straightforward 'home international' model used by the Welsh Office (now the office for the National Assembly) has little validity, not taking into account the significant differences between the two regions. In fact, research in Scotland has suggested that high-attaining students, of the kind correlated with privileged socio-economic status, boost school examination scores by more than their own contribution (Willms and Echols 1992). If so, this halo effect could also be taken into account when assessing the effectiveness of a school.

Methods Used

The study uses three main sources of information about LEAs: the examination results for 1993/4 in England (DfE 1994) and Wales (Welsh Office 1995c), and the equivalents for 1997/8 (DfEE 1999b; Welsh Office 1999), the percentage of children taking free school meals in England and Wales, the percentage of school-age children in fee-paying schools, the percentage of householders in each social class and the population and area of each LEA (Census 1991). The results for 1994 are used since they are from the last complete academic year before the local government reorganization into unitary authorities in Wales (see Welsh Office 1996b). The results for 1998 are used since they are the most recently available at the time of writing.

The chief performance measure chosen is the GCSE benchmark of the percentage of the relevant age cohort gaining five or more grades A–C, and as usual the figure for both years is lower for Wales than that for England. This benchmark figure is used for several reasons. It is the most commonly quoted, used in government publications, in league tables, by press and other media, and by many of the articles cited above. Above all, it is the one used in 'home international' publications such as *A Bright Future* (Welsh Office 1995a) and by the Education and Training Action Group of the new National Assembly (ETAG 1998). There is an established tradition of LEAs and researchers using public examination results as performance indicators at the school level (e.g. Gray and Wilcox 1995). This is not to say that another examination measure, such as the percentage gaining no qualifications aged sixteen, GCSE points per student or even a performance indicator other than examinations, would not also be useful. There are, however, problems in using the percentage leaving with no qualifications or points per student as indicators, since children in Wales can take the very elementary Certificate of Education, which is only recently available in England. The growing use of GCSE points per student involves distorting the ordinal grade scores into supposedly equal-interval points (see Chapter 9). The purpose of the analysis described here is merely to show that basing educational policy initiatives on simple comparisons of raw scores between regions, the 'home internationals', is unhelpful.

The independent variables used to characterize the LEAs are social class, low income and population density. These are used for two main reasons. They are conveniently available at this level of disaggregation from census data and Welsh Office STATS1 forms, and they have been linked to school performance both by this study and others (Sammons et al. 1994; Gray and Wilcox 1995). Family social class has been shown to be strongly linked to school performance, therefore the proportion of families in each LEA with social class I and II backgrounds is linked to LEA performance (Bellin et al. 1996). Similarly, poverty as assessed by free school meal provision is an excellent indicator of examination performance (Lake 1992). The geographical features of each LEA are used to distinguish urban, suburban and rural areas, which have been shown to be relevant to educational achievement (Gordon 1996). Population density in particular can be seen as relevant to school outcomes in a market system of schooling, while the area of the LEA gives an indication of the time children might spend travelling each day. Although there are other factors that could be built into the model, some of which were tried and rejected in this study, many are highly correlated with each other, such as the proportion of lone parents and free school meals. Others, such as differential selective school policies and proportions of children at fee-paying schools or opted-out schools, have been found to be insignificant in previous analyses of LEAs in England (e.g. Gordon 1996). Although several of the variables require caution in their use, they have the major advantage of having no missing values and being available in a standard format for both England and Wales.

The secondary data were collected for all 107 English LEAs (excluding the micro-LEA of City of London and combining the Scilly Isles with Cornwall) and the eight Welsh LEAs in 1994 and the twenty-two Welsh unitary authorities (UAs) in 1998, and converted to percentages where necessary. Since all data were real numbers, the correlations between them were calculated using Pearson's r. The data were further analysed in two ways. For each Welsh LEA, the most similar English LEAs on each measure were identified as being potential candidates for comparison. Secondly, a multiple linear regression analysis was used to explain the variance between all 107 English LEAs in terms of the independent variables (Achen 1982). This is similar to the method used more recently in the *Observer* school league tables (1998) where school outcomes are related to student poverty, special need, first language and school selection, and in the report by Hackett (1999) of contextualizing Key Stage 2 results by an index of poverty per LEA.

All of the independent variables correlate significantly with the GCSE benchmark at LEA level, with the percentage taking free school meals accounting for 75 per cent of the variance in results between schools by itself in both 1994 and 1998 (see Figure 5.1). The relationships between all of the predictors and the dependent variable are approximately linear (Maxwell 1977), although the natural logarithm of the GCSE benchmark figures was also plotted

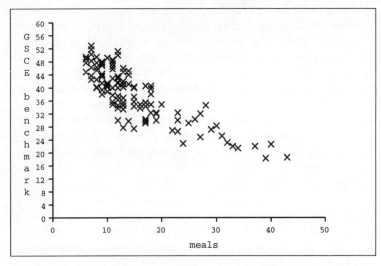

Figure 5.1. Scatterplot of GCSE benchmark 1998 against eligibility for FSM

against the independent variables, and the relationships were if anything even more clearly linear (see Gorard 1998b for a full comparison).

Both the log results and the untransformed data were tested using multiple linear regression. It does not really matter whether regression is used in order to predict or explain LEA performance (Gorard et al. 1997a). The essential question to answer is what can be expected of each English LEA, given its determining characteristics, and from this to extrapolate what can be expected of each Welsh LEA. Multiple regression is similar to a series of individual analyses but with the added advantages of parcelling out the variance between potentially interacting predictors, so reducing the amount of unexplained variance (Pedhazur 1982), and limiting the repetition of tests designed for one-off use (Stevens 1992). The relationships between all of the predictors and the dependent variable are approximately linear (Maxwell 1977), and other diagnostics suggest that the other major assumptions underlying regression also hold (see for example Figure 5.1), although even where they do not the results can still be used with care (Berry and Feldman 1985). The variables were added to the model using forward stepwise entry which maximizes efficiency (Norusis 1994). The results from both years are described in the next section.

Re-evaluating the Welsh School Effect

This section outlines the results obtained from the data and methods described above. These are used as an extended case study of 'international' comparisons, to emphasize the importance of socio-economic context in evaluating the performance of educational systems. The supposed Welsh school effect is demonstrated by the fact that schools in Wales generally have lower school outcome measures compared to England. The results here demonstrate some of the weaknesses in this position and suggest an alternative way of analysing the school performance data which leads to the opposite conclusion on both propositions. Schools in Wales are doing reasonably well in comparison with equivalent schools in England, and there is no evidence of children being disadvantaged by a Welsh education.

Tables 5.1 to 5.7 show the GCSE benchmarks for each of the eight LEAs in Wales in 1994 alongside the benchmarks of all LEAs in England with the same percentage of students eligible for free school meals (FSM). Thus, unlike the 'schooled for failure' comparison by Bellin et al. (1994: see Chapter 4) these comparisons are more like-with-like, at least in terms of poverty. Tables 5.1 and 5.2 show that Powys and Mid Glamorgan do indeed have lower scores than all equivalent LEAs in England.

Table 5.1. Comparison of LEAs with 6% FSM

LEA	Benchmark
Buckinghamshire	49%
North Yorkshire	49%
Surrey	48%
Powys	**45%**

On the other hand, Tables 5.3 and 5.4 suggest that West Glamorgan and Clwyd both obtain around average scores for equivalent LEAs, while Gwynedd obtains better than average scores.

Table 5.2. Comparison of LEAs with 19% FSM

LEA	Benchmark
Oldham	32%
Rochdale	32%
Mid Glamorgan	**30%**

Table 5.3. Comparison of LEAs with 18% FSM

LEA	Benchmark
Camden	40%
Wirral	40%
West Glamorgan	**38%**
Cleveland	35%
Walsall	32%

Table 5.4. Comparison of LEAs with 12% FSM

LEA	Benchmark
Barnet	51%
Richmond	50%
East Sussex	43%
Gwynedd	**43%**
Wigan	42%
Dudley	41%
Clwyd	**40%**
Kirklees	37%
Leeds	36%
Durham	35%
Humberside	34%
Gateshead	33%
Sunderland	30%

Tables 5.5 to 5.7 show that Gwent, South Glamorgan and Dyfed are at or near the top of their respective 'leagues' of equivalent LEAs. Viewed as a whole, then, these figures provide no evidence of a general underperformance of the schools and students in Wales, relative to England (perhaps even the reverse).

Table 5.5. Comparison of LEAs with 16% FSM

LEA	Benchmark
Gwent	**35%**
Doncaster	34%

Table 5.6. Comparison of LEAs with 15% FSM

LEA	Benchmark
Hounslow	40%
South Glamorgan	**40%**
Croydon	37%
Sheffield	36%
Tameside	34%
Sandwell	27%

Table 5.7. Comparison of LEAs with 13% FSM

LEA	Benchmark
Cornwall	46%
Dyfed	**45%**
Bolton	42%
North Tyneside	41%
Bedfordshire	40%
Enfield	40%
Calderdale	37%
St Helens	36%
Nottingham	35%
Merton	33%
Barking	28%

This analysis can be repeated for each available measure of socio-economic context individually, so that similar tables can be created using the percentage of families in social class I and II as a criterion, for example. Similar, but small-scale, analyses have been conducted by statisticians at the WJEC and by ESIS (1998). In each case, the prevalence of FSM is used to set a socio-economic 'context' for each LEA, leading to a comparison between similar

LEAs. Although the precise results alter each time, none of them provide any evidence of a negative school effect for LEAs in Wales. Nevertheless, the presentation of such an analysis is confusing, especially when two or more background variables are used to match LEAs in England and Wales (although in fact there is no match for an LEA with a population density as low as Powys). This is the main reason why multiple regression is used below (see also Chapter 7). The logic of using matched English and Welsh LEAs as the basis for a fair comparison remains, but in the regression analysis all of the socio-economic characteristics are matched simultaneously.

Results for the 1994 Local Education Authorities

Although it is true that several of the independent variables used in this study are correlated, their correlation coefficients are much less than that between each independent variable and the dependent variable of examination scores. For example, the social class of residents and eligibility for FSM only correlate at –0.22, whereas the social class of residents and the GCSE benchmark correlate at +0.44. There is, therefore, little collinearity in any of the regression models used below, as each of the predictor variables is apparently measuring a different factor (Norusis 1994). This is evidenced by the elevated class profiles combined with relatively high FSM figures for some London LEAs. These two figures together may give an indication of the range and diversity of social conditions in each area. Some areas have consistently high-income profiles (for example, Kingston-upon-Thames), while some have consistently low-income profiles (for example, Tower Hamlets). Other areas have polarized incomes with a high proportion of both 'privileged' and poor families (for example, Westminster), and a few have homogeneous populations with few professionals and also relatively few families in poverty (for example, Sunderland). These variations are also differentiated in terms of urban/rural locations. Multiple regression is, therefore, a useful analysis for these complex relationships since it takes all variables into account simultaneously. and partitions the explained variance between them.

The best and most parsimonious model for predicting the 1994 GCSE benchmark figures for each LEA in England used only three of the potential predictors: the percentage of secondary-school children taking free school meals, the percentage of householders in social classes I and II and the population density. The resulting model was an excellent one with high tolerance for all predictors (R square of 0.85, F of 214, probability of 0.000). The model is:

GCSE benchmark = 31.52 – 0.59*meals – 0.055*density + 0.45*class

The relevant characteristics of the eight Welsh LEAs can then be substituted in this model, and their predicted results are presented in Table 5.8. On this analysis, Wales as a whole is doing as well as, perhaps better than, can be expected in comparison with equivalent LEAs in England. Four LEAs in Wales are doing better than the model predicts, one is breaking even and three come out worse (although in each case the residuals are small and unlikely to be either significant or constant over time). There is no evidence here that children in Wales as a whole are being schooled to fail. In fact, schools in Dyfed, West Glamorgan and Gwynedd ought perhaps to be congratulated. If the school population of each LEA is taken into account (by being multiplied by the size of the residuals) then slightly more children appear to gain by being at school in Wales than not.

Table 5.8. Predicted GCSE benchmarks for Welsh LEAs, 1994

LEA	Predicted	Observed	Residual
Dyfed	39.28	45	+6
West Glamorgan	35.23	38	+3
Gwynedd	40.78	43	+2
Clwyd	39.08	40	+1
South Glamorgan	40.35	40	0
Gwent	36.47	35	–1
Mid Glamorgan	32.78	30	–3
Powys	47.51	45	–3

Results for the 1998 Unitary Authorities

Similar models have been created using a dataset with results from all secondary schools in England for 1998 (the most recently available figures at the time of writing). The dependent variables are the percentage of students in each of the 118 unitary authorities (revised LEAs) obtaining one GCSE grade G, five GCSE grade G, five GCSE grade C, and the average number of GCSE points per candidate in each UA. The independent explanatory variables are the local population density, the percentage of local residents in social classes I and II and the percentage of students eligible for free school meals, as before. For each dependent variable a very similar model emerged for 1998 as for 1994. The most powerful and parsimonious model is that relating the GCSE benchmark of percentage attaining 5+ GCSEs A*–C to the percentage eligible for FSM and the percentage of local residents in social classes I and II (adjusted R square of 0.74, F of 180, probability of 0.00). Therefore, nearly 75 per cent of the variance in examination scores for each area can be explained by these two variables alone. Also, although too much should not be read into this, since population density is not significant, it suggests that the differences in performance between urban and rural areas may have declined since 1994. The model is as follows:

GCSE benchmark = 37.68 – 0.46*meals + 0.38*class

Using this model it is possible to calculate predicted scores for each of the current twenty-two unitary authorities in Wales, and again address the question of whether there is any evidence that schools in Wales are underperforming in relation to those in England. For example, Flintshire in Wales has 34.4 per cent social class I and II residents, according to the 1991 census, and 12 per cent of the students at school in Flintshire are eligible for FSM. Thus, the model predicts a GCSE benchmark as follows:

37.68 – 0.46*12 + 0.38*34.4 = 45.23%

The actual score in 1998 was 45 per cent, so the residual is an insignificant –0.23 points. Schools in Flintshire are, therefore, obtaining exactly the level of results predicted from using scores for equivalent students in England. Of twenty-two UAs in Wales, only six had a negative residual, and only two of these were more than 5 per cent of the observed score. Caerphilly has a residual of –4.5 points and Blaenau Gwent has a residual of –5.4, suggesting that, for the 1998 figures, schools in these two authorities are underperforming in relation to their peers in England. However, several UAs in England have even larger negative residuals. The achieved score for both Bristol and North East Lincolnshire is 9.1 points lower than predicted. Of all the 140 UAs in England and Wales, the highest positive residual is for Tower Hamlets (+10.2 points), while the second highest is for Ceredigion in Wales (+9.3). Over all, there is no evidence from 1998 that schools in Wales are underachieving, and in general their results are in line with expectations derived from the characteristics of their student intakes. This is confirmed by a t-test for independent samples, using the standardized residuals for each 'home nation'. The findings for other outcome measures are similar.

The Implications

The findings above, revealing the powerful link between the characteristics of students in each LEA and their results in public examinations, have been replicated in many studies and at many different levels of aggregation (from classroom to international). Clearly these findings do not imply that children from families in poverty are unable to obtain good examination results, especially since the analysis is not conducted at the level of the individual student. They *do* reveal how little of the variation in school outcomes can be attributed to school systems and processes themselves. In the context of the comparison between England and Wales, this means that there is no realistic evidence for the 'schooled to fail' thesis. Schools and students in Wales are attaining pretty much the level of results that would be expected from their socio-economic make-up, and there is no reason at present to suggest that schools in England and Wales are differentially effective with equivalent students.

How then can we construe the continued use of raw-score data by officials and by some academics, when in other arenas the latter have been highly critical of analyses which do not feature at least some kind of 'value-added' account? How should we interpret the overly negative assessment of Welsh schools when other measures demonstrate that the Welsh–English gap in school performance does not exist? It appears that a loose alliance of researchers, journalists and policy-makers have established what can only be described as an official discourse about the performance of schools in Wales. The set of public meanings constituting this discourse promotes the idea of underachieving Welsh schools and the relatively greater effectiveness of the English schools which might serve as a model for schools in Wales. It is both important and dangerous that this discourse involves a disregard of scrupulous and careful analysis of the input data which show that the differences in outcomes are not as great when social factors are accounted for (as they have been here).

There are several reasons why it is important that a clearer and fairer picture of comparative performance in the two home countries emerges. Perhaps first and foremost, it is important that the teachers in Wales gain the credit that they deserve as much as their colleagues in England, particularly in view of the strong criticisms of Welsh schools and teachers voiced by more than one former Secretary of State for Wales, and which have now become almost an article of faith for Welsh Office commentaries and policy statements for the new National Assembly (see, for example, ETAG 1998). The myth of poor Welsh schools may discourage families from moving to a fast-growing economic region in Britain. It may also encourage the setting of unrealistic performance targets or the setting of overly demanding standards by OHMCI who 'are being targeted to reinforce action on these publications' (Jones 1996, p. 30). Finally and most directly, there are the effects on the current market in schools. Families may be encouraged to send their children to schools over the border for example, as the mine-owners of south Wales have traditionally done (Gorard 1997c), or to the expanding *ysgolion Cymraeg* which are currently outper-forming English-medium comprehensives in terms of raw-score indicators (see Chapter 6).

One of the prerequisites necessary for the current competition between schools to lead to an improvement in educational stand-ards is the correct mixture of 'alert' and 'inert' clients (Hirschman 1970). Those parents who are more alert to educational rights, problems and opportunities provide the stimulus for change either by exercising their 'voice' to the governors of the school, or by signalling their dissatisfaction through exit. Unfortunately, it may be the parents most likely to bring about change who are also those most likely to leave (Willms and Echols 1992). 'Choosers tended to select schools with higher mean socio-economic status and higher mean levels of attainment' (Cookson 1994, p. 92), which may be a rational attempt to boost a child's attainment (Echols et al. 1990). In terms of student ability, a 'favourable school context' measured by mean student SES is a 'zero-sum resource' (unless society becomes more affluent over all). What one school gains, the other loses. The policy of parental choice may, therefore, benefit choosers in relation to everyone else without necessarily improving standards overall, and as the number of alert families increases, the proportion gaining any benefit at all may drop. Worse, since much of feedback to schools based on migration could anyway be incorrectly based on raw data, it might encourage the wrong changes. Effective schools in disadvantaged areas may be tempted to change, in a hopeless attempt to prevent the loss of students, while less effective schools in better areas might be made complacent by the attractiveness of their high mean SES (Willms and Echols 1992). This could be the true damage done by the 'schooled to fail' myth.

It is not suggested that the variables used here are the only ones, or even the best, available, nor that the model and its residuals would be identical if further measures were available (although the model is similar for different years, and using alternative measures of attainment). Since comparisons, however fruitless, will inevitably continue to be made, further analysis needs to be done with other indicators, other years and a larger basket of predictors, such as ethnicity, first language, proportion of lone parents, educational qualification of the adult residents, absences from school, SEN and unemployment. The use of schools in one LEA by residents in another, perhaps even in another home nation, the examination results of those in fee-paying schools and the comparability of examination results between boards, modes and years also need to be taken into account in a larger and more complex analysis. However, the purpose of this part of the book has been to question the wisdom of simple international comparisons of raw indices of academic attainment wherever they occur. It bears repeating at this stage that there is no indication that schools in Wales are generally performing any worse than schools in equivalent parts of England. This alternative analysis also has implications for the prevalent use of league tables of international school performance, and the resultant impetus towards policy-borrowing from the educational systems of rapidly growing Pacific economies. The claim that schools in Wales are underperforming may have encouraged the setting of unrealistic performance targets, such as those in the *People and Prosperity*, *A Bright Future*, and *Building Excellent Schools Together* publications (e.g. Welsh Office 1995a, 1995b, 1996a, 1997a, 1997b), which have already been 'down-sized' once as the impossibility of their attainment began to dawn on politicians.

Since outcomes are so clearly predictable from school intakes it is important that we arm ourselves against ever again accepting 'evidence' of the supposed superiority of one national school system over another when the analysis does not take this proportionate relationship into account. Of course, the precise nature of the relationship between economic conditions and educational success is yet to be determined. For example, is it likely on this evidence that nations gain economic prosperity from having a school system which produces high raw-score indicators of attainment? Or is it more likely that what is perceived as a successful school system is actually a result of a healthy economic situation? A tentative answer to these questions about the economic value of investment in 'human capital' is presented in Chapter 10.

6

Differences between Groups of Schools

This section of the book examines the oft-quoted claims that particular types or sectors of schools are more effective than others, and that the clear differences in outcomes between such groups of schools are primarily related to school processes rather than the characteristics of their student intake. To some extent, therefore, this section simply redefines the debate about the relative effectiveness of national education systems in Chapter 4 at a lower level of analysis, and all the methodological points made there still apply. This chapter considers the differences in terms of examination outcomes between the best and worst LEA-controlled comprehensives, and between comprehensives and grant-maintained (GM) schools, fee-paying schools, grammar schools and *ysgolion Cymraeg* (where instruction is in the medium of Welsh). It has been suggested that the gap between the best and worst performing of these schools is increasing over time (that is, their results are becoming polarized). In addition, using the local coeducational LEA-controlled comprehensive school as the basis for comparison, it has been variously suggested that single-sex, fee-paying, grammar, grant-maintained and Welsh-medium schools are more effective with similar students. As with the international and home-international comparisons in Chapter 4, these sectoral comparisons lead to pressure for the 'failing' sector to copy some aspects of their more successful peers. The chapter examines the evidence for each of these comparisons in turn.

Best and Worst

'The gap according to Woodhead is widening' was the headline for a 1998 article in the *Times Educational Supplement*, while 'Tory market theory widened schools performance gap' was the *Guardian* headline for the same story, based on the comments of Her Majesty's Chief Inspector for Schools in England. This conclusion

is backed up by a recent report from the Institute of Public Policy
Research comparing the performance of the top and bottom
scoring schools (Robinson and Oppenheim 1998), and these, in
turn, are supported in their conclusions by a similar analysis from
the Liberal Democrats and the lobby group Article 26 (*TES* 7
August 1998, p. 4). As an example of the evidence on which this
widening gap between supposedly good and bad schools is based,
'OFSTED cite figures showing the top and bottom 10% of schools
had average GCSE points scores of 46.1 and 15.7 respectively in
1992. Comparative 1996 figures were 51.8 and 19.8, a gap of 30.4
points in 1992, growing to 32 in 1996' (*TES* 12 June 1998, p. 5).
These figures are summarized in Table 6.1. According to the
Guardian, 'the better schools improved faster than their weaker
rivals' (Carvel 1998a, p. 5), leading to increasing polarization of
student attainment. Chris Woodhead has blamed the widening gap
on those head teachers who do not focus on their own school's
problems and attempt to sort them out educationally. He therefore
argued that market theory did not work in education, while at the
same time somewhat confusingly suggesting that 'parents do not in
fact have the right to choose schools' (Carvel 1998a, p. 5).
OFSTED's findings are already being used as the basis for plans
and new policies to improve schools, and are part of an ongoing
process of naming and shaming those schools regarded as 'failing'.

Table 6.1. *Gap in GCSE point scores between 'top' and 'bottom' schools*

Decile	1992	1996	Difference (pts)
'Top' score	46.1	51.8	30.4
'Bottom' score	15.7	19.8	32

As stated in Chapter 2, some commentators are using this
increasing polarization of outcomes between the best and worst
schools to argue backwards that therefore schools are likely to be
becoming more polarized by intake as well. For example, Gibson
and Asthana quite reasonably claim that *if* socio-economic
segregation between schools was decreasing then one would expect
the patterns of attainment linked to socio-economic factors to be
converging also. In fact, they go so far as to claim that 'if schools
with poor GCSE results . . . [and associated SES measures] can be

shown to be improving their performance and social composition relative to those with good GCSE results . . . then the polarization thesis will have to be dismissed' (1999, p. 14). There is, of course, not much likelihood of this, in their opinion, since they claim in the same article that the actual results of schools are tending to widen the gap between the best and the worst (Table 6.2). Gibson and Asthana therefore support the OFSTED conclusions for very much the same reasons. For example, Gibson and Asthana (1999) claim that the gap, in terms of GCSE performance, between the top 10 per cent and the bottom 10 per cent of English schools has grown significantly from 1992 to 1998. Table 6.2 shows the proportion of students attaining five or more GCSEs at grades C or above (the official Key Stage benchmark), for both the best and worst attaining schools in their sample from England. It is clear that the top 10 per cent of schools has increased its benchmark by a larger number of percentage points than the bottom 10 per cent. On the basis of these calculations they conclude that schools are becoming more socially segregated over time. In fact, they comment, 'within local markets, the evidence is clear that high-performing schools both improve their GCSE performance fastest and draw to themselves the most socially-advantaged pupils' (in Budge 1999, p. 3).

Table 6.2. Changes in GCSE benchmark by decile

Decile	1992	1994	1998	Gain 94–98	Gain 92–98
Top 10%	60.0	65.0	71.0	6.0	11.0
Nine	48.2	54.0	59.1	5.2	10.9
Eight	42.0	47.7	53.1	5.4	13.1
Seven	37.1	42.5	47.2	4.7	10.1
Six	32.8	37.5	41.6	4.1	8.8
Five	28.2	32.9	37.2	4.3	9.0
Four	23.8	28.4	32.2	3.8	8.4
Three	19.3	23.7	26.8	3.1	7.5
Two	14.7	18.2	21.4	3.1	6.7
Bottom 10%	7.9	10.6	13.1	2.5	5.2

Fee-paying and State-funded

In addition to the alleged gaps between state-funded schools discussed above, the difference between the outcomes of fee-paying and state schools has been described as growing, with the first group emerging more and more favourably from the comparison (Jones and Reynolds 1998, *TES* 12 June 1998, p. 18). This is a particularly interesting proposition since, in considering the relative effectiveness of schools over time, it may be possible to use the fee-paying sector as a control group. Advocates of explicit parental choice of schools have suggested that allowing families to choose which school they use will help lead to a rise in standards. Fee-paying schools in England and Wales have been relatively unaffected by legislation such as the Education Reform Act 1988 and have always been in a market for students, often a very competitive and volatile market (Gorard 1997a). Therefore, if explicit choice policies were to lead to an improvement in school standards, one would expect the state sector to improve its performance relative to the established market of fee-paying schools.

The last intake of students to enter secondary school before the Education Reform Act 1988 sat for their GCSEs in 1992. In that year, as in every year since, the average public examination results for those students at fee-paying schools were better than for students at LEA and GM schools (Table 6.3). For example, the difference between fee-paying and state-funded schools in Wales was 36 percentage points in 1992, but this had risen to 40 by 1997. Thus, using the logic applied by Chris Woodhead and others above, the gap between state and fee-paying schools has widened. Specifically, since the introduction of explicit school choice policies in 1988 which left fee-paying schools unaffected, the relative effectiveness of state schools appears to have declined, and, therefore, the policy of school choice appears to have failed in terms of improving standards (even if schools themselves have become more socially mixed, see Chapter 3).

Grant-maintained and LEA-controlled

Similarly, using the DfEE figures for the average GCSE point score per student at LEA-controlled, grant-maintained and independent

Table 6.3. Exam scores by type of school (Welsh Office figures)

	% GCSE A*–C		% GCSE A*–G		A-level points	
	LEA/GM	Fee	LEA/GM	Fee	LEA/GM	Fee
1992	34	70	76	86	13.4	17.3
1993	36	73	77	86	13.6	17.7
1994	39	75	80	87	14.5	20.0
1995	40	80	80	90	14.9	19.2
1996	41	79	80	91	15.5	19.3
1997	43	83	81	89	16.0	19.9

Source: Welsh Office.

schools, the differences in terms of attainment between each sector appear to have grown over time (from DfE 1994, 1995; DfEE 1996, 1997, 1998). In 1993 independent schools scored 16.2 points per average student higher than LEA schools, while GM schools scored 4.5 points higher (Table 6.4). By 1997 these differences had grown to 16.4 and 5.9 points respectively. These changes may not be large (in fact, in raw scores the state-funded sector as a whole is catching up with independent schools), but they form a key part of the crisis account, showing the increasing polarization of student results depending on the type of school attended.

Table 6.4. GCSE points by type of school (England)

Sector	1993	1994	1995	1996	1997
LEA	31.1	32.3	32.6	33.4	33.8
GM	35.6	37.0	38.1	38.8	39.7
All state	31.7	33.1	33.6	34.4	34.9
Independent	47.3	48.6	48.6	49.8	50.2

Coeducation and Single-sex

Another gap between types of schools often put forward is that between mixed and single-sex provision. The standard argument is that single-sex schools are more effective for girls, whereas mixed schools are more effective for boys. For example, as discussed in

Chapter 1, Arnot et al. argue that 'it is possible that gender segregation has a substantial influence on gender performance' (1996, p. 42) and that 'girls in single-sex schools might be at a substantial advantage' (p. 43). They back their claims up with the GCSE benchmark figures for 1994, using seven types of schools each divided into mixed, boys and girls schools. By separating the analysis into categories they hope to avoid the charge that single-sex girls schools are, by their very nature, more socially selective than the more commonly supported mixed schools. They discover that 'all-girls schools obtain higher ratings than all-boys schools in all seven categories' (p. 42), as well as scoring higher than mixed schools.

English- and Welsh-medium

A similar logic is used by the Institute of Welsh Affairs in Jones (1996) with respect to Welsh- and English-medium secondary schools in south Wales (those schools using Welsh and English respectively as the chief language of instruction). Basing their argument on the work of Reynolds and Bellin (1996), they conclude that English-medium schools in Wales are performing worse than their Welsh-medium peers, and consider the possible explanations for this. As evidence of this differential attainment, they present the GCSE results of seven schools in Rhondda Cynon Taff LEA (Jones 1996) in which there are undoubted differences in outcome measures (see Table 6.5). The three Welsh-medium schools all have a higher percentage of students achieving five or more GCSEs at grade C than the four English-medium schools selected for comparison. The relative position of the schools is similar in terms of other measures such as A-level results, and the percentage of school leavers with no qualifications. Jones suggests that these differences are unrelated to differences in the characteristics of the students attending both types of school, and offers two justifications for this position. First of all, as the schools are close together, their catchment areas must overlap, and second there is evidence that Welsh-speaking and social advantage are anyway unrelated (Bellin et al. 1999). In this way, the comparison in Table 6.5 is seen as a comparison between matched schools with similar intakes, which differ chiefly in their language of instruction.

Table 6.5. Comparison of schools in Rhondda Cynon Taff, 1996 and 1997

School	GCSE benchmark '96 %	GCSE benchmark '97 %
Ysgol Gyfun Cymer	50	64
Ysgol Gyfun Llanhari	49	48
Ysgol Gyfun Rhydfelen	35	46
Porth	31	27
Treorchy	29	34
Tonypandy	26	22
Ferndale	23	27

The possible explanations of these differences, as given by Reynolds and Bellin, include the extra stimulation stemming from a bilingual education, a greater clarity of educational goals in Welsh-medium schools, the range of activities on offer, higher staff motivation, and greater parental involvement, forming an 'interlocking, overlapping community of interest'. The Institute of Welsh Affairs comments: 'no research has been done to identify factors which account for these differences . . . It could prove useful to English Medium schools in Wales' (Jones 1996, p. 31). Therefore, the raw scores of Table 6.5 are being used to assemble and promote models of school improvement, along the lines that all schools should emulate *ysgolion Cymraeg*. This approach is further propagated through the research literature, where there is a widespread belief that Welsh-medium schools are 'better' (for example, Jones 1997), and through the media, where only Welsh-medium schools have been referred to as 'Welsh' schools, and the users of English-medium schools in Wales are described as being 'English' (*Western Mail* 1997c). This is in a similar vein to previous claims by some language activists that the majority of Welsh people are not 'really Welsh' as they are unable to speak Welsh (in Giggs and Pattie 1994). In effect it has become a key element of the 'official discourse' about schools and schooling in Wales. For example, a *Western Mail* leader column commented: 'only more intensive research will discover how and why the success of Welsh medium schooling could be applied to its English medium equivalent' (*Western Mail* 1998, p. 10). The Welsh-medium sector is therefore growing, not necessarily because demand for Welsh-speakers is growing, but because parents in non-Welsh-speaking areas are encouraged to see the Welsh-medium sector as better for both standards and discipline (Passmore 1998).

An Alternative Comparison of the Sectors

On the other hand, when many of the figures cited above are examined in light of the criticisms made in earlier chapters (especially Chapter 1), a different conclusion emerges in each example. Where the crisis account portrays large differences in the effectiveness of types of school, and growing gaps in attainment between sectors, this alternative account shows the reverse. Even more interestingly, the alternative account does so using the same figures as the crisis version. For example, on closer examination of the figures used by Chris Woodhead and OFSTED to portray a growing discrepancy in the outcomes of the best and worst schools, it can be seen that these schools are actually getting closer in attainment over time (Table 6.6).

Table 6.6. The proportionate gap between 'top' and 'bottom' schools

Deciles	1992	1996	Ratio '92–'96
'Top' score	46.1	51.8	1.12
'Bottom' score	15.7	19.8	1.26
Gap	49%	45%	

Using the proportionate method of calculating attainment gaps described in Chapter 1, the relative improvement in the scores for the 'bottom' 10 per cent of schools is greater than for the top 10 per cent. The bottom group gained 4.1 points from a base of 15.7 (26 per cent improvement), whereas the top group gained 5.7 points from a base of 46.1 (12 per cent improvement). If the 1992 and 1996 scores are converted to achievement gaps, the same conclusion emerges. The gap between the top and bottom schools, far from increasing, has actually declined since 1992, from 49 to 45 per cent. This is, of course, good news but it is totally the opposite of the official and media commentaries based on the same figures.

What appears to have misled the inspectorate, and many other commentators, is the increase in the size of the gap in percentage point terms. All of the numbers in 1996 are larger than in 1992, including the scores for both groups. Since all of the numbers have increased, the question is not whether the difference in percentage points has grown but whether it has grown faster than any of the other numbers involved in the calculation. It has not. Proportionately, the growth in outcome scores for both groups is larger than the growth from 30.4 to 32 in the percentage point difference between them. Confusing as it may seem, if both groups of schools continued to increase their scores at the same rates as in Table 6.6, then within three cycles the bottom group would be recording a higher percentage point increase than the top group (as well as a superior improvement rate). To continue this thought experiment, in time the score for the bottom group would eventually overtake the score for the top group. Of course, it is not suggested that this will happen, any more that it is intended to suggest by this reanalysis that GCSEs are a good measure of school outcomes, or that converting the categorical grades from GCSEs into pseudo-interval points scores is a valid statistical operation. The point to be made here is that the 'politician's error' made by Chris Woodhead (and others) has real consequences. Policies to ameliorate this gap will be justified on the basis of the invalid OFSTED conclusion.

It is of course particularly ironic that Chris Woodhead provides this example of analytical confusion, since he has been so vociferous in his condemnation of the standard of much British educational research, even to the extent of misrepresenting the more balanced findings of the research he commissioned into the state of other people's research. For example, he is quoted as saying that educational researchers 'produce little more than badly written dross' (Woodhead 1998, p. 51), whereas the report from which he was drawing his evidence found much to celebrate as well as criticize (Tooley and Darby 1998).

A similar argument can be presented in relation to the findings of Gibson and Asthana about the increasing polarization of schools by outcomes. Their figures (Table 6.2 above) use differences in GCSE scores from 1992 and 1994 to 1998 for each decile of schools (ranked by GCSE results). The differences are expressed in their publication using the symbol '%'. For example, a change from a benchmark of 60 to 71 is expressed as 11%. This appears to mislead the authors into thinking that the differences are expressed as percentages rather than as percentage points. If percentage points were a form of 'common currency', and in themselves proportionate figures, then perhaps no more complex analysis would be necessary.

However, to accept this would lead to a paradox in achievement-gap research, since the standard method used in reputable research calculates the change over time in proportion to the figures that are changing. A simple example of the correct use of percentages appears in a recent NIACE report that 'there has been a 20% fall in participation by retired people over the last 3 years from . . . 20% to 16%': in this analysis, Tuckett and Sargant (1999, p. 5) do not claim that participation has declined by 4 (percentage points), but by one-fifth of the 1996 base figure. A similar approach is used by Charles Newbould and Elizabeth Gray in the widely admired EOC study of gendered attainment (Arnot et al. 1996). For them, an achievement gap is the difference in attainment between boys and girls, divided by the number of boys and girls at that level of attainment (see Chapter 9).

If such a standard method of expressing differences in scores over time is used with the Gibson and Asthana figures, the conclusions from Table 6.2 are reversed. For the purposes of this illustration the assumption is made that there are no entry gaps (that is, equal numbers in each decile). Although the difference between the deciles grows larger in percentage points over time, this difference grows less quickly than the scores of the deciles themselves. Table 6.2 is reproduced below, with the addition of columns showing the proportionate change over time, calculated as the difference in points, divided by the initial or base score (Table 6.7). As can be seen, this flattens the differences between deciles so that from 1994–8 (the best estimates available) most bands improve their initial score by approximately the same proportion. However, in both years the lowest gain is in the highest scoring bands while the highest gain is in the lowest scoring bands (improving approximately three times as quickly as the top schools). The bottom schools improved their 1992 score by an impressive 66 per cent. If this were a trend, as Gibson and Asthana suggest, the implication would be that the lowest decile would eventually match the highest decile in theory (although in fact the top schools would hit the barrier of 100 per cent before that happened).

Table 6.7. Proportionate changes in GCSE achievement gaps by decile

Decile	1992	1994	1998	Gain '94–'98	Propn	Gain '92–'98	Propn
Top 10%	60.0	65.0	71.0	6.0	.09	11.0	.18
Nine	48.2	54.0	59.1	5.2	.10	10.9	.23
Eight	42.0	47.7	53.1	5.4	.11	13.1	.31
Seven	37.1	42.5	47.2	4.7	.11	10.1	.27
Six	32.8	37.5	41.6	4.1	.11	8.8	.27
Five	28.2	32.9	37.2	4.3	.13	9.0	.32
Four	23.8	28.4	32.2	3.8	.13	8.4	.35
Three	19.3	23.7	26.8	3.1	.13	7.5	.39
Two	14.7	18.2	21.4	3.1	.17	6.7	.46
Bottom 10%	7.9	10.6	13.1	2.5	.24	5.2	.66

Therefore, according to their own argument, as schools with poor results have been shown by their own data to be improving their performance relative to schools with good results, 'the polarisation thesis will have to be dismissed' (Gibson and Asthana 1999).

A similar approach can be taken with the claim that the results from fee-paying and state schools are diverging over time (see Jones and Reynolds 1998). In 1992 an average 13 per cent more students at fee-paying schools gained five or more GCSEs grades A–G than those at state schools (86 versus 76 per cent), while 106 per cent more (over twice as many) gained five or more GCSEs grades A–C (70 versus 34 per cent). In 1994, when that same year group took A and AS levels, students at fee-paying schools gained an average 38 per cent more A-level points per candidate than those at state schools (Table 6.8). However, it should be noted that the official figures for fee-paying schools do not include the students at schools such as the small Christian fee-paying schools who do not enter any candidates for traditional examinations (Gorard 1997a). Therefore, the official figures for results at fee-paying schools should always be treated as slightly inflated.

By 1997, when the limited market in the state sector had been running for ten years, and six complete year groups had moved through the secondary school system since 1988, the differences were as follows: 10 per cent more students at fee-paying schools gained five or more GCSEs grades A*–G, 93 per cent more gained

Table 6.8. Exam scores by type of school

	% GCSE A*–C		% GCSE A*–G		A-level points	
	LEA/GM	Fee	LEA/GM	Fee	LEA/GM	Fee
1992	34	70	76	86	13.4	17.3
1993	36	73	77	86	13.6	17.7
1994	39	75	80	87	14.5	20.0
1995	40	80	80	90	14.9	19.2
1996	41	79	80	91	15.5	19.3
1997	43	83	81	89	16.0	19.9

Source: Welsh Office.

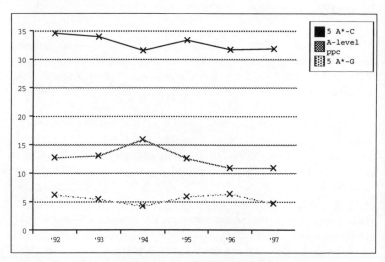

*Figure 6.1. The fee-paying/state school gap, Wales 1992–1997 (the
gap is calculated as the percentage for fee-paying minus the
percentage for state-funded, divided by the percentage for fee-paying
plus the percentage for state-funded, multiplied by 100)*

five or more GCSEs grades A–C, while students at fee-paying
schools gained an average 24 per cent more A-level points per
candidate. Thus, on all three measures of attainment, the gap
between state-funded and fee-paying schools appears to have
closed slightly (Figure 6.1). It is interesting to note and speculate on

the reasons for the gaps at A*–C GCSE and A level, which are the most quoted entries on league tables of school examination results, closing more dramatically than at A*–G GCSE. Perhaps this finding is partial evidence that schools are now playing the 'market game' successfully, and that this has led to a relative improvement of standards in LEA and GM schools, but that the improvement is not uniform across all levels of attainment (and non-attainment). Either way, the crucial finding for this part of the book is that, far from moving apart over time, the results from state-funded schools are actually catching up with those of fee-paying schools.

These findings are confirmed by a comparison of the independent and maintained sectors in England (Table 6.9). The improvement in average GCSE point score per student is greater in the state-funded sector than the independent sector from 1993 to 1997, when the figures are viewed proportionately (DfEE 1998c). Therefore, the differential attainment (or gap) between the two sectors has declined. As in Wales, the state schools are improving their results relative to independent schools. In fact, using matched students, it has been suggested that, despite the higher raw-score results for students in British fee-paying schools, high-ability students actually perform better in comprehensive schools, even though these have lower overall results (see Redpath and Harvey 1987). *Within* the state sector, however, the situation is more confused. Grant-maintained schools (as they then were) not only have a higher GCSE score per candidate than LEA-controlled schools, but are also improving those scores more quickly. Thus, the gap between LEA and GM is increasing. It should be noted that this is not evidence of differential performance between the sectors, and it is shown in Chapter 7 how these differences can be explained in terms of school intakes. Nevertheless, this is the first example encountered in this book of genuine evidence of increasing segregation between schools in England. It is, therefore, important to note it, and to return to it in the conclusion.

The finding by Arnot et al. (1996) that the raw scores for attainment in girls-only schools are higher than for coeducational and boys-only schools should not surprise most readers of their book. The first part of the same chapter in their book is devoted to the 'growing' gender gap in favour of girls in most subjects at GCSE (but see Chapter 9). Thus, if girls are generally doing better than boys, one would expect schools containing a high proportion of girls, such as

Table 6.9. GCSE points by type of school (England)

Sector	1993	1994	1995	1996	1997	Improvem.
LEA	31.1	32.3	32.6	33.4	33.8	1.09
GM	35.6	37.0	38.1	38.8	39.7	1.12
All state	31.7	33.1	33.6	34.4	34.9	1.10
Independent	47.3	48.6	48.6	49.8	50.2	1.06
LEA/GM gap	6.8	6.8	7.8	7.5	8.0	
State/Ind gap	19.7	19.0	18.2	18.3	18.0	

girls' schools, to attain a higher benchmark figure than schools of the same type containing a high proportion of boys. The question is: is the difference between the results at girls' schools and mixed (or boys') schools greater than the difference one would naturally expect? Despite their own conclusions, the answer on the data provided by Arnot et al. (1996) for 1994 would appear to be 'no'.

In 1994, the published DfE figures for the attainment of five GCSEs at grade C or above in LEA comprehensives are 35.9 per cent for boys and 45.1 per cent for girls. These give a realistic estimate of the predicted performance of girls in girls-only schools and boys in boys-only schools, assuming that the children in single-sex schools are no different in any other relevant way from the majority of children in mixed comprehensives. Of course, if the type of children attending single-sex schools differs, for example in occupational class backgrounds or eligibility for free school meals, then a raw-score comparison of the type made by Arnot et al. would be inappropriate anyway. Under the assumption of no difference between intakes except by gender, one would expect girls in girls-only schools to have an average benchmark of 45.1 per cent. In fact, according to Arnot et al., they achieve 41.1 per cent, which is less than the national average for girls in all LEA comprehensives. Thus, *if* the two sets of figures are comparable, the findings of the EOC study are actually that girls in single-sex schools are underachieving (the complete opposite of the reported conclusion).

Another way of looking at this is that Arnot et al. give the figures of 29.9 per cent achieved in single-sex boys' comprehensives and 41.1 per cent in single-sex girls' comprehensives in 1994. Under the assumption that the children in these schools are comparable in every way to those in mixed schools, and since the cohort is divided almost 50:50, these figures can be used to estimate the achievements of mixed schools. Mixed schools should have an average benchmark of (29.9+41.1)/2, or 35.5 per cent. In fact the mixed LEA comprehensives had a benchmark of 36.3 per cent in that year, according to Arnot et al., and 40.5 per cent according to the DfE (1995b). Whichever figure is correct, there is no indication here that girls perform better in single-sex schools and some evidence that they might do worse. It could be argued that a higher proportion of high-ability girls use single-sex fee-paying schools instead of local comprehensives and that therefore the single-sex comprehensives have an academically depressed intake. However, once this line of reasoning is advanced, the whole argument for basing the superior performance of single-sex girls' schools on raw scores falls apart. As stated above, the argument assumes an unbiased distribution of students. If this assumption is false, for whatever reason, then evidence must be sought of the actual characteristics of the different types of schools as is done in the following chapters.

As an example of what this logic entails, Caerphilly LEA has two single-sex comprehensives and nine mixed comprehensives. For all nine years from 1988 to 1996 both of the single-sex schools had a significantly lower proportion of students eligible for free school meals than the average for the LEA. Of the two schools, the girls-only schools also consistently had a lower proportion of children with this indicator of poverty than the boys' school. The relationship between eligibility for free school meals and examination outcomes is already well-documented (also see Chapter 7), and thus one would expect the single-sex schools to produce better results than the average for Caerphilly, and the girls' schools to produce better results than the boys' schools. In addition, since girls are achieving more C grades at GCSE overall, one would expect the raw figures from the girls' school to be substantially better than average for the LEA. They are, but this, of itself, implies nothing about the relative *effectiveness* of mixed and single-sex schools.

Conclusion

On closer inspection, much of the evidence for the polarization of school sectors is insignificant at best, or simply wrong at worst. In this light it is interesting that a recent large-scale study at Lancaster University concluded that 'schools with the worst performances in 1993 have, in general, improved the most' (Sutcliffe 1999, p. 2). According to this alternative picture, schools in general now appear to be run more efficiently with improved performance and better attendance. In terms of the outcomes measures used in this chapter, all qualities and types of schools appear similar in terms of effectiveness, and where there are attainment gaps in raw scores between types of schools these are getting smaller over time. Again the crisis account of British education appears to be misdirected. In comparing the best and worst schools, coeducational or single-sex, state-funded or fee-paying, grant-maintained or fee-paying, there is no clear evidence to suggest that any of them are more or less effective than any other for equivalent students. The question of the relative effectiveness of types of schools, and how one makes decisions about the performance of schools, is looked at in more detail in the following chapter, using a more detailed case study of English- and Welsh-medium schools.

7

Investigating Differences between School Sectors

This chapter addresses the issue of using simple raw-score indicators, such as the percentage of students attaining the GCSE benchmark, to compare the performance of groups of educational establishments. Despite the growth of sophisticated, some might say oversophisticated, ways of estimating the value-added to a performance by an institution such as a school, raw-score comparisons continue to be made by researchers, journalists and by policy-makers. In Wales, programmes of improvement measures and targets have been predicated upon the unproved notion that the majority of secondary schools in Wales (English-medium comprehensives) should be looking to Welsh-medium schools for their models of improvement strategies. The substantive purpose of this chapter is to argue that such a comparison is rhetorically misleading, and to show that under closer analysis the differences and effect-sizes claimed by the advocates of this position are statistically insignificant. The lack of difference between the sectors is so easily discernible in the light of background factors that one wonders why politicians, some academics and the media continue to cite the alleged poor performance of the majority of schools in Wales in support of their preferred programmes of action. This chapter, therefore, could have been entitled 'in defence of local comprehensive schools' (see Gorard 1998a).

The Nature of the Intake at Welsh-medium Schools

In one recent survey, 5,790 employers in Wales were offered a choice of languages in which to be interviewed. Of these, nine (or 0.16 per cent) chose to be interviewed in Welsh (Future Skills Wales, see ETAG 1998). A similar choice was given to the 6,164 residents of Wales in the survey. Of these, eleven (or 0.18 per cent) chose to be interviewed in Welsh. In another recent survey of 1,104 residents in industrial south Wales, just over 1 per cent described themselves as speaking Welsh or both Welsh and English at home (Gorard et al. 1997b). This figure probably gives a more accurate account of Welsh usage than the census figure for the same area of around 8 per cent of the population able to speak some Welsh. For example, an even larger proportion of the population may be able to speak *some* French, although the question was not asked in the census, but without using French in the home as a language of communication. In the survey, the Welsh-speakers are significantly older than the average, all describe themselves as white – that is, none of the ethnic-minority respondents spoke Welsh – and they are also predominantly male, from a chapel or Nonconformist family background. They are generally better educated than average for the sample, having remained longer in full-time education than their contemporaries, spent longer in lifetime learning and gained higher qualifications. The Welsh-speakers are, in general, of much higher occupational and social status, and these benefits are also shared by their children. Given these figures, it might be the case that those using designated Welsh-medium schools today are more socially advantaged than those using local comprehensives, and this might explain at least some of the apparent differences in the performance of the students. It is certainly true that previous analysts have found an over-representation of Welsh-speakers in the highest social classes in south Wales (Giggs and Pattie 1994). Of course, not all users of *ysgolion Cymraeg* in south Wales are themselves Welsh-speaking (Packer and Campbell 1993), but given the small proportion of the population speaking Welsh it could not be otherwise. There are more places at Welsh-speaking schools than there are Welsh-speakers to fill them. This situation has led to a myth that the English-speaking users of Welsh-medium schools are the same kinds of parents as those using English-medium schools (*Western Mail* 1997c; see also *TES* 1997b). It is against this background, then, that the sustaining myth, of Welsh-medium schools being more effective than their 'English' counterparts, needs to be examined.

An example of an argument for this myth is advanced by Jones (1996), without citing any substantive evidence. The basis of that argument is that, since Welsh- and English-medium schools in Rhondda Cynon Taff LEA, for example, are 'cheek by jowl', taking students from overlapping catchments of similar socio-economic characteristics, then the undoubted differences in their outcome measures must be due to something that is happening in the schools concerned. This position is partly based on earlier studies suggesting that Welsh-medium schools perform better, even when the type of intake factors described above have been taken into account. The chief basis for the 'cheek by jowl' argument about equivalent intakes is apparently provided by the principal components analysis in Bellin et al. (1996), and the variant which appears in Higgs et al. (1997) and later in Bellin et al. (1999). This analysis of the relationship between school intake characteristics and outcome measures produced three factors underlying all of their variables. These factors are unrelated to each other by definition, since orthogonal rotation was used to obtain the solution. One of these factors, the only reliable one on the basis of the number of variables with high loadings according to most sources (e.g. Stevens 1992), is a combined measure of social advantage/disadvantage (such as parental occupational class) and school outcomes (such as GCSE results). The high loadings of several variables (e.g. father's unemployment and GCSE results) on this factor suggest that they are all alternative 'pure factor' measures (Comrey 1973), and therefore that both school intake and school performance are in fact measuring the same underlying variable. This, in itself, is a fascinating finding. In statistical terms school intakes and outcomes are identical. The fact that scores on this performance factor do not correlate with the scores on the other two – speaking Welsh and ethnic-minority origin – show that speaking Welsh is actually unrelated to examination performance once other socio-economic differences have been accounted for.

Unfortunately, Bellin et al. do not draw either of these conclusions, but try to argue that the independence of Welsh-speaking and social advantage shows that those using Welsh-medium schools are of similar social advantage or disadvantage, and that the market is not 'creaming off' privileged parents for *ysgolion Cymraeg* (Bellin et al. 1996, p. 19). They therefore ignore the fact that the independence of the two factors is a mathematical outcome of their choice of rotation, rather than an empirical finding, and that their Welsh factor only represents that variance attributable to Welsh-speaking *after* socio-economic advantage has been isolated. They also ignore the empirical fact that simple observation of the intake characteristics of students in different types of school in Wales shows that the schools in their comparisons are not equivalent (see below). For some reason, and despite their otherwise complex analysis, they do not attempt simply to measure whether the intakes to the various schools in their study are balanced or not. This may be another example of researchers needing to find a use for their expensive Geographical Information Systems (GIS) even when higher quality data is available at the school level (see also Chapter 2).

Method for Investigating Differences between Sectors

The present study uses data from the school-level database for all 357 secondary schools in Wales created from data supplied by the Welsh Office Statistical Directorate and Welsh Office (1998). Each record contains the number on roll in each school, the number of students eligible for free school meals (FSM), the age range, the type of school (LEA, GM, fee-paying, Catholic, and so on), the number of students with statements of special educational need (SEN), percentage unauthorized absences and a range of attainment outcomes, such as the number of the fifteen-year-old cohort entered for any qualification, the number obtaining no qualifications and the number obtaining at least one GCSE grade G, at least five GCSEs grade G, and at least five GCSEs grade C, and the number of GCSE points per candidate (where G=1, F=2, and so on).

The data for 1995/6, 1996/7 and 1997/8 are used to predict outcomes for the Welsh-medium schools in the dataset in terms of their student background characteristics. The model used is created using the equivalent data for all English-medium schools. The year 1996 was chosen to coincide with the picture presented by the Institute for Welsh Affairs in Jones (1996). Incidentally, it is in order to counter this unfair picture that the seven schools named (and especially the four schools shamed) in Jones (1996) are also named in this book, with the agreement of Rhondda Cynon Taff LEA. The year 1998 was chosen for analysis as the most recently available at the time of writing. Additional characteristics about the locality of each school were obtained from the census (1991, via NOMIS).

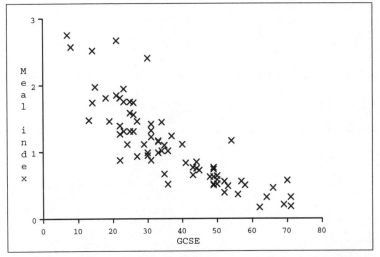

Figure 7.1. School GCSE benchmark 1998 and ratio of poverty
(FSM)

The use of FSM, as a proxy indicator of poverty and social disadvantage, has been long standing within 'the political arithmetic' tradition of social research. More recently, however, a new derivative of this measure, the FSM segregation ratio, has been employed to investigate and report on the comparative performance of secondary schools in Wales and England, and the effectiveness of state schools compared with their counterparts in the private sector. These studies give weight to the previously established strong link between the socio-economic characteristics of school intakes and later public examination results, but have also challenged other orthodoxies, and have, therefore, received considerable publicity locally and nationally (being well received by local LEAs and the schools themselves). The FSM segregation ratio, then, has proved to be a remarkably flexible and useful measure and has been shown to be more powerful, even in isolation, for contextualizing school outcomes than a variety of other indices devised for that purpose.

At the school level, all of the independent variables correlate significantly with the GCSE benchmark for all three years, with the segregation ratio of free school meals accounting for 75 per cent of the variance in results between schools by itself (see Figure 7.1 for

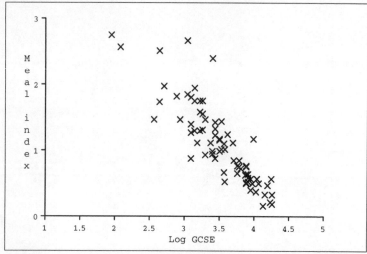

Figure 7.2. Log GCSE benchmark 1998 and ratio of poverty (FSM)

example). The relationship between student poverty and school examination results is so clear and so powerful that it is almost impossible to believe that policy-makers do not take it into account but continue with an official line of 'poverty is no excuse for failure'. Perhaps this refrain is a simple device to enable politicians to appear to be tackling the symptoms of failure while accepting the underlying problem of poverty to which it is related as though it were an integral and incorrigible part of our society.

The relationships between all of the predictors and the dependent variable are approximately linear (Maxwell 1977). In fact, if the GCSE benchmark scores for each school are converted to natural logarithms, then the slight curve in Figure 7.1 is eliminated, and the linear fit between the two variables is even better (Figure 7.2). Thus, in the analysis, both GCSE and Log GCSE are used as independent variables in different models. Both the log results and the untransformed data were tested using multiple linear regression (Pedhazur 1982).

Multiple regression is a useful analysis since it takes all variables into account simultaneously and partitions the explained variance between them (Achen 1982). Multiple linear regression analysis was used to answer the question of what can be expected of each school, given its determining characteristics. Diagnostics suggest that the major assumptions underlying regression hold in these two examples. The results are described in the next section.

The Relative Effectiveness of Two Types of School

It is quite clear that, for each school in the study, their ratio of segregation by poverty (see Chapter 3) is strongly related to the proportion of the fifteen-year-old cohort gaining five or more GCSEs at grade C, and to all the other outcome measures tested here as well. The usefulness of this segregation ratio devised by Gorard and Fitz (1998b) is, therefore, further validated by its ability to predict GCSE results even more accurately than has been achieved in the past by the simple proportion of students eligible for free meals. This is especially significant since although the mean ratio of social disadvantage as assessed by FSM in the schools of south Wales is 1 (by definition), the mean ratio of disadvantage in English-medium schools is 1.14, while in Welsh-medium the ratio is 0.59. In general Welsh-speaking schools therefore take about half as many children from families in poverty as English-speaking schools. Thus, using a model based on social disadvantage, Welsh-medium schools would be expected to gain significantly better results simply to display the *same* level of performance as the majority of schools in south Wales.

The 1996 Model

The best and most parsimonious model for predicting the 1996 GCSE benchmark figures for each of the 116 secondary schools in south Wales used only one of the potential predictors, the segregation ratio in terms of students eligible for free school meals. The resulting model was an excellent one with high tolerance for all predictors (R square of 0.88, F of 93, probability of 0.0000). Local population density, the size of the school, the percentage of local householders in social classes I and II, the percentage of householders with a qualification from higher education and the number and proportion of children eligible for free school meals were not used by the resulting model, since they contributed nothing further to the accuracy of predictions once the impact of

FSM segregation was taken into account (using forward stepwise selection). The competing indicators are anyway partially collinear (see Table 7.1) which can cause bias when all are included in the same solution (Menard 1995).

Table 7.1. Correlations between variables at the school level

	Class	Density	HE qual.	NOR	FSM ratio	GCSE	Qual. rate
Class		+0.9	+1.0				
Density	+0.9		+0.9				
HE qualif	+1.0	+0.9					
NOR					–0.5	+0.4	+0.3
FSM ratio				–0.5		–0.9	–0.7
GCSE				+0.4	–0.9		+0.8
Qual. rate				+0.3	–0.7	+0.8	

Class= the percentage of local householders in occupational class I and II; density= local population density; HE qual.= the percentage of local householders with qualification higher than A level; NOR= number of pupils in school; FSM ratio= school's ratio of 'ideal' number of pupils eligible for free meals; GCSE= the percentage of students gaining 5+ GCSEs A*–C; Qual. rate= the percentage of students gaining any qualification.

Thus, the relative poverty of a school's intake explains nearly 90 per cent of the variance in its GCSE results. Of course, this figure leaves 12 per cent of the variance in examination outcomes to be explained by other factors, but these other factors also include an error component. Therefore, it is probably true to say that the results of any school in the study are basically a reflection of the prevalence of poverty among their student intakes.

The resulting model is:

$$\log(\text{GCSE benchmark}) = 4.3 - 0.74 * \text{FSMratio}$$

This model can be used to predict the expected outcomes from any school in the dataset. Table 7.2 shows this for the same seven schools as in Table 6.5. It is worth recalling that the first three schools are Welsh-medium and the other four, held up by Jones (1996) as examples of poorly performing schools, are English-medium. Interestingly, Ferndale which had the lowest raw score in the original table is the school which appears to have the largest positive school-effect. Only one of the Welsh-medium schools has a positive impact, while one of the others is apparently the worst performing school of the seven, using this model. There is no clear evidence here that children are advantaged by attending either type of school in general (although Jones might actually have been on slightly safer ground in suggesting that Welsh-medium schools might use English-medium schools as a model for improvement rather than vice versa). There may be individual school effects (although the model using only the proportion of children in poverty is remarkably accurate), but there is certainly no clear school-type effect in Rhondda Cynon Taff. In 1996, there are *ysgolion Cymraeg* elsewhere in south Wales achieving rather better results than might be expected, such as Ysgol Gyfun Gŵyr, but there are English-medium schools performing just as well, such as Bishopston, and some doing much better, such as Aberdare Girls'. A t-test for independent samples showed no significant difference in the mean residuals between the different types of schools. There is no difference between the performance of Welsh- and English-medium schools in 1996.

Table 7.2. Observed and expected outcomes

School	GCSE benchmark '96	Expected	Difference
Ysgol Gyfun Cymer	50	48	+2
Ysgol Gyfun Llanhari	49	50	–1
Ysgol Gyfun Rhydfelen	35	46	–9
Porth	31	29	+2
Treorchy	29	33	–4
Tonypandy	26	29	–3
Ferndale	23	18	+5

Several other models have been created and tested in the same way. Variations include using other benchmarks as the dependent variable (for example, the percentage of students gaining any qualification, or the average GCSE points per candidate). The primary relevance of poverty as a predictor remains constant across all models. Similar results are obtained using figures for examinations in 1997 as well as 1996 (see Gorard 1998b for a fuller comparison). None of the models suggests that children attending

Welsh-medium schools gain any kind of competitive advantage in public examinations.

The 1998 Model

The analysis using data for 1998 involves a larger dataset of all 357 secondary schools in Wales. These are assessed in terms of six outcome measures: the percentage of the fifteen-year-old cohort entered for examinations, percentage gaining one GCSE grade G, five GCSE G, five GCSE C, the GCSE points per candidate and the percentage of unauthorized absences. The full range of independent variables (such as the proportion of children with a statement of special educational need) is described above.

In all of the resulting models there are several consistencies. First, the age range of the school (for example, eleven to sixteen) makes no difference to the GCSE or other outcome scores. Similarly the size of the school makes no difference. Most importantly, the type of school (fee-paying, Catholic, Church in Wales, Special, and so on) makes no difference to the outcomes once all other factors have been accounted for. This is crucial evidence that the different sectors of schooling in Wales are *not* differentially effective with equivalent students. Second, as in 1996 and not surprisingly, the relative ratio of families in poverty is the key indicator for all models. The 'weakest' model is that using the percentage gaining one or more GCSEs grade G or above (adjusted R square of 0.65, F of 112, probability of 0.00). The percentage for each school is predicted to be:

Qualification rate = 100.69 – 7.92*FSMratio – 0.41*SEN

Put simply, this means that each school would expect 100 per cent of their intake to gain a minimum GCSE qualification, unless they had at least some students eligible for free school meals or with a statement of SEN. The more of these disadvantaged students there are in any school, the lower the qualifications would be expected to be. Some fee-paying schools, for example, have no FSM and no SEN, and, therefore, using this model one would expect all of their students to gain some qualifications. In fact all such schools in Wales do (some of the 'famous' fee-paying schools, for example).

However, this is more a comment on the relatively privileged nature of their intake than any compliment to their teaching and learning.

The 'strongest' model is that using the standard GCSE benchmark at grade C (adjusted R square of 0.80, F of 166, probability of 0.00). The percentage gaining five or more GCSEs A*–C is predicted to be:

$$\text{Benchmark} = 68.28 - 13.83*\text{localratio} - 9.23*\text{nationalratio}$$

This means that each school would expect around 70 per cent of their intake to achieve the GCSE benchmark, unless they had at least some students eligible for free school meals. Again, the higher the ratio of FSM, the lower the expected results for the school. School intake is assessed in this model in terms of two very similar indicators. The 'localratio' is the proportion of its fair share of students in poverty that a school takes in comparison to other schools in the LEA. The 'nationalratio' is the proportion of its fair share of students in poverty that a school takes in comparison to all other schools in Wales. For example, St Illtyd's is an LEA-controlled Catholic school in Cardiff. In 1998 29 per cent of its fifteen-year-old cohort attained the benchmark, which is significantly less than 68 per cent. However, St Illtyd's takes one and a half times as many children from poor families as you might expect from the number in Cardiff as a whole, and over 1.7 times as many as expected for Wales as a whole (assuming an even spread of poverty across Wales). The model therefore predicts that the results for St Illtyd's would be:

$$68.28 - 13.83*1.5 - 9.23*1.73 \text{ or } 31.57\%$$

In this year, and using this model which is only 80 per cent accurate, the results for St Illtyd's are pretty much as expected. There is a negative residual (the difference between expected and observed) of 2.57 points. This is unlikely to be significant.

Of the 357 secondary schools in Wales, forty-seven teach primarily through the medium of Welsh. In general, these all have relatively high raw-score GCSE results. *All* of these forty-seven schools have fewer than their fair share of students from poor families, and this is true even in predominantly Welsh-speaking areas such as Gwynedd. Most Welsh-medium schools actually have less than half the usual proportion of FSMs, while Penweddig, as an extreme example, has fewer than one-quarter. When these figures are taken into account, the picture of the relative effectiveness of Welsh- and English-speaking schools alters considerably. Of these forty-seven schools, thirty-five do not have significant residuals in terms of the model above. Put simply, most Welsh-medium schools are obtaining GCSE results exactly in line with national expectations once the relatively privileged nature of their intake is recognized. This finding also confirms the general accuracy of the model used. Of the remaining twelve, six have significant positive residuals (that is, they appear to be overachieving), and six have negative residuals (that is, they appear to be underachieving). For example, Llanhari is a Welsh-medium school in Rhondda Cynon Taff and one of the schools held up by the Institute of Welsh Affairs as an exemplar for English-medium schools to emulate. In 1998 44 per cent of its fifteen-year-old cohort attained the GCSE benchmark. Llanhari takes around half as many children from poor families as you might expect from the number in Rhondda Cynon Taff, and just over half as many as expected for Wales as a whole (assuming an even spread of poverty across Wales). The model therefore predicts that the results for Llanhari would be:

$$68.28 - 13.83*0.48 - 9.23*0.59 \text{ or } 56.20\%$$

The residual is −12.20 points, suggesting that, given the nature of its intake, the results in Llanhari would be expected to be significantly higher than actually obtained. Glantaf, on the other hand, is a Welsh-medium school in neighbouring Cardiff with almost exactly the same intake proportions as Llanhari. In 1998 69 per cent of its fifteen-year-old cohort attained the benchmark. The model predicts that the results for Glantaf would be:

$$68.28 - 13.83*0.47 - 9.23*0.55 \text{ or } 56.70\%$$

In this case the residual is +12.30 points, suggesting that given the nature of its intake the results in Glantaf would be expected to be significantly lower than actually obtained. While these individual differences between some schools do exist in 1998, there is no reason to believe that the residuals are constant from year to year, and overall there is no clear evidence of differential effectiveness between any two sectors of schools in Wales. Of course, these differences can be construed as evidence that the model omits a crucial additional variable. However, if these calculations are accepted, an individual student in Wales would obtain a similar set of GCSE results whichever type of school they attended: 80 per cent of the variance in results comes from the student characteristics, not from the religious basis, funding regime or language of instruction in the school. The implications of these findings are discussed further in the next section.

The Implications

There is no evidence from this analysis of any systematic difference between the performance of Welsh- and English-speaking schools, or indeed between any types of school. What then does this matter? There appear to be four main conclusions to be drawn from this extended case study: for policy-makers, for schools, for researchers and for the crisis account generally. This 'value-added' comparison of two competing sectors of schools shows that the widely accepted view of the superiority of one sector over the other is suspect. By implication, all other such comparisons based on raw-score indicators are equally suspect. This should matter to policy-makers and target-setters, and it should matter to families making choices of school. Above all, it should matter to commentators on the education system generally. As perhaps predicted by Chapters 4 and 6, there is little convincing evidence anywhere that different types of schools, perhaps even individual schools, are any more or less effective than any other.

Implications for the Assembly
Discourses are forged and sustained by an ensemble of field positions and field occupants. Clearly the latter may wish to defend the boundaries of their field, the values embedded in their discourse and their own position as judges of what is counted as valid or legitimate knowledge about schools in general, and Welsh schools in particular. This chapter will therefore be seen as an uncomfortable challenge both to the discourse and to those who

have invested in it politically, academically and administratively. For example, the chairman of Cardiff Education Committee recently stated that 'there is a growth in the Welsh language in all parts of the city, so the language can no longer be seen in Cardiff as something which is very middle-class' (Passmore 1998, p. 6). According to him, demand for Welsh-medium primary education is growing in Cardiff at just over 6 per cent per year, even from English-speaking homes. This is because *ysgolion Cymraeg* are seen to have both higher standards and better discipline than English-speaking counterparts. Thus, rather than defend the majority of the schools in his LEA, the Cardiff chairman is promoting a discourse of the superiority of one type of LEA-controlled school over another.

It may be that such supporters of this sectoral 'effect' represent an alliance between those whose policy presupposed that education in Wales is generally poor (such as previous Secretaries of State for Wales) and those who want to elevate the performance of the *ysgolion Cymraeg*, seeking more general approval for their existence in terms of such schools' relative effectiveness, rather than using the more obvious (but not necessarily straightforward) argument based upon a choice of the medium of instruction. In fact, the evidence for either proposition is very weak, as it is for the proposition that GM schools or fee-paying schools *per se* are performing better than their competitors.

Implications for schools
It is also important to point out the harmful and divisive effects of the standard discourse for schools, teachers, parents and students. By claiming that most schools in Wales are not doing a good job, the crisis account denies the people involved with the majority of schools the credit that they deserve, and head teachers of English-medium schools in Wales have been rightly annoyed with the prevailing discourse about their inferiority. Moreover, in a 'market' where student recruitment is vital and loss of students endangers institutional survival, the notion of superior Welsh-speaking schools skews current choices, encouraging the use of Welsh-medium schools by non-Welsh-speaking families. This is a policy with potentially serious equal-opportunity implications for ethnic minorities in Wales (Gorard 1997c). It also encourages the

use of schools across the border in England, and other forms of harmful market migration based upon creating complacency in schools with high mean SES, or encouraging unnecessary changes in policy by schools in relatively disadvantaged areas (as predicted by Willms and Echols 1992).

Implications for researchers

These results show that research based on the assumption that Welsh-medium and English-medium schools are equivalent in their student intake is simply incorrect. If instead of using census data and artificial catchment areas (e.g. Bellin et al. 1996) researchers use the characteristics of students actually attending each school, then the picture is very different. These findings have important implications for those using Geographical Information Systems (GIS) to track educational changes. On some occasions, such as this, GIS data are not even grossly accurate. It should also be noted that the analysis by Bellin et al. (1999) is anyway fatally flawed even in its own terms (see above). On p. 192 they state that 'factor analysis with orthomax rotation would allow indicators to load on more than one factor', but on pp. 183–4 they assume that the factors they produce are unrelated and orthogonal. This orthogonality is the basis of their argument that the Welsh-speaking factor is unrelated to the social advantage factor ('cutting across social class', p. 183). Yet their third factor termed 'ethnicity' could be substituted in the same argument. Surely Bellin et al. do not wish to suggest that Welsh-speaking cuts across ethnicity, and that families of Punjabi origin, for example, are just as likely as local-born Welsh to speak Welsh at home? Yet this is the implication of their interpretation. This conclusion warns of the dangers of such artificiality in research. The best assessment of the character of a school intake is based on analysis of the school intake, not of the residents surrounding the school.

Implications for the crisis account

This extended case study has, like those in previous chapters, been made possible because of public access to high-quality data. Proportionate analysis of this school-level data has transformed the traditional account of the relative performance of Welsh- and

English-medium education. This finding does not, in itself, provide evidence that all such sectoral comparisons would lead to similar conclusions, but the evidence so far presented suggests that the actual impact of schools on their examination outcomes is far less than in popular imagination. The key predictors of examination success derive from the background characteristics of the student, and this is true *regardless* of the type of school attended. To put it another, perhaps more helpful, way, the inequalities in society far outweigh any differences between schools.

Of course, such a conclusion provides both good and bad news. The good news is that, contra the crisis account, there is no genuine reason to believe that any children are unduly disadvantaged by attending any particular type of school. Once the context (or student mix) of schools has been taken into account, there is no difference in the performance of different sectors (see Levačić and Hardman 1999 for example). The level of poverty among students is not simply the best indicator of school examination outcomes, it has also been found to be the best predictor of OFSTED inspection grades (Cassidy 1999d). Even trained school inspectors, therefore, appear to be making judgements about the quality of schools and their teachers chiefly on the basis of the family characteristics of the students. Once the full implications of this finding have registered it can be seen that there can, therefore, be little evidence of school improvement (or disimprovement) except in terms of attracting a more 'desirable' intake. Currently, the best way for a school to rise in the league tables and in OFSTED's estimation is to attract more students who are liable to do well in examinations, and deny entry to those who are not. This last strategy is a zero-sum game for the education system as a whole, and may have many undesirable outcomes in terms of social justice.

The bad, or rather the perplexing, news is that schools do not seem to make much difference at all to outcomes. Does that mean that we as educators should not bother overmuch with the quality and nature of schools? Two points can be made here. First, the emphasis of this chapter, indeed of the whole book, has been on academic outcomes. This is chiefly because it is comparisons of these outcomes that have been used as the foundation of the crisis account, and of recent official discourse about schools (e.g. Barber and Sebba 1999). It is to be hoped that the full experience of school for a student is actually about a lot more than this. Even in its own terms, the official human capital approach to education may be flawed (see Ball 1999). Second, all of the evidence in this book so far points to societal injustices as the root problem in education, and as one that is, therefore, unlikely to have a purely educational solution. Of course, it would be better not to have socially advantaged and 'sink' schools present in the same area, and it might be better for them to become more mixed by a process of choice (or busing or allocation of places by lottery), but the evidence presented so far and in the remainder of the book is that such a transformation may make little difference to the actual life chances of the individuals involved. Disadvantage remains disadvantage wherever students are taught how to read and write. Perhaps what the results of this chapter are suggesting is that policy-makers should not accept the serious inequality in society as a given phenomenon and then try to engineer a solution solely through school improvement, but that they should also tackle the inequality. In fact, education may be far from the best economic policy we have. Both of these points are developed further in Chapter 10.

8

Achievement Gaps between Groups of Students

This chapter continues the consideration of 'gaps' that was started in Chapters 4 and 6, but at an even lower level of aggregation (that of the individual student, and groups of similar students). There are clear and systematic differences between the examination performance of various identifiable groups in society. The examples used here stem from differences by occupational class, ethnicity and the gender of the students involved in assessment. These differences are outlined at the start of the chapter, and then considered in more detail. The 'crisis' account of recent British education reveals significant growth over time in the size or scale of these gaps between groups of students, leading to the apparently inevitable conclusion that the educational system is becoming more and more divisive by class, race and gender. The point here is that even if national and regional systems, or sectors of schools, or schools themselves are not becoming more polarized over time, it is still possible for the results of individual students to be polarizing in terms of gender, class or ethnicity but across institutional or geographical boundaries. A final possibility to be considered is that the performance of the 'best' and 'worst' students is polarizing (even though these students may be becoming more mixed throughout the school system, see Chapter 3).

Growing Gaps in Attainment

A recent review of secondary data from the Youth Cohort Study summarized the standard crisis view of differences between groups by concluding that deprived children, ethnic minority students and boys have all 'fallen behind' their comparators in recent years (Slater et al. 1999). Quoting a study by S. Demack, D. Drew and M. Grimsley, the claim is made that 'the gulf in performance between rich and poor pupils in England and Wales has been widening for at least a decade', and Demack is quoted as saying that 'the groups that were doing relatively well in 1988 have improved at a much swifter rate. The gap has widened' (Slater et al. 1999, p. 1). The kind of evidence on which these claims is based, as cited by the authors in the article, is reproduced here as Table 8.1. In this table the percentage of students attaining five or more GCSEs at grade C or above (hereafter referred to as the GCSE benchmark) is compared for two occupational class backgrounds over time. The difference apparent in 1988 is, therefore, said to be worse by 1996, since the results of children from professional/ managerial backgrounds have improved faster than those from non-employed backgrounds. This is clear, in their version of the findings, because 58 (the percentage point difference between the two groups in 1996) is a larger number than 48 (the equivalent for 1988).

Table 8.1. The gap between professional and unemployed families

Occupational class	1988	1996
Professional	59%	77%
No paid employment	11%	19%
Difference	48	58

Such systematic differential attainment between groups of students has been frequently cited as a major problem in British schools, and one that is apparently getting worse over time. Another example relates to attainment and ethnicity from the work of Gillborn and Gipps (1996). Their work articulates to a long-term ongoing dispute over school effects and 'methodological purity' represented by Hammersley and Gomm (1993), Gomm (1995) and Foster and Hammersley (1998) on the one hand, and Gillborn and Drew (1993), Troyna (1993) and Gillborn and Gipps (1998) on the other. The first group are seen as 'realists', believing that the most important attribute of any research is its truthfulness, whereas the second group are more concerned with the socio-political impact of any research findings (or even its commissioning). This issue is discussed further in Chapter 10.

In a review of research on the differential attainment of ethnic minority students, Gillborn and Gipps (1996, p. 21) present evidence that in Brent LEA 'the gap grew between the highest and lowest achieving groups (Asian and African Caribbean respectively)'. An example of their evidence is reproduced here in Table 8.2, which shows that in terms of percentages attaining the GCSE benchmark, the gap between African Caribbean students and Asian students increased from 1991 to 1993. Gillborn and Gipps make similar claims on the basis of similar evidence about other outcomes measures, and about other LEAs, and about the gaps between White and Asian/African Caribbean students.

Table 8.2. The gap in GCSE benchmark between ethnic groups in Brent

Ethnic group	GCSE 1991	GCSE 1993
Asian	30.0%	38.0%
African Caribbean	19.1%	25.6%
Difference (points)	10.9	12.4

As with the differences by occupational class background, school outcomes as analysed by ethnic background therefore also appear to be growing in their systematic division into 'winners' and 'losers'. Again both groups in the comparison have 'improved' their score (or at least the score for both groups has risen), but according to the researchers children from an Asian background in terms of the census of population have improved their score more rapidly than those from African Caribbean families. Again the logic is simple. The 1993 difference in percentage points (12.4) is larger than the 1991 difference (10.9).

It should be noted that neither of these examples of research findings, nor many of those outlined below, are used here because they should be construed in any way as 'straw' targets. The researchers involved are among the best known and most respected in their fields. Many other lesser known examples could have been used, because in the area of education and social justice stories of the increasing unfairness of the educational system for any disadvantaged group are, unfortunately, plentiful.

In a less well-researched but nevertheless influential and widely read book, Phillips (1996, p. 4) reveals that

a core of about 20% of 7-year-olds have failed to reach the standard for their age since the first of these tests . . . was held in 1991 . . . The first tests for 11-year-olds held in 1995 revealed that more than half were not up to scratch.

Although this is clearly presented by Phillips as a criticism of the overall standard of British education, the implication is that a subgroup of each age cohort is being left behind. As Barber (1996, p. 27) puts it, there is indeed a crisis in education where 'we have rising standards and falling standards at the same time. While they are rising for the many, they are low for perhaps 40% and falling for a significant minority. In this failing group white working-class males are predominant.' He is therefore pointing out that, whereas standards have risen for many, they have risen faster for the already advantaged. Bentley (1998), a policy consultant for the current Labour administration and widely cited author on education and society, claims that the statistics from education reveal a large-scale problem of underachievement. This underachievement is manifested by limited standards of literacy, school leavers who lack any qualification, and a growing gap between boys and girls even up to A-level standard, coupled with increases in the figures for truancy and exclusions.

Gender gaps
One of the clearest issues of differential attainment between groups of students in recent years is that currently construed as a 'gender gap'. Perhaps the most widely shared image of the 'gender gap' relating to achievement in schools is that the performance of girls is improving more rapidly than that of boys. Therefore, the gap between the achievement of boys and girls at school is increasing over time. This is a view held by academics such as Speed who states in this context that 'girls' performance has increased more rapidly than that of boys' (1998, p. ii), Arnot et al. (1996) who have shown how 'female students have improved their performance markedly, whereas male students have not shown a similar improvement' at GCSE (Speed 1998, p. 1), Stobart et al. who described 'increasing gender differences in performance' (1992, p. 261) and Brookes of the NFER who is quoted as saying that the 'gap is more marked than ever before' (Carvel 1998b, p. 19). The view is shared by government departments and officials such as those from the Department for Education in Northern Ireland who

believe that their data shows 'the rate of increase on measured educational attainment levels for females has tended to be faster' (DENI 1997, p. 1), and OHMCI (1997) who describe an annual increase in the number of schools in Wales where the percentage of boys gaining five GCSE grades A*–C (the GCSE benchmark) is 20 or more points below that for girls.

At least some politicians seem to agree with this picture, and Stephen Byers, then schools standards minister in England, has spoken of a 'growing gender gap' (Carvel 1998b). It is, therefore, not surprising to find that the media generally share this vision (*Independent* 1998). At GCSE 'girls have accelerated ahead much faster' than boys and the 'gap has widened' (*Guardian* 1998, p. 12), and the 'latest GCSE results showed girls achieving increasingly impressive results at the expense of boys' (Petre 1998). According to one newspaper, in 1988 the gap between boys and girls at the GCSE benchmark was 4 per cent, but by 1997 it was 9 per cent, always in favour of girls, and 'boys' underachievement at school has reached crisis point' (Bright 1998, p. 13). Similar claims have been made about gender differences in the results at Key Stages 1 to 3 and at A level, with the even more alarming suggestion being made that the gender gap is not only increasing over time at any level of assessment, but that it also increases with the age of the child. According to Gubb (1999), for example, the national gap in literacy scores widens as students get older from Key Stage 1 assessments to Key Stage 4. This is supported by another report (Cassidy 1999e), which also points out that girls are now outscoring boys at A level as well for the first time, and that a larger number of boys than girls are gaining no A-level points at all.

Another common belief is that the gender gap is primarily driven by a group of 'disaffected' boys, influenced by the 'new lad' culture (Chaudhary 1998), and, therefore, the lower down the achievement range from grade C at GCSE one considers, the worse the situation is, and with more serious consequences (Bright 1998). The most worrying *under*achievement is apparently among boys from low-income homes (Baker and Jones 1993), and by the end of 1998 failing boys were being described as the 'public burden number one' and 'one of the most disturbing problems facing the education system' by OFSTED's chief inspector for schools in England (Dean 1998, p. 1). Other reports have suggested that the underachievement of boys is as much a middle-class as a working-class phenomenon because the percentage point gap in favour of girls was 15 in both Richmond and Hackney for example (Carvel 1998b). Richmond is a relatively wealthy area with high raw-score student results in its schools, while Hackney is a relatively poor area, also in London, with much lower raw-score results. Therefore, the fact that the gap between boys and girls is identical in the two areas is seen as evidence that gender gaps are not class-related. This is the position taken by the then minister for schools, Stephen Byers.

The kinds of evidence advanced to support this account of a growing gender gap should be familiar to readers by now. The most widely used example is reproduced here as Table 8.3 (from DfEE 1997, table 2a). While it was the case that a larger proportion of girls than boys obtained five or more GCSEs at C or above in 1990, by 1997 that difference had apparently grown. Again the logic is as follows: 7.6, the difference in percentage point terms in 1990, is smaller than 8.9, the difference in percentage point terms in 1997.

Table 8.3. The gap in GCSE benchmark between boys and girls in England

Gender	GCSE 1990	GCSE 1997
Boys	30.8%	41.9%
Girls	38.4%	50.8%
Difference (points)	7.6	8.9

An Alternative Interpretation of the Gaps

There is no suggestion here that the differences between students described above do not actually exist, and no attempt should be made to minimize their significance for the relationship between education and social justice. It is important to state this at the outset of the reanalysis below since the author has observed a tendency for people to confuse 'growing' with 'large' and 'shrinking' with 'small' (in the same way, incidentally, as low achievement is now often confused with 'underachievement'). To repeat: the alternative explanation of these systematic differences does not suggest that differential attainment by students in Britain is small, but that it is in general getting *smaller* over time. This, of course, is in direct contradiction of the crisis account. In terms of social justice, however bad (or good) things are, they *were* worse and are now getting better. How is this possible? The general problem with simple comparisons over time using percentage points is described in Chapter 1. The specific examples are dealt with here in the same order as above.

Dealing first with the observation by Demack et al. (reported in Slater et al. 1999) that differences in attainment by occupational classes are increasing, it is necessary to repeat the figures from Table 8.1. Here, however, the differences between groups are represented as achievement gaps, which are calculated relative to the attainment of both groups (Table 8.4). The changes over time are also represented by ratios, where the new scores for each group are compared with the old scores for the same group. Both of these indicators clearly show that the improvement in the GCSE benchmark for children from families with non-employed adults has been greater than those from professional/managerial backgrounds. Put another way, the indices show that the attainment of both groups has grown faster than the differences between them. Difficult as this may be to envisage without completing the necessary iterative calculations, on the basis of the figures described by Slater et al., if this trend continued then the difference between the occupational classes would eventually disappear. Whereas in 1988 children from professional backgrounds scored 69 per cent better than average at the GCSE benchmark, by 1996 their advantage had declined to 60 per cent (further details of these calculations are given in Chapters 1 and 9). This decline may be small, and it may be considered insufficient as yet from the point of view of social justice, but it is clearly in the opposite direction to that claimed by the original authors. Similarly, whereas the score for students from professional families increased by 31 per cent from 1988 to 1996, the score for the students from non-employed families increased by 73 per cent.

A similar reanalysis of the figures presented by Gillborn and Gipps can be used to show why it is not true that 'in many LEAs the gap between the highest and lowest achieving groups has increased' (see above). The example they give is for Brent LEA. The figures for Table 8.2 are reproduced here (Table 8.5), but again using proportionate achievement gaps, and ratios of improvement. Viewed proportionately, the gaps between students of different

Table 8.4. Proportionate gap between professional and unemployed families

Class	1988 %	1996 %	Ratio 1996:1988
Professional	59	77	1.31
Non-employed	11	19	1.73
Achievement gap	69	60	

ethnic background in Brent are actually *decreasing*. The ethnic group with the highest proportionate improvement are African Caribbeans. The attainment of students from Asian backgrounds is 27 per cent higher in 1993 than it was in 1991, and the attainment of students from African Caribbean backgrounds is 34 per cent higher.

Table 8.5. The proportionate gap between ethnic minority groups in Brent

Ethnicity	1991 %	1993 %	Ratio 1993:1991
Asian	30.0	38.0	1.27
African Caribbean	19.1	25.6	1.34
Achievement gap	22	19	

If the score in Table 8.5 for African Caribbeans increased every two years by the same proportion as it did from 1991 to 1993 (that is, by 34 per cent of the original figure), and assuming the score for Asian students increased in the same way, then within six years the improvement in percentage points would be approximately equal in the two groups. In the longer term, the score for African Caribbeans would, theoretically at least, overtake the score for Asians. Of course, it is not suggested that this has happened, will happen or even can happen. Both groups would hit the 100 per cent mark long before their scores matched. The point is that, in the two snapshot years given as evidence by Gillborn and Gipps (1996), the opposite is happening at that time to what they describe. This is the 'politician's error' *par excellence*.

Several other examples given by Gillborn and Gipps (1996), when reanalysed in this way, suggest that the apparent under-achievement of African Caribbean pupils is declining over time.

While this is good news for those who care about social justice, it is not the intention of this reanalysis to downplay the importance of the gaps that obviously do exist, nor to cast doubts on the value of the research as a whole. The points that Gillborn and Gipps make are not solely dependent upon the existence of a *growing* gap. However, it is suggested here that Gillborn and Gipps have also unwittingly become confused between percentage points and percentages, and therefore converted some encouraging signs of improvement into a more depressing educational trend.

Similar reanalyses reveal the same basic problem with the figures used by both Barber (1996) and Bentley (1998). In fact, this error is widely propagated in the media, the research literature and in policy documents (see Gorard 1999a for further examples). Bentley describes the difference in attainment between boys and girls as the underachievement of boys, without defining what that under-achievement is in relation to. In fact, he is unable to explain the term 'underachievement' without using the term in its own definition. It is clear from the examples he uses, such as lack of qualification or limited literacy, that he is actually writing about low achievement, and he presents no evidence that these low-achieving students could or should do better, any more than students of average or even high achievement should. This again is a common error. A recent Welsh Office circular sent to LEA directors of education defines underachieving students as those 'leaving school without GCSEs/GNVQs' (Welsh Office 1999, p. 12), without any attempt to explain why these students are underachievers rather than simply low achievers, nor what their underachievement is in relation to. Phillips (1996, p. 4) has fallen into a similar trap (see above). How can an expected standard be defined in the first tests for seven-year-olds without reference to the *actual* results of the children of that age? It cannot. Similarly, how is it possible for more than half of the eleven-year-olds not to be of the standard of eleven-year-olds? There *are* no other eleven-year-olds by whom to set the standard. Just as Thorndyke suggested that the concept of 'underachievement' was merely evidence of the failure of our predictive instruments, it is possible to suggest to Phillips that, if over half of the age cohort did not reach a predefined level on an assessment, then it is the assessments and not the students that are in error. Unfortunately, such a conclusion does not make such a good story for the crisis account.

It is worth noting two points about the claim made by Gubb (1999) that the national gap in literacy scores for boys and girls widens as students get older (see above). First, how is it possible to calculate such a phenomenon? The scores to be compared at different Key Stages would have different metrics, different distributions and different absolute sizes. A plausible calculation using standardized figures (of multiples of deviations from the mean) may be possible, but not in the way presented by Gubb which simply uses percentage point differences between the benchmarks for each assessment. Second, there is another article in the same newspaper which reports national figures for English at Key Stages 2 to 4. This article completely contradicts the assertion that gaps in literacy grow with age (Ghouri 1999a, p. 9). However, neither of the articles nor the editorial comment on this discrepancy. This recent example provides a revealing demonstration of how confused commentators are in this area of comparing performances between groups over time (or age, or place).

Returning more fully to the question of differential attainment by gender, which has been reported as growing over time as the performance of girls outstrips that of boys, it is suggested here that these claims are at least partially a result of the same tendency for observers to confuse percentages and percentage points. To refute the specific example given earlier in the chapter, it is not true that the gender gap at the GCSE benchmark in 1997 was 9 per cent in favour of girls. The aggregate score for girls may have been 9 percentage points higher than that for boys, but this means that the girls' score was much more than 9 per cent larger than the boys. It also means that, as the percentage of both boys and girls achieving the benchmark has increased annually (DfEE 1997), so the significance of any gap expressed in percentage points has decreased. To put it simply, a percentage point difference of 10 would represent an enormous gap in a year in which 0 per cent of boys and 10 per cent of girls reached the benchmark; but it would be much less in a year where 60 per cent of boys and 70 per cent of girls did so. To consider the 10 percentage point difference to be constant over time (cf. Welsh Office 1998; or OHCMI 1997, p. 7, the 'boy/girl differential has . . . usually run at 10 to 15% in girls' favour'), or between LEAs with differing levels of achievement (Stephen Byers in *Independent*, 5 January 1998, p. 8), or between different assessments at different ages (the QCA and Wragg in *TES*, 30

January 1998, p. 22) is to ignore the significant changes over time in the base figures on which the percentages are calculated. In the same way, when Hargreaves and Comber (1998) talk of a 5 per cent gap between the performance of boys and girls at Key Stages 1 and 2, they are actually referring to 5 percentage *points*.

When sociologists calculate changes in social class mobility over time, or geographers calculate changes in ethnic segregation over time, they generally use 'multiplicative' models of change that consider the changes between groups (class, ethnicity or gender) in proportion to the changes across the groups. Only apparently in education is it considered normal practice to present 'additive' percentage point differences as though they were proportionate changes. Using the figures cited by Cassidy (1999f), the gap between boys and girls is actually declining over time since the percentage point difference between them is growing more slowly than the overall annual increase in examination scores. Seen proportionately, the trend is the exact opposite of that previously described. The figures from Table 8.3 are reproduced in Table 8.6, with the addition of proportionate achievement gaps for each year, and improvement ratios for each gender. In terms of the GCSE benchmark, the gap between boys and girls in England has not grown since 1989/90, rather it has decreased. While the percentage of girls gaining five or more GCSEs A*–C has grown by 32 per cent over seven years, the percentage of boys with the same results has grown by 36 per cent. As with the examples of ethnicity and class above, the problem of differential attainment by gender may be becoming smaller over time.

Table 8.6. Proportionate GCSE gap between boys and girls in England

Gender	GCSE 1990 %	GCSE 1997 %	Ratio 1997:1990
Boys	30.8	41.9	1.36
Girls	38.4	50.8	1.32
Achievement gap	11	10	

A similar picture of convergent results by gender appears at several levels of analysis. Table 8.7 shows the changes over time in the proportions of boys and girls gaining five or more GCSEs

A*–G (a lower level benchmark than the more usually cited A*–C). Even incorrectly assessed in percentage points (as is usual in the crisis account), there is no reason for commentators to believe that there is a growing gap between boys and girls at these lower levels of qualification (figures from DfEE 1997). Viewed proportionately, the gap between boys and girls has halved over the period covered in the table.

Table 8.7. Proportionate 5+ A–G gap between boys and girls in England*

Gender	A*–G 1990 %	A*–G 1997 %	Ratio 1997:1990
Boys	77.0	87.2	1.13
Girls	83.7	90.0	1.08
Achievement gap	4	2	

Table 8.8 shows changes over time in the percentage of boys and girls obtaining no GCSEs at grade G or above (DfEE 1997). The gap between boys and girls has more than halved, and while the percentage of girls with no qualifications in 1997 is only 93 per cent of the 1990 figure, the equivalent drop in unqualified boys is to 74 per cent of its original figure.

Table 8.8. Proportionate no-GCSE gap between boys and girls in England

Gender	GCSEs 1990 %	GCSEs 1997 %	Ratio 1997:1990
Boys	8.7	6.4	0.74
Girls	5.8	5.4	0.93
Achievement gap	20	8	

Cassidy (1999e) claims that girls now beat boys at A level, since 'Boys also account for some of the weakest performances. While 4 per cent of girls scored no points at A-level, the figure for boys was one in 20.' Yet the claim itself reveals substantial arithmetic confusion. Why are decimal and vulgar fractions used in the same sentence? One reason may be that 4 per cent and 5 per cent (one in twenty) do not sound alarmingly different. However, even accepting this discrepancy in presentation, the figures are simply not true. A much larger percentage than this gain no A-level points since only a subset of the relevant age cohort takes any A/AS levels. If the story means that the percentages are from A-level candidates *only*, then (a) the story should make this clear, and (b) the fact that entry rates at A level are differentiated by gender would need to be factored into the calculation before claims of this nature are made.

Given publicly available results such as these, it is difficult to conceive how the crisis account, of the gender gap at least, has much foundation. Since the gender gap is the focus of the case study in Chapter 9, nothing further is added to the reanalysis here.

Assessing the Polarization of Students

Of course, in the final analysis, it is individual students, rather than areas, nations, genders, schools or sectors, that matter for the purposes of increasing social justice. It may be that, even though the distribution of disadvantaged students is now more even between schools (Chapter 3), and relative performance is now more equal as assessed by nations or regions (Chapter 5), sectors (Chapter 7) and groups of students (see above), some forms of unfairness in the system are still growing. Given the foregoing evidence of desegregation and declining gaps at all levels such a conclusion might be thought unlikely. However, this concept is worth further attention for two reasons. The increasing polarization of student results at a level below the institution has been suggested as a fall-back position by some of those cited in previous chapters who wish to maintain the credibility of their version of the crisis account. It is also possible that an increased emphasis by policy-makers on raw-score indicators of school 'performance', coupled with the increasing popularity of the GCSE benchmark, and the pressures of parental choice and pupil-related funding, may have produced a situation where increasing polarization is taking place within schools but is not discernible *between* them. For example, schools may be encouraged to concentrate their resources on those students considered to be on the 'cusp' between GCSE grade C and D (or between G and fail). The long-term impact might be to improve the results of relatively 'high-ability' students at the expense of relatively low achievers, producing 'winners' and 'losers' in each school.

Happily, a robust dataset is available to test such an idea. Since 1994 the DfEE have published the average GCSE points scores for all students in the appropriate fifteen-year-old cohort in England, disaggregated by ranked twentieth parts (DfE 1994, 1995a; DfEE 1996, 1997). In other words, the points score of the top twentieth of the population (as measured by GCSE outcomes) can be compared to the bottom twentieth, and to every 5 per cent of the population in between. Each twentieth part represents around 22,000 students per year. These figures are also broken down by type of school, and from 1995 the figures have been presented for boys and girls separately. The advantage of the GCSE point score (where G=1, F=2, E=3, and so on) over the more usual GCSE benchmark is that it measures across all levels of attainment better, rather than focusing unduly on GCSE grade C. The disadvantage is that it is an artificial measure created by converting an ordinal value (ranked grades) into a pseudo-interval value in which a C grade is worth five times that of a G grade. There is no mathematical, philosophical or educational justification for this. It is simply convenient, and, therefore, any conclusions based on such a measure must always be tempered with caution. It is also important to recall that figures from a maximum of five years have been published in the most basic format, and only from three years separated by gender.

In summary these figures provide no basis for a worsening crisis account of polarization by individual students. Although the variation between the absolute GCSE points scores for each twentieth of the population is large, and indicative of a highly polarized examination system, this in itself is no surprise. In a sense the whole examination system is currently based on discriminating between the performance of individuals. Whether this should be so is considered in Chapter 10. The important finding for present purposes is that, over time, the differential attainment of the highest and lowest scoring groups is decreasing. This is true for all students, and for each school type, and for both boys and girls (with just one possible exception dealt with below).

The point about the disparity in scores between the top and bottom groups is well made in Tables 8.9 and 8.10. These differences in attainment are enormous. However, there are other points to notice as well. For both boys and girls, the achievement gaps are not getting any larger over time. This finding, among others, therefore shows the theory of increasing polarization by student outcomes to be incorrect. In fact, there are small decreases in achievement gaps over time, and the proportionate improvement scores for the lowest achieving 10 per cent is markedly higher than for any other decile. It is interesting that the relative improvement for poorly performing boys is so much better than for girls, since this confirms the findings about gender gaps in Wales (Chapter 9), but is totally contrary to the commonly held view that 'underachievement' is worsening among boys. Girls do have higher GCSE points scores than boys for every decile but these gender differences, like the differences between the deciles, are getting smaller over time. Polarization in performance among boys is greater than among girls, but again is decreasing over time.

Table 8.9. Gap between top and bottom 10% by GCSE points – boys

Boys	Points 1995	Points 1996	Points 1997	Improvement
Bottom 10%	0.10	0.15	0.20	2.00
Top 10%	64.70	66.45	66.95	1.03
Achievement gap	99.7%	99.5%	99.4%	

Table 8.10. Gap between top and bottom 10% by GCSE points – girls

Girls	Points 1995	Points 1996	Points 1997	Improvement
Bottom 10%	1.30	1.45	1.55	1.19
Top 10%	65.95	68.25	68.80	1.04
Achievement gap	96.1%	95.8%	95.6%	

A very similar picture appears at each level of aggregation. Tables 8.11 and 8.12 show differences in GCSE points scores for the top and bottom 25 per cent and 50 per cent of students respectively. These are not separated by gender, and it is therefore possible to use the figures back to 1993. They show a remarkably consistent pattern. The gaps in attainment between the top and bottom groups, whether quarters or halves of the school population, are closing at about the same rate. The improvement in the lowest attaining group is markedly greater than for the highest.

While these findings may come as no surprise to those who have read this far in the book, it is worth recalling here that we are talking about points per student, and that the figures can be used to decide whether the attainment of students *within* schools is becoming increasingly polarized. It is not.

Table 8.11. Changes in gap between top and bottom 25% by GCSE points

All	Points '93	Points '94	Points '95	Points '96	Points '97	Improvemt.
Lower 25%	7.22	7.74	7.84	8.24	8.56	1.19
Top 25%	57.14	58.50	59.16	60.26	60.72	1.06
Gap	77.56%	76.63%	76.59%	75.94%	75.28%	

Table 8.12. Changes in gap between top and bottom 50% by GCSE points

All	Points '93	Points '94	Points '95	Points '96	Points '97	Improvemt.
Lower 50%	16.97	18.09	18.34	18.8	19.22	1.19
Top 50%	49.25	50.81	51.35	52.07	52.56	1.07
Gap	48.74%	47.48%	47.36%	46.94%	46.44%	

As schools become more similar in composition, their overall results are converging and these new findings show that results within schools are converging also. This is all good news as far as it goes. Two problems remain. First, despite the figures in the four tables above, if the same analysis is done for the top and bottom 5 per cent, an increasing separation of results is uncovered. This is because the bottom 5 per cent average 0 points per candidate (to the accuracy published by the DfEE), which appears to be constant over time. Of course, it may be that with more accurate figures for that 5 per cent, although their score is only a fraction of a point per student, they are also found to be catching up with the rest of the cohort. Nevertheless, a significant number of students in every year gain no GCSE/GNVQ points at all. This leads on to the second problem. The disparity is very large.

9

Investigating the Differential Attainment of Boys and Girls

This chapter describes a recent study of the differential attainment of boys and girls at school. It is used as a detailed example case study to demonstrate how a proportionate analysis can transform our understanding of one of the most deeply entrenched components of the crisis account of British education: the growing gap between the achievement of boys and girls. For interested readers, the methods used are described in more detail in Gorard et al. (1999b).

Methods Used to Investigate the Gender Gap

The data used in this study are the Key Stage (KS) statutory assessment, GCSE, A- and AS-level examination results for all students at school in Wales from 1992 to 1997, provided by the Welsh Joint Education Committee (WJEC) and the Welsh Office. All figures relate only to students from the appropriate age cohorts (not, for example, including mature-age students retaking GCSEs at further education colleges). The quality of the data for Key Stages 1 to 3 (KS1 to KS3) until 1995 is relatively poor, with limited returns due to the problems encountered during the early years of SATs implementation, including the initial 'non-cooperation' of teachers. Therefore, the analysis of KS1 to KS3 results is presented for the years 1995 to 1997 only. Apart from the introduction of the A* grade at GCSE, there are no substantive changes in the forms of assessment during the six years of the study. The results for each assessment are broken down by gender, subject of entry, year and grade or outcome. It is doubtful whether such a complete dataset has been made available to a researcher in this field before.

Some of the records were collapsed prior to analysis. Some individual subject entries have been grouped via a standard classification (see Appendix D) in records where the number of entries per year is too small to allow reliable conclusions to be drawn (for example, the number of candidates taking economics at GCSE is too small for serious analysis). Some outcomes have been collapsed, again on the grounds of small numbers and relevance, where distinctions were originally drawn within the dataset between different classes of 'failure' in an assessment (for example, at KS3 the distinction between levels 'W' and 'D' is not preserved).

The analysis here focuses on the gap in achievement between boys and girls (the 'achievement gap') at each age for each grade or level and subject. The achievement gap has been calculated at each grade level for each subject individually, for each year, for all of Wales; and for all subjects combined, at each grade level, for each year, for all of Wales (and for each LEA in Wales). Therefore, although the method is the same as that used by Elizabeth Gray in Arnot et al. (1996) to calculate gaps in GCSE at C or above, in this study it is possible to examine the differences in gaps at all grade boundaries. Accordingly, this study provides a more detailed analysis of patterns of relative performance, using the higher-quality data on the relevant age cohorts that is now available, than most previous studies have done, not only in Wales but also elsewhere in Britain.

Calculation of the achievement gap requires a preliminary analysis of the patterns of entry for boys and girls in each subject, which give rise to an entry gap. The *entry gap* for an assessment is defined as the difference between the entries for girls and boys relative to the relevant age cohort for KS1 to KS3; and relative to the entries from the age cohort for GCSE. The result is the difference between the percentage of the entry for any assessment who are girls and the percentage of the entry for any assessment who are boys.

$$\text{Entry Gap} = (GE-BE)/(GE+BE).100$$

where GE = number of girls entered (or in the age cohort); and BE = number of boys entered (or in the age cohort). For example, if 700 girls and 300 boys enter English A level, the entry gap would be 40 per cent.

The *achievement gap* for each grade within an assessment such as GCSE is defined as the difference between the performances of boys and girls, relative to the performance of all students achieving that grade (or level), minus the entry gap. The achievement gap is thus a measure of the relative achievement of each gender for any grade level.

$$\text{Achievement Gap} = (GA-BA)/(GA+BA).100 - \text{Entry Gap}$$

where GA = the number of girls achieving that grade or better; BA = the number of boys achieving that grade or better. For example, if 500 girls and 500 boys enter Italian GCSE, while 300 girls and 200 boys get graded C or above, then the achievement gap at grade C or above is:

$$(300-200)/(300+200).100 - 0 = 20\%$$

(since the entry gap is 0 and where a positive value is in favour of girls). To put this in plainer terms, 50 per cent of all candidates attained a C or above. If there was no gender gap, we would expect 250 girls to attain a C or above. In fact 300 did, or 20 per cent more than we expect. Similarly, we expect a figure of 250 for boys, and the actual 200 is 20 per cent below what we expect. Therefore, the achievement gap is 20 per cent.

Previous studies, such as DENI (1997), have presented the differences in achievement between genders as pairs of columns representing the percentage of each gender attaining each grade (see Figure 9.1). This approach has the major disadvantage that it does not give the reader an easy overall impression. Even in a simple case such as Figure 9.1, where more girls are achieving high grades and conversely more boys are achieving low grades, it is not easy to answer questions such as: are the same proportion of boys and girls getting a grade G or above? To take another example, if in 1997 more boys than girls gained grade C in maths GCSE, it is not clear whether this means that boys are doing better or worse than girls. On the other hand, if it is known that more girls than boys are gaining grade C *or above* in maths GCSE, then it is clear that girls are doing better than boys. Thus, in most cases, the analyst does not want to know the proportion of each gender attaining each grade in isolation, but the proportion attaining each grade or better (in exactly the same way as in benchmark figures and in previous studies such as Arnot et al. 1996). The data from Figure 9.1 as above are thus presented cumulatively in Figure 9.2. Working from the left, the bars in Figure 9.1 are simply placed on top of each

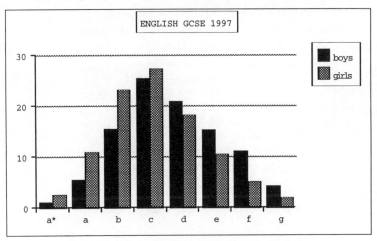

Figure 9.1. Percentage attaining each grade in Wales

other. In this way, it is easier to gauge the gap at grade G or above, for example. Unfortunately, this graph is still as potentially misleading as Figure 9.1, since an unwary reader may believe that it is the difference in height between the pairs of bars that is the gap for each grade. In fact, as has been seen above, the significance of such a percentage point difference varies depending on the overall height of the bar. For example, the achievement gap at grade B in Figure 9.2 is proportionately much larger than at grade C, even though the graph makes them look similar, because the gap at grade B is in relation to a much lower percentage overall.

In order to avoid misleading the reader in this way, and to simplify the graph further, the same data can be presented as in Figure 9.3. The bars in Figure 9.3 represent only the differences between heights of the pairs of bars in Figure 9.2. However, they have been scaled to take into account the total heights of the bars in which they appear. For example, the gap at grade D is 10, meaning that boys account for 45 per cent of those attaining grade D or above, while girls account for 55 per cent. This is the form in which the majority of results are presented, either graphically or in table summaries (further discussion of the derivation of achievement gaps appears in Appendix E).

A similar approach is used with the aggregate results for individuals, such as the proportion attaining the GCSE

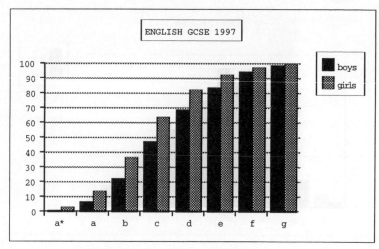

Figure 9.2. Percentage attaining each grade or above in Wales

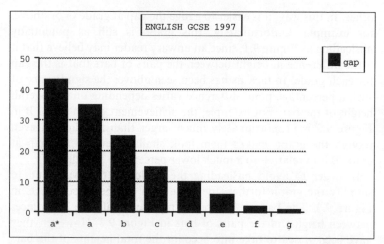

Figure 9.3. Achievement gap in favour of girls at each grade or above

benchmark. The gap between boys and girls is expressed in relation to the entry and to the overall performance. The common use of simple differences in percentage points takes entry differences into account but not the annual changes in performance. This is how it is possible for a naïve observer to conclude that the gap is growing when it is actually static or shrinking (see Table 9.1). In Wales, the

Table 9.1. *Percentage gaining five GCSEs at grade C or above in Wales*

Gender	1992 %	1997 %	Ratio
Boys	28	39	1.39
Girls	38	49	1.29
Achievement gap	15	11	

'gap' between boys and girls in terms of percentage points, of the kind used by Stephen Byers (see Chapter 8), was 10 in 1992 and 10 in 1997. However, since the overall level of attainment rose between 1992 and 1997, the actual achievement gap has fallen between 1992, where girls were doing 15 per cent better than boys on average, and 1997, where girls were doing 11 per cent better on average. The same conclusion is drawn by looking at the improvement in the boys' and girls' scores separately. The boys' score in 1997 was 1.39 times as good as their score in 1992, while the girls' was only 1.29 times as good. Thus, boys are 'catching up' with girls on this measure of attainment. The next section summarizes the most significant results obtained by using these proportionate methods of analysis and presentation.

Subject-specific Findings

Mathematics

In mathematics at Key Stage 1, there is no difference between the proportion of boys and girls in the age cohort who attain at least level 1 (Table 9.2). There is a small gap in favour of girls at level 2 (the 'expected' level for this assessment) and a small gap in favour of boys at level 3 (exceeding expectation). The figures for level 3 are slightly more volatile from year to year, as they represent such a small fraction of the cohort. Otherwise the picture is relatively static, even showing a gradual change towards a totally 'gender neutral' assessment. The figures for Teacher Assessment (TA) and Task or Test (TT) are in close agreement, but it is worth noting at this stage that, where there is a difference, the gap is larger using TA.

Table 9.2. Achievement gap in favour of girls: KS1 mathematics

Attainment	1995	1996	1997
Level 1 TA	1	1	1
Level 1 TT	0	1	1
Level 2 TA	4	4	3
Level 2 TT	3	3	3
Level 3 TA	–6	–4	–3
Level 3 TT	–2	–5	–2

At KS2 in mathematics, where larger numbers in the age cohort attain levels 3 and above, there are no large gaps at any level (Table 9.3). It is still the case that boys are slightly more likely to attain the highest levels at KS1 and KS2, despite the recent reports of the relative underachievement of boys. The relationship between TA and TT is now more complex. It does not appear that TT is necessarily more gender neutral than TA *per se*, but that, where there is a difference, TT tends to produce results more favourable to boys.

Table 9.3. Achievement gap in favour of girls: KS2 mathematics

Attainment	1995	1996	1997
Level 1 TA	–	0	0
Level 1 TT	–	0	0
Level 2 TA	–	–3	–3
Level 2 TT	–	–3	–3
Level 3 TA	–	2	1
Level 3 TT	–	1	1
Level 4 TA	–	–2	–1
Level 4 TT	–	–4	–3
Level 5 TA	–	–3	–3
Level 5 TT	–	–4	–4

At KS3 in mathematics there are no significant gaps at any level using Teacher Assessment, and no significant gaps at levels 5 and 6 (the 'expected' outcome) and below in Task or Test (Table 9.4). Again, there is a suggestion that TT produces results more favourable to boys and that, despite the recent furore in the press the results of boys in mathematics are actually marginally better than those of girls.

Table 9.4. Achievement gap in favour of girls: KS3 mathematics

Attainment	1995	1996	1997
Level 1 TA	–	–2	–2
Level 1 TT	–	–2	–2
Level 2 TA	–	–2	–2
Level 2 TT	–	–2	–2
Level 3 TA	–	–1	–2
Level 3 TT	–	–2	–2
Level 4 TA	–	0	–1
Level 4 TT	–	0	–2
Level 5 TA	–	2	0
Level 5 TT	–	1	–1
Level 6 TA	–	2	0
Level 6 TT	–	1	–2
Level 7 TA	–	0	–5
Level 7 TT	–	–2	–9

There is currently no clear gender gap in either entry or achievement in mathematics at GCSE (Table 9.5). There has not been an entry gap since 1992, although there has until recently been an achievement gap in favour of boys at grades A and then A*. This gap has disappeared at all grades below A*, without there being a clear trend towards a gap in favour of girls. The gap at A* is, as previously noted, very volatile, being attained in 1997 by twenty-five more boys than girls from an examination cohort of 32,000. As with KS1 to KS3, mathematics at GCSE is close to neutral in gender terms, and the differences, such as they are, tend to favour boys slightly at higher grades. Since 1994, there has consistently been no difference in the attainment of boys and girls at grade C and above (the benchmark grade). In terms of differential attainment, the situation has, therefore, improved marginally over time.

The situation at A level is almost identical to that at GCSE. There is not and never has been any difference between the proportion of boys and girls achieving a recognized grade of E or above, and there is little difference at any grade below A (see Table

Table 9.5. Achievement gap in favour of girls: GCSE mathematics

Attainment	1992	1993	1994	1995	1996	1997
Entry	0	1	1	–1	0	1
A*	–	–	–19	–2	–16	–11
A	–7	–2	–11	–2	–5	0
B	–3	–1	–5	0	2	3
C	–3	–2	–1	1	1	1
D	–2	–2	–1	0	1	1
E	–2	–2	0	1	1	1
F	–2	–1	0	1	0	1
G	–1	–1	0	1	0	1

9.6). The gap at grade A in favour of boys has recently disappeared. At present the only clear difference relating to gender in mathematics is an entry gap of around 30 per cent in favour of boys. Of course, if this entry difference were reduced it *might* lead to an achievement gap in favour of boys in its place (if it assumed that in general the strongest candidates are already more likely to be taking any subject).

Table 9.6. Achievement gap in favour of girls: A-level mathematics

Attainment	1992	1993	1994	1995	1996	1997
Entry	–37	–32	–32	–25	–30	–25
A	–7	–15	–5	–3	–5	0
B	–4	–9	–2	–2	2	1
C	–2	–5	0	–2	–2	0
D	–1	–3	0	0	0	0
E	1	–1	0	0	0	0
F	1	–1	0	0	0	0

Sciences

As in mathematics at KS1, the same proportion of boys and girls attain level 1 in science (Table 9.7). There is a small gap in favour of girls at level 2 (the 'expected' level for this assessment), and until 1997 there was a small gap in favour of boys at level 3 (exceeding expectation). Again, as with mathematics, the picture is relatively

Table 9.7. *Achievement gap in favour of girls: KS1 science*

Attainment	1995	1996	1997
Level 1 TA	0	1	1
Level 2 TA	2	3	3
Level 3 TA	–5	–5	0

Table 9.8. *Achievement gap in favour of girls: KS2 science*

Attainment	1995	1996	1997
Level 1 TA	–	0	0
Level 1 TT	–	0	0
Level 2 TA	–	–3	–3
Level 2 TT	–	–3	–3
Level 3 TA	–	1	1
Level 3 TT	–	1	1
Level 4 TA	–	–1	–2
Level 4 TT	–	–2	–3
Level 5 TA	–	–4	–1
Level 5 TT	–	–1	0

static, or even showing a gradual change towards a totally 'gender neutral' assessment. At KS2, there are no large differences in attainment in science between boys and girls at any level, and this picture is remarkably constant across two years (Table 9.8). It would be unwise to read very much into the minor differences from 1996 to 1997 at levels 4 and 5 (although it would be wise to monitor them for the future). In 1997, using Task or Test, exactly the same proportion of boys and girls in the age cohort attained level 1 and level 5. At KS3 science, the results are similar to those for mathematics (Table 9.9). In general, the same proportions of boys and girls attain levels 1 to levels 5 and 6 (the 'expected' outcomes). The gap in favour of boys is larger using TT than TA, but is smaller in 1997 than 1996.

At GCSE there is a constant entry gap of less than four units in favour of boys, and until recently a small achievement gap in favour of boys at the higher grades (Table 9.10). However, neither of these gaps is very large, and they are decreasing over time,

Table 9.9. Achievement gap in favour of girls: KS3 science

Attainment	1995	1996	1997
Level 1 TA	–	–2	–2
Level 1 TT	–	–2	–2
Level 2 TA	–	–2	–2
Level 2 TT	–	–2	–2
Level 3 TA	–	–1	–2
Level 3 TT	–	–2	–2
Level 4 TA	–	–1	–1
Level 4 TT	–	–2	–1
Level 5 TA	–	0	0
Level 5 TT	–	–3	0
Level 6 TA	–	1	–1
Level 6 TT	–	–7	–1
Level 7 TA	–	–5	–2
Level 7 TT	–	–24	–8

Table 9.10. Achievement gap in favour of girls: GCSE science

Attainment	1992	1993	1994	1995	1996	1997
Entry	–4	–4	–4	–4	–5	–2
A*	–	–	–11	–5	–3	3
A	–4	–3	–6	–4	–1	0
B	–2	–2	–3	–3	0	1
C	–2	–2	–2	–2	–2	0
D	–1	–3	–1	–1	–1	–1
E	–1	–2	0	–1	0	0
F	–1	–1	1	0	0	0
G	0	0	0	0	0	0

suggesting that gender is not a clear problem in the sciences. There are, of course, differences within the sciences but they generally fall into two patterns. In double-award and physics and chemistry, there is no clear gap in either entry or achievement. In biology to some extent, in other sciences, and especially in single-award, there is an entry gap in favour of boys and an achievement gap in favour of girls. Since the number of entries for other sciences and single-award are small, these differences do not appear when the science

Table 9.11. *Achievement gap in favour of girls: A-level science*

Attainment	1992	1993	1994	1995	1996	1997
Entry	−16	−15	−13	−13	−17	−15
A	−11	−4	−9	1	1	6
B	−6	−5	−4	1	1	5
C	−4	−3	−2	1	1	3
D	−3	−2	−2	1	1	2
E	0	−1	−3	0	0	1
F	−1	−1	−1	0	0	0

figures are combined. Overall, GCSEs in the sciences are now *precisely* gender neutral at grades E, F and G (the lowest level of pass grade).

At A level the entry gap is more marked than at GCSE, running in favour of boys at around fifteen units. Boys began the period of this study gaining better grades than girls overall, but this achievement gap has now been eliminated and perhaps even reversed (see Table 9.11). Either way, it is the case that sciences at A level are now more gender neutral than in 1992.

English

The picture for English is like the other two core subjects at KS1 in some respects. It is still true that approximately similar proportions of boys and girls attain level 1 (Table 9.12). Again, there are no indications that gaps are growing over time. Where the assessments differ, then Task or Test in Reading leads to smaller gaps than Teacher Assessment or TT Writing. Unlike mathematics and science, there is a significant gap in favour of girls at level 2 (the 'expected' outcome), and a large gap at level 3.

By KS2, approximately equal proportions of boys and girls are attaining level 3 (Table 9.13). A significant gap in favour of girls now appears at level 4 (the 'expected' outcome), and a much larger gap at level 5. The figures are fairly similar over the two complete years, but where changes have occurred they tend towards reducing the size of the gaps. In this case, as with KS1 Writing, the gaps are larger using Task or Test.

Table 9.12. Achievement gap in favour of girls: KS1 English

Attainment	1995	1996	1997
Level 1 TA	0	2	2
Level 1 TT Reading	1	2	2
Level 1 TT Writing	2	3	3
Level 2 TA	7	8	7
Level 2 TT Reading	7	8	7
Level 2 TT Writing	8	8	7
Level 3 TA	25	24	25
Level 3 TT Reading	19	20	20
Level 3 TT Writing	34	28	39

Table 9.13. Achievement gap in favour of girls: KS2 English

Attainment	1995	1996	1997
Level 1 TA	–	0	0
Level 1 TT	–	2	0
Level 2 TA	–	–2	–2
Level 2 TT	–	–4	–2
Level 3 TA	–	3	2
Level 3 TT	–	5	2
Level 4 TA	–	6	6
Level 4 TT	–	6	5
Level 5 TA	–	20	19
Level 5 TT	–	26	19

By KS3 English the gap in favour of girls has grown to thirty-five units at level 7, and around fifteen to twenty-five at levels 5 and 6 (the 'expected' outcomes). While the assessment for English is clearly gender neutral at the lower levels, as with mathematics and science, the relative 'underachievement' of boys is marked in this subject alone of the core subjects at the higher levels (Table 9.14). However, even here some doubt can be cast on the substantive importance of this gender gap in educational terms. In a recent study by the Qualification, Curriculum and Assessment Authority, a closer examination of the written papers at both KS3 and KS4 showed boys actually using more sophisticated (ambitious) words than girls but nevertheless making no more spelling mistakes (Cassidy 1999g). Boys also generally used punctuation better than girls, and wrote more complex sentences. While the writing of boys focused on action rather than elaboration, the writing of girls tended to include more dialogue. It could be on the basis of factors such as these that girls achieve higher grades.

Table 9.14. Achievement gap in favour of girls: KS3 English

Attainment	1995	1996	1997
Level 1 TA	-	-2	-2
Level 1 TT	-	-1	-1
Level 2 TA	-	-1	-2
Level 2 TT	-	-1	-1
Level 3 TA	-	1	0
Level 3 TT	-	1	1
Level 4 TA	-	5	4
Level 4 TT	-	6	4
Level 5 TA	-	15	14
Level 5 TT	-	14	15
Level 6 TA	-	25	26
Level 6 TT	-	23	26
Level 7 TA	-	35	34
Level 7 TT	-	33	35

At GCSE there is a very small entry gap for English language in favour of girls, hovering since 1992 between one and two units, but there are large gaps in achievement at grade D and above (Table 9.15). While this clear evidence of differential attainment may be alarming, it should be noted that, apart from the attenuation at high grades caused by the introduction of the A* grade in 1994 (which affected the gender gap in all subjects), there is no evidence here of any increase in the gap, and some evidence of the reverse. Overall, 1997 was the most gender-neutral year for English GCSE since these records began in 1992.

The situation of English literature at GCSE is similar, but even more favourable for girls, since although the gaps are of the same order of magnitude as in English language, these figures are on top of a marked entry gap in favour of girls of around ten units per year (Table 9.16). As with all subjects, at every level of assessment

Table 9.15. Achievement gap in favour of girls: GCSE English

Attainment	1992	1993	1994	1995	1996	1997
Entry	2	2	3	1	1	2
A*	–	–	43	44	43	43
A	27	31	34	35	36	35
B	23	24	27	24	25	25
C	16	16	18	16	16	15
D	10	10	11	8	9	9
E	5	5	5	4	4	5
F	1	2	1	1	1	2
G	0	0	0	0	0	1

Table 9.16. Achievement gap in favour of girls: GCSE English literature

Attainment	1992	1993	1994	1995	1996	1997
Entry	9	9	11	9	9	10
A*	–	–	22	35	37	34
A	27	29	19	26	31	29
B	22	22	16	18	21	21
C	15	14	11	12	11	12
D	9	9	7	6	7	6
E	5	4	3	3	3	2
F	2	1	1	1	1	1
G	1	0	0	0	0	0

so far, there is no evidence of a deteriorating position, and no evidence that the assessment favours either gender at low levels of attainment.

At A level the entry gap rises to around fifty units in favour of girls; however, the achievement gap then disappears, and is even reversed to some extent (Table 9.17). At high grades boys are doing slightly better than girls. As with A-level mathematics and science, there is now little evidence of a gap below the highest grades, but in this subject there is still no clear evidence of the small gap in favour of boys at the highest grades disappearing. To some extent, the achievement gap at high grades might be reduced by balancing the entry gap.

Table 9.17. *Achievement gap in favour of girls: A-level English*

Attainment	1992	1993	1994	1995	1996	1997
Entry	49	49	46	47	50	51
A	–1	–5	–1	–8	–11	–6
B	3	–2	–1	–3	–7	–2
C	5	–1	0	–1	–4	0
D	2	1	1	0	–2	–1
E	2	0	0	1	–1	0
F	1	0	1	1	0	0

Other subjects

No data are available in Wales relating to KS1 to KS3 in subjects other than the core subjects. At GCSE the humanities and design-related subjects are taken by more boys, and show no achievement gap at low grades, but a disproportionate number of girls gain grades A*–B in these subjects. Modern languages, including Welsh, and minority subjects like economics, are taken by more girls. These subjects also display no achievement gap at low grades, but a disproportionate number of girls gain grades A*–B. At A level, this position changes significantly. In modern languages and minority subjects, the entry gap rises to around sixty units in favour of girls, but the results show no gender gap at any grade. More girls take these A levels, but proportionately they do no better or worse than boys. Humanities A levels are taken by approximately even numbers, while design-related subjects are more popular with boys. In both groups, there have been no significant achievement gaps at any grade until recently. In humanities the gap in favour of girls at A grade rose from two to twenty-one units, and in design-related subjects the gap at A grade rose from zero to twenty. In both cases the change is only apparent at the highest grade, but the situation should nevertheless be monitored for the future.

Aggregate Findings

All subjects combined

If the results of all subjects are combined to give an assessment of the examination system for each age group as a whole, the rather complex details above can be simplified somewhat (Table 9.18). This table shows the achievement gap in favour of girls at the benchmark for each assessment (level 2 KS1, level 4 KS2, level 5 KS3, grade C GCSE, grade C A level). Given that the entry gap at GCSE remains constant at around three units in favour of girls (taking more GCSEs), and at A level at around ten units, it is clear that the differential attainment of boys and girls has not changed much over the past six years. Indeed, on these figures, it would be difficult to 'extrapolate' to a time when the situation was much different. Girls in any year group are proportionately more likely to achieve any individual benchmark grade (taking into account entry gaps which could themselves be the result of prior differential attainment in the immediately receding stage of education), but there is certainly no backing here for the *recent* moral panic about failing boys.

Table 9.18. Achievement gaps in favour of girls for each 'benchmark'

Benchmark	1992	1993	1994	1995	1996	1997
KS1	–	–	–	4	5	4
KS2	–	–	–	–	2	0
KS3	–	–	–	–	5	5
GCSE	7	7	8	8	8	8
A level	1	–1	0	2	0	2

Official indicators

When the official government benchmarks of aggregate profiles for individuals are examined, the situation is even more markedly different from the standard accounts outlined in the introduction (Table 9.19). The 'difference' between boys and girls in percentage point terms remains at around 10 for every year. However, this point difference is not the gender achievement gap, which must be calculated proportional to the overall annual achievement. The achievement 'gap' – or point difference divided by the overall attainment – takes these annual changes into account and shows a somewhat different pattern. It is the confusion between percentages and percentage points that may have led observers to conclude that the gap was static or increasing when it is actually decreasing.

Table 9.19. *Percentage gaining five GCSEs at grade C or above*

	1992	1993	1994	1995	1996	1997
Boys	28	32	35	36	37	39
Girls	38	42	44	46	47	49
Difference	10	10	9	10	10	10
Gap	15	14	11	12	12	11

If the achievement gap in favour of girls is not growing but is actually declining, this raises the question: when were boys ahead (and it should be noted that other official indicators show the same picture of decreasing gender gaps)? There are no data to answer the question from this study, but two points should be noted. If extrapolation was done only using the above data, there would be no reason to assume that there had ever been a gap in favour of boys. In addition, the figures from the DfEE (1999b), using the percentage of school leavers as an estimate of the age cohort size, show a small gap in favour of girls at O level stretching as far back as 1974 for England (the earliest records available from this source).

Local and regional differences
From an initial analysis of those gender-based assessment results that have been published for England, there is no reason to suppose that the situation in England is very different from that described here. Although a full analysis, with access to the 'raw' data for England, should be completed, using an appropriate proportionate method of calculating gaps, it is very likely that the findings reported here present another example of the usefulness of Wales as a coherent but diverse 'social laboratory' (see Gorard 2000), in the sense that full results for England can be predicted from the more manageable figures for Wales. Nevertheless, it is likely that there are differences *within* England and Wales which are much larger than any differences between them (see below).

In making sense of local differences in the differential attainment of boys and girls, it is necessary first to address a contradiction (presumably unnoticed by its perpetrators) that has been creeping into reports and policy decisions in this area. It is perhaps most obvious as presented by Stephen Byers as the school standards minister. The gender gap, according to this account, is the same 'across the country' (*Observer* 4 January 1998, p. 1), and not related to local differences in indicators such as male unemployment. Stephen Byers argues that the gap is as much a middle-class as a working-class phenomenon, and the evidence presented for this is the observation that the percentage point gap in favour of girls is 15 in both Richmond and Hackney, even though both areas have markedly different socio-economic profiles (Carvel 1998a). However, he goes on to say that further down the achievement range from the 5+ benchmark (that is, at lower grades) the problem of boys' underachievement is worse, with more serious social consequences (Bright 1998). Thus, his 'analysis' leads to the contradiction that the gap is not seen as class related, but is smaller at the higher grade levels generally obtained by students of elevated class status, and larger at the low levels associated with indicators of poverty.

The present study may have the means to resolve this contradiction. First, it is clear that the notion of boys' underachievement being worse at low levels of attainment is simply incorrect. There are, of course, differences in the number of boys and girls with statements of special educational need, and there may be non-academic behavioural reasons for these. However, the number of such children is small. In terms of the entire age cohort, the achievement gap *only* appears at high grades, while the proportions of boys and girls 'failing' any examination are similar, and constant over time. Given the established link between socio-economic conditions and examination success, this does make it highly unlikely that the gender gap is primarily to do with disaffected boys from economically depressed families. The second problem leading to the contradiction is that the figures used are percentage points, and not percentages, and they need to be placed in the context of the base figure from which they are taken. Put simply, since Hackney and Richmond have a gap of 15 percentage points, but the benchmark figure for attainment in Hackney is much lower, this portrays how much more serious the actual achievement gap is in Hackney than Richmond. A similar mistake is made in the report by Cassidy (1999f) when describing an increase in the 'literacy' gap between boys and girls, and suggesting that the regions of greatest improvement are those where boys are 'falling furthest behind'. Nevertheless, when the actual gender gap is compared with the overall level of attainment of official benchmarks in an area (and indeed over time in the same area), there is no obvious relationship, and scatterplots reveal only a uniform distribution for LEAs in England.

There are no substantial differences between the results examined at the level of the eight old LEAs in Wales, in terms of any GCSE measures below grade A (Table 9.20). Approximately equal numbers of boys and girls enter all GCSEs combined, and equal numbers gain the minimum pass grade. At grade C, the national achievement gap in favour of girls is constant across LEAs. Only at grade A are there marked differences between LEAs (which do not therefore show up in benchmarks using grade C). The pattern is broken and weak at this level of aggregation, but in general the gap at high levels is larger in more densely populated regions, with higher unemployment and lower overall GCSE results. Powys, the LEA with the most elevated socio-economic status (in terms of eligibility for free school meals) has the smallest achievement gap at grade A, despite having the highest overall GCSE results as well. The regions with the lowest population densities generally have the lowest gaps. The position at A level is less clear. There is a significant entry gap in favour of girls in each LEA of the same order of magnitude as for Wales overall. The achievement gaps at the lowest grade are small. At A grade, most LEAs have had years since 1992 when the achievement gap was in favour of boys and years when the gap was in favour of girls, but all now have a smaller gap than in 1992.

Clearly, more data are necessary and more work is required on local variation using the twenty-two new unitary authorities, but one working hypothesis to be tested by any extension of this study would be as follows. It is possible that the gendered achievement gap is larger in areas in which schools are more likely to be seen as underperforming using value-added analyses. For example, four characteristics of LEAs have been found, in combination, to be related to the size of the gap at GCSE level: the overall GCSE results, the percentage of householders in social class I and II, the percentage of children eligible for free school meals and the population density. Together they can predict/explain around 50 per cent of the variance in the size of the gaps at LEA level (in both Wales and England). When these are combined in such a way that

Table 9.20. Mean achievement gap at GCSE, 1992–1997

LEA	A	C	G	Entry	FSM%	Density	Class I/II
Powys	5	7	–	–	6	0.2	43
Dyfed	14	8	–	4	13	0.6	37
Gwent	14	8	–	2	16	3.2	32
Gwynedd	15	8	–	–	12	0.6	36
Clwyd	17	8	–	2	12	1.7	34
W. Glam	17	9	–	1	18	4.4	32
Mid Glam	17	7	–	2	19	5.2	28
S. Glam	19	7	–	3	15	9.4	40

the total variance is partitioned between them, a region with a lower gap would have a low population density, low proportion of free school meals, few 'professional/executive' families and a relatively high GCSE benchmark. This description applies to Powys and to a lesser extent to Dyfed, which in a previous study was shown to have slightly better GCSE results than would be predicted from a simple value-added model (see Chapter 5). A mirror area with a higher population density, and a more 'polarized' population (in terms of free school meals and occupational class), such as South Glamorgan, may have lower overall as well as lower than expected GCSE results, and also a larger gender gap.

Summary of Findings

The analysis presented here suggests a more complex pattern of school performance by boys and girls than is widely portrayed. When examined at an all-Wales level, using total subject entries, it is clear that girls perform slightly better than boys in the system of statutory assessment and examination at KS4. For example, girls tend to enter more, and more varied, subjects at GCSE, achieving more higher grades overall. At A level, where students exercise a greater choice of subjects, entry gaps tend to be larger, whilst the achievement gaps tend to be smaller than in GCSE. In general, gender appears to play less of a role in attainment at A level. When broken down into subject groups, achievement gaps are largest in English (and Welsh) at KS1 to KS4. There are also significant achievement gaps in some other subject groups. These gaps appear year after year, and they are nearly always in favour of girls. The exceptions to this pattern are mathematics and sciences, which constitute the majority of core subjects, where there are *no* systematic differences at any age between the performance of boys and girls.

There are also no systematic differences at any age between the performance of boys and girls at the lowest level of *any* measure of attainment, such as level 1 KS1 or grade G GCSE. The overall conclusion is, therefore, that the system assesses girls and boys equally at the lowest levels. This finding is in direct contradiction to theories that the achievement gap is primarily a problem at lower levels of attainment and among lower ability or 'demotivated' boys. The achievement gap in favour of girls (in subjects where it exists) is actually largest at the highest levels of attainment. In general, the size of the achievement gap gets larger at successive attainment levels. The gap in favour of girls at middle levels of attainment, in subjects where it exists such as grade C in GCSE English, has been constant for the past six years. In contrast to reports of a growing overall achievement gap, even in the subjects where girls' superior performance is most marked, the differential attainment of boys and girls remains static or even reduces over time when considered at the benchmark levels, such as level 2 at KS1 or grade C in GCSE.

The achievement gap between boys and girls in terms of aggregate measures, such as the percentage attaining five or more GCSEs at grades A* to C, has declined since 1992. These findings provide an important corrective to many previous accounts of boys' 'underachievement'. Of course, it remains a matter of concern that, in general terms, boys are performing less well than girls in any subjects (and vice versa), and also if any students of either gender are underachieving. Nevertheless, in terms of the pattern of achievement gaps identified here, it is important that the scale and nature of this 'underachievement' is clearly understood, in order for research on the reasons for the gaps to be useful, and for appropriate policies to be drawn up to deal with it.

The Implications

Of course, the picture of gender gaps painted by this study in Wales could be very different from England and elsewhere. It could be that the gender gap in England is uniformly distributed along the ability and achievement range, or even that it is larger at the lower levels. The analysis simply has not been done, although there are a few commentaries involving England which *do* use proportionate figures, and therefore tell a story compatible with this one, of 'stabilized disparity' between boys and girls, and smaller differences at lower grades (e.g. Paechter 1998, Hillman and Pearce 1998). A reduction in the gender gap in reading at KS2 was recently reported for 1999 (Bunting et al. 1999). Several other current analyses suffer from at least one of three defects: they are small-scale snapshots of single grades or years; they do not calculate the gap as proportionate to the overall achievement (the 'politician's error'); or they consider the gap at snapshot grades rather than at each grade and above. In fact, the analysis so far of data from England suggests that the picture there is the same as in Wales – perhaps a case of 'for England see Wales'? It is interesting how often the small and manageable but diverse national dataset for Wales has recently been used to uncover educational processes that are only later discerned for England.

If one accepts as broadly true the notion that quantitative analysis is good at establishing what the differences actually are in the attainment of boys and girls, and that qualitative analysis is better at explaining how and why these differences occur, then qualitative research in this area has a problem derived from its quantitative analytical framework. The majority of British work has been attempting to explain a pattern that does not, in fact, exist. This finding may have implications for the conduct of educational research in general, as well as specific points to make about the apparent underachievement of boys. This point is picked up again in Chapter 10.

In fact, the results in this chapter lead to several important conclusions: for the value of regional studies, for the conduct of educational research, for the crisis account of increasing differential attainment between students and for policies to deal with the gender gap.

Policies to counter the gender gap
General research literature attempting to explain the determinants of the gaps is relatively plentiful, but recent work is overwhelmingly concerned with a pattern of boys' 'underachievement' which

is conceptualized as a general phenomenon, applying to boys as a relatively homogeneous category (or perhaps slanted towards lower levels of attainment). For a detailed review of this literature see Salisbury et al. (1999). Given the nature of these previous research findings, it is not surprising that proposals with respect to ameliorative action have focused on raising the level of boys' performance generally. Younger and Warrington (1996, p. 312), for example, on the basis of extensive empirical analysis, set out a pretty typical agenda for remedial action. They suggest the use of more interactive teaching–learning styles and resources, and differentiation of teaching materials and approaches; a renewed focus on the dynamics of the classroom, and the nature and quality of teacher–student interactions; improvements in the functioning of the tutorial/pastoral system in the school, to ensure that all students feel valued and supported; monitoring of the structure and nature of coursework assessment at GCSE, to ensure variety, equal access and renewed opportunities, within an integrated teaching programme; a focus on the goals and aspirations of students, and how these might be raised; an analysis of the ways in which the school contributes to and can influence the self-concept and self-image which students develop.

More focused proposals have also been advocated. OHMCI (1997) has recommended, for example, that particular attention be paid to issues such as identifying and supporting underachieving individuals at KS3 and KS4; improving classroom management with the specific objective of integrating boys and girls more effectively; setting targets both for individual students and subject departments; monitoring the effects of setting arrangements; and so on. A number of action-research projects have adopted strategies of mentoring to improve the performance of boys. Similarly, considerable attention has been directed at strategies for enhancing boys' language competencies.

The evidence is simply not available as yet to allow judgements to be formed on the effectiveness of these kinds of measures. It would be difficult to argue against them in general terms, but it is important to emphasize that they are not directed – and presumably are not intended to be directed – at addressing the complex pattern of differential attainment which this study has revealed. The conclusions of much of the relevant work are in the form of suggested explanations. Some have very little empirical basis, many are based on very small-scale work and nearly all are directed at explaining the prevalent picture of gender gaps in school performance. Since that picture has been found to be false, even the most convincing explanations of that false picture are in doubt, and their implications for remedial action inappropriate.

Recommendations with respect to ameliorative policies are very different where the problem to be tackled is defined in closely specified terms. Extensive further research aimed at understanding actual patterns of differential attainment is a necessary pre-condition of effective intervention to reduce it. The research would need to explain the differences in achievement gaps between subjects and between levels of attainment. For example, it appears that the effects of different forms of literacy are felt especially where students are attaining above a given threshold of performance. It may be that some students – both boys and girls – are disadvantaged sufficiently by, for example, their family backgrounds to obscure the effects of gender differentiation. Hence, only where students do not experience this disadvantage, and are thus achieving higher levels of attainment, does gender differentiation occur. This is consistent with the general research on the influences of home backgrounds and the actual distribution of achievement gaps identified in this study, but further research is required to develop a proper understanding of the specific processes at work here.

Again, if the dynamics of classroom interaction between student and teacher are significant in affecting student motivation, engagement and achievement, then, to the extent that this interaction is differentiated by gender, it provides a possible explanation of differential attainment by boys and girls. However, it is clear that further evidence is required to clarify these effects of student–teacher interaction. Evidence from Wales is very limited (although, see, for example, OHMCI, 1996; WSSA/OHMCI, 1996). More-over, how gendered patterns of classroom interaction operate with students at different levels of attainment remains to be explored. In this context, it is instructive that Younger and Warrington (1996) identify poor student–teacher interaction as affecting achievement for both boys and girls at lower attainment levels. It may be, therefore, that gender differentiation in respect of classroom interaction operates only at higher attainment levels. If this proves to be the case, then teachers need to develop their pedagogies and classroom management to take account of this characteristic pattern of differentiation.

There are currently numerous other initiatives aimed at ameliorating the incidence of achievement gaps through various approaches to mentoring, the targeting of 'underachievers', the enhancement of boys' language competencies, single-sex setting and so on. It is clearly important to monitor the results of these programmes. However, in many cases, it seems unlikely that adequate data will be made available to allow proper evaluation. Even so, the desperate need for such studies may be glimpsed in the way in which a study of two teachers in one school (Woolford and McDougall 1998) was built by the media into a panacea requiring immediate changes in policy (*Western Mail* (5 February 1998) p. 1; *TES* (6 January 1998), p. 21). There is a case, therefore, for the implementation of properly constituted action-research projects designed to investigate the true impacts of these kinds of initiative. At the most basic level, there is a clear need to monitor the differential performance of boys and girls in assessment over time. In some areas, such as GNVQ, this will entail the generation of more detailed information than is currently available. The current confusion in this field is helping to build a moral panic about the underachievement of boys. Left unchecked, this panic might (and in some cases already does) influence the allocation of government and local authority finance, or even the funding of educational research.

The chief focus of this chapter has been on gendered attainment in compulsory schooling. Although examination performance at age sixteen is clearly a determinant of later academic route, the apparent advantages enjoyed at school by some high-performing girls are not always 'cashed out' into later advantage in higher education and beyond (e.g. Riddell 1992). This needs to be considered by those 'social engineers' wishing to intervene to make academic assessment gender neutral in the same way as psychometrics strove in the past to make IQ tests gender neutral (in Stobart et al. 1992). Having statistically balanced results at GCSE, for example, may look neat, but intervening to achieve that neatness has potential knock-on effects for the relative position of men and women in society.

10

Putting it All Together: Education and Social Justice

If the foregoing reanalysis of the crisis account is accepted, then the immediate implications are mostly pleasant ones (and it is important to note that in each of the case studies presented there is no issue of sampling error, and the data presented are official statistics: so that, in terms of the indicators used, this *is* what happened). In each of the themes discussed, the situation for schools and education more generally is better than it appears on first acquaintance. Readers may care to take a moment to reflect on that. For adherents of the crisis account, except perhaps for journalists, this book contains good news. Social justice in British education is growing, as divisions between the home nations, between school sectors, between schools and between students are declining. Of course, this does not mean that there is much room for complacency, since the divisions are still large and injustice in the education system is still rife. The remainder of this chapter is devoted to a consideration of the implications stemming from the substantive findings presented in this book, which are summarized here for convenience:

- Schools are becoming more socially mixed over time, as students of differing social and ethnic backgrounds are becoming more evenly spread between schools (Chapters 2 and 3).
- International variation in the standard and effectiveness of education systems is exaggerated (Chapters 4 and 5).
- There are no clear differences between the effectiveness of different types and sectors of schooling (Chapters 6 and 7).
- Gaps between the attainment of different groups of students, and between the highest and lowest attainers, are decreasing over time (Chapters 8 and 9).

Was there a Golden Age?

Progress in the twentieth century has led to considerable improvements in social inclusion and opportunities by gender, ethnicity and class, and these improvements apply to education as much as any other social phenomenon. It would be inappropriate to deny, or downplay, this progress. Whatever our complaints may be in retrospect, the 1944 Education Act, the comprehensivization of schools, perhaps even the 1988 Education Reform Act and a host of other initiatives, have all attempted to produce greater social justice in our education system, and to some extent they have all succeeded. To admit these improvements is not to deny the existence of the remaining problems, but to help describe the current situation more precisely and so define those problems more closely.

Reasonably authoritative sources can be cited to show that people of all periods in the twentieth century were worried about standards, underachievement, literacy and inequality in education, pretty much as they are now. This is certainly true of 1904 and 1943 (in Lestor 1979). There may be a tendency for each generation to perceive a decline in standards. Perhaps it is simply that more and more is expected from education over time.

In fact, some evidence is available that schools are not only improving their statutory assessment scores over time, but that other problems such as truancy are declining, while schools are becoming more efficient in economic terms (Bradley et al. 1999). If true, it is welcome that these general improvements in the standards of, and outcomes from, education also appear to be reducing the educational inequalities between different social groups and geographical regions. Kelsall and Kelsall (1974) present some evidence that the gap between the top and bottom of the social scale in economic, power and status terms was being reduced by the 1970s. Although inequality and injustice for the socially disadvantaged has always existed, in fact, 'if you take a long-term historical perspective of the provision of education in the UK throughout its entire statutory period . . . you could say that a constant move towards greater justice and equity has been the hallmark of the whole process' (MacKay 1999, p. 344).

Plethora of Remedies

In Britain there are presently many active projects, programmes and policies intended to improve the education system. Most are in the form of initiatives to raise examination/test scores, and even where they are attempts to improve equity and justice they mostly plan to achieve this by relative improvements in examination scores. Some of these plans have appeared in the chapters of this book, including calls for the reduction of selection in GM schools, for literacy and numeracy hours, citizenship, national targets, homework clubs, male primary teachers, summer schools, teacher 'Oscars', the University for Industry, educational action zones, the abolition of the Assisted Places Scheme, individual learning accounts, a ban on calculators and the 'national curriculum for teacher training'. A recent scheme is a revision of the GCSE examination timetable, allowing subjects with large numbers of entries to be tested later, so allowing more revision time for most candidates (Cassidy 1999h). A survey by the NFER of 245 schools found that they had introduced no fewer than 630 separate approaches to raising scores at Key Stage 2 alone (Sharp 1999). There is truly a plethora of remedies for education and social justice.

Unfortunately, the basis for many of these plans, in addition to the reason why we have so many, is the standard crisis account of British education: standards are falling, gaps are growing and inequality is rising. As this book has, I hope, made clear, this account is far from proven. Since the diagnosis may be wrong, the remedies are often not appropriate, being based on incomplete or incorrect knowledge of the educational problem to be solved.

At best, an inappropriate 'remedy' will be ineffective. Research findings indicative of the ineffectiveness of some of these recent policies already exist. On the return to basics, international studies have failed to unearth much evidence that style of teaching has a significant impact on attainment. Nor has any relationship been found between test results and the time spent on topics in class. We generally teach as we do on faith alone, since 'education is still in the dark ages' (Kelley 1999, p. 2). Policy-makers have used the apparently poor showing of British schools in international comparisons to introduce a return to traditional classroom practices, despite the fact that British students already had more skills practice than most countries and that pupils using calculators performed better (Brown 1998a). Recent evidence suggests that, despite the introduction of twenty minutes' homework per day for eight-year-olds, homework actually does little to raise standards (Cassidy 1999i). Teachers and their styles, qualifications and skills have been found to make little difference to results (Kelley 1999), perhaps not surprisingly, given the strong and consistent relationship between attainment and socio-economic background. Large-scale longitudinal studies, such as the Youth Cohort Study, the Labour Force Survey and the National Child Development Study, all show this strong relationship between socio-economic disadvantage and educational attainment. They provide no indication yet that factors such as pre-school experience, class size, teaching methods, homework policy, streaming or setting have any impact on literacy or numeracy skills.

Educational improvements resulting from changes of policy or practice are anyway slow to impact, and generally incremental (e.g. McPherson and Willms 1987), but few policy-makers will have the patience or political lifetime to see them through. If changes do not work immediately, a new or revised plan can be added and advertised. Therefore, there is little need, nor apparently any time, for painstaking research findings to underpin any changes. Perhaps policy-makers believe that policy changes will produce results quicker than a proper programme of research. In effect, Britain may now have two levels of educational research: academic studies, and what could be termed policy-based action-research.

At worst an inappropriate remedy can cause new problems, perhaps without even affecting the problem it is introduced to solve. Those who advocate sitting boys and girls alternately in class for the benefit of the boys do not appear to consider the possible impact on the girls. Studies in New Zealand and Australia found that computational skill was negatively correlated with the frequency of skills practice in class (Brown 1998a). The literacy hour, which actually requires disproportionate class time, may be an inadvertent threat to the acknowledged international excellence of science teaching in primary schools (Cassidy 1999j). More frequent homework in primary schools may actually be associated with lower levels of attainment (Farrow et al. 1999).

Of course, none of the evidence of the ineffectiveness or dangers of recent remedies is necessarily any better than the evidence of the problems for which the solutions are devised. Nevertheless, the fact that these points are still debatable suggests that insufficient basic research may have been done. It is, of course, not unusual for researchers to call for more research to be done. The point here is that the identifiable requirement is for a specific form of research, but not necessarily the kind that recent public reports have been advocating (Hillage et al. 1998; Tooley and Darby 1998).

Educational Research

As is shown in Appendix C, alternative ways of analysing the same dataset are not new. Bowen (1972) gives an illustrative example of contradictory conclusions drawn from apparently similar analyses of similar data. In a 1962 House of Commons debate, Gaitskell (opposition) reported the student population divided by the total population for several countries to show how poor the equivalent position in Britain was. Brooke (government) replied with the percentages of the relevant age group graduating from universities in these same countries to show how good the position in Britain was. Such differing interpretations are not a new phenomenon. However, in an era when expenditure on educational research is being closely audited, amid claims that much research is not helpful, not practical or is ideologically driven, the implications for researchers are considerable. The majority of British researchers seem to use what they term a 'qualitative' approach (although ironically it is clear from some methodological writings that this is still seen as a radical and minority stance). Some of these appear simply to take on trust any findings involving numeric analysis, while others seem to reject all research involving numbers as somehow untrustworthy (what Mortimore and Sammons, 1997, p. 185, call 'crude anti-quantitative attitudes'). Neither of these approaches leads to the rigorous checking necessary for the cumulation of knowledge. Accounts based on numeric and qualitative analyses, therefore, too often lead to an apparent contradiction (Riddell 1992, p. 46), because the qualitative analyses are attempting to explain a situation based on flawed numeric reasoning. Qualitative researchers are, therefore, doing themselves a disservice by engaging insufficiently with the descriptive statistical data on which their explanatory research is often based (such as those attempting to explain a 'growing' gender gap through a close examination of classroom processes). On the other hand, researchers using a 'quantitative' approach, such as those in the school effectiveness movement, appear to be drawn to more and more complex methods of analysis, leaving consideration of such simple issues as the misuse of proportionate data to others.

This book, therefore, leads to a further plea for a middle way in educational research: numerate, rational, empirical and balanced (Gorard 1998e). If the research community does not respond to this call, then the reputedly poor quality of much educational research may continue to be used to justify the curtailing of academic freedoms in this area, making research subservient to the needs of the government or one of its client groups such as teacher trainers (see Hillage et al. 1998). Of course, research probably needs policy-makers as much as policy-makers should need research, since unless the research eventually leads to practical outcomes, it is unfettered by reality and, therefore, untestable. Once these constraints of testability are removed, 'researchers' can write pretty much what they want (and on the evidence presented in this book, at least some may already be doing so). The outcome is no longer accounted research and, therefore, probably rightly, is ignored by policy-makers (Hargreaves 1999). It is already evident that public bodies are prepared to ignore or withhold research findings that would threaten their planned budgets. This may be one further reason why bad news is apparently preferable to good news. No one votes funds for institutions to tackle good news. On the other hand, research cannot be simply subordinated to the needs of policy-makers and political agitators without being in danger of becoming contract 'research' which may be used to justify already prepared programmes of action. In order to avoid this, the British educational research community probably needs to start policing itself better before someone else is appointed to do the job for them (cf. Brown 1998b). Recognizing this could be a good start in navigating a course between the Scylla of ineffectuality and the Charybdis of intellectual censorship.

The second major improvement that could be achieved, in addition to the removal of the over-used distinction between qualitative and quantitative approaches, would be the weakening of political pressure on researchers. The government wishes such pressure to increase, to control research both financially and intellectually, but perhaps the greatest pressure is coming from researchers themselves. Lauder (whose work is criticized in Chapter 2) has devoted a lot of effort to defending his own study and, as is right and proper, looking for potential flaws in work with which he disagrees. Yet he seems to have accepted the conclusions of Gibson and Asthana, with which he agrees, uncritically and despite the clear problems with their methods. The fact that this is so could be indicative of a 'political/personal' rather than a methodological or substantive motivation, which though understandable cannot be allowed to alter social science facts (such as they are). Vance Randall et al. (1999, p. 14) point out that 'in part the political reaction to unpopular research is a defense mechanism and a signal that research has hit a nerve . . . [A]reas of study . . . provoke passionate responses, even anger and controversy.' Surely, unless researchers can greet all possible outcomes of their empirical investigations with at least equal respect, are prepared to be surprised by what they find, and apply the same standards of rigour to other people's work regardless of whether they approve of the findings or not, then they are not behaving as researchers but as political agents.

A famous example of the difficulties of behaving as a researcher, rather than an agent, come from the findings of James Coleman in the USA. In 1966 Coleman was hailed by a majority of liberal commentators for finding out about the academic success taking place in Black and White integrated classrooms – for proving, perhaps, that ethnic integration was not only morally approved, but also educationally effective. Then, having used almost identical techniques of large-scale data analysis, in 1981 he was vilified by the same establishment for suggesting that disadvantaged children, including many of those of Black or Hispanic origin, did better at Catholic private schools than they did at schools in the state sector. The point here is not to claim that either study was beyond criticism but to suggest that, when we as peers say 'I really like this work', we are all too often saying that we approve of the findings rather than admiring the rigour of the analysis or the replicability of the data collection or the logic involved in drawing the conclusions.

A more recent example explains part of why this might be so. Thrupp (1998) has raised concerns about the political implications of school effectiveness work in New Zealand by Harker and Nash (1996) which suggests that there is no school mix effect. In other words, a large-scale study has suggested that there is no 'halo' effect, whereby having large proportions of privileged or underprivileged children in a school would disproportionately increase or decrease (respectively) the school achievement scores. Despite this, Thrupp claims that the school mix effect must exist, on the basis of his own small-scale study of processes in schools which actually took as its starting assumption (that is, before collecting any data) that the school mix effect existed. The original purpose of his study was to establish a possible explanation of the mechanics of the effect, yet the work has now been turned around to be used as primary proof that the effect exists. Nash (1998) disputes this 'proof' on the basis of his much larger numeric analyses designed specifically to measure the effect. This may be another example of spurious but plausible qualitative results based on flawed quantitative reasoning. Nash is taking a pedantic 'realist' position in arguing for the evidence about what is actually happening in the education system, 'supporting coherent and honest argument as a means of discovering what the world is really like, in order to be better able to act within it' (Nash 1998, p. 223). Thrupp, like Griffiths (Chapter 1), is taking a political stance by stating: 'research issues . . . *are* important but we should not lose sight . . . of the urgent social justice concerns which are at stake' (Thrupp 1998, p. 234). In fact, he goes on to suggest that Nash should not say what he does about there being no school mix effect, *not* because it may be wrong, but in case it leads to increasing polarization in schools. This is at least partly why I quote Winston Smith (from the novel *Nineteen Eighty-Four*) at the end of Chapter 1. Words may be powerful things, but surely as social scientists we cannot be scared of saying anything if it is true? The main political argument used in the field of social justice is that we must not publish findings that suggest good news in case they are used as a justification to make things worse again. Thrupp is not alone in this approach, and it is one that has to be jettisoned by all of us to some extent.

It has been suggested elsewhere that research findings do not really matter, in the sense that actors take so little note of them (Gazial and Blass 1999), and this is clearly a powerful idea. However, as I hope to have suggested so far, at least part of the reason for this lack of impact is the lack of substance in some educational research. Perhaps this is the same idea that makes other commentators push for concentration on classroom interaction and the processes of teaching and learning (e.g. Whitehead 1998), but, rather than delimit what could and could not be researched in this way, perhaps we could return to an updated form of 'political arithmetic' as a first basis for educational research. This is clearly an ideal, but then the search for social justice is full of ideals. If research is to be cumulative, we should start with the basics, get the simple things correctly set down and move on from there. This is clearly going to involve numbers, but not necessarily difficult calculations. Of course, social processes such as education are complex, and the findings of research based on them are also often complex, but this should not be used as a practical justification for starting where the complexity is greatest – rather the reverse.

Problems that Remain

Claiming that inequality in education, or the standard of education generally, is bad and getting worse over time provides a hostage to fortune for critics of the crisis account. As this book has made clear, the problems of education are *not* getting worse over time. Perhaps they are simply becoming less acceptable. The danger then is that, as these problems are not getting worse, people will believe the problems are also not that bad (the author has had personal experience of this, for example, when a sub-editor headlined a newspaper article about *increasing* comprehensivization with 'Divisions not very deep'). It is sometimes hard to separate the absolute and the proportionate in this area, but the improvements charted in this book should not be allowed to obscure the deep divisions that remain in education today. Even if things are getting better perhaps they are not improving quickly enough, and the remainder of this chapter is devoted to a brief consideration of what can be done to remedy the situation. It is important to get to this stage of a closer definition of the problems for education and social justice in order to be able to begin to describe reasonable solutions, and a 'beginning' is all that is possible here.

It has been shown that the only worsening crises in British education are relatively minor ones, such as the possible polarization of results between GM and LEA-controlled schools and the possibly growing discrepancy of those with no qualifications. Both of these require further work, involving the investigation of fairly closely defined questions. In general, however, it is not clear how to deal with social justice issues of this type. Inequalities in education (usually expressed as differential attainment by groups) can be classified in several ways. This book has presented these inequalities at different levels of aggregation, from international comparisons to achievement gaps between groups of students. Another way of classifying the same inequalities would be in terms of the natural response to alleviate them. In some cases the differences between groups should be tackled at source. For example, if families in poverty are less likely to achieve high grades in any scholastic assessment it would be an inexplicable, although relatively common, reaction to accept the poverty and try to change the nature of the assessment. Neither the poverty nor the educational inequality are acceptable, and both should be tackled. However, poverty has a prior place in the hierarchy of needs, both for a society and for the individuals concerned. Compare the comment of one respondent who describes a clear hierarchy of needs, 'I can cope with the old man knocking me about a bit, but I can't cope with not feeding my kids' (Ghouri 1999b, p. 14), and imagine how she feels about class sizes, for example. In the same way, if those in poverty are found to be less likely to have life insurance, it might not be considered an appropriate use of public funds to provide free life insurance for those without decent homes or food.

As another example, if boys are less likely to achieve high grades in any scholastic assessment, it is not necessarily possible to deal with the problem directly through a change in society, or the distribution of economic rewards. In this case, therefore, the natural reaction is to intervene to equalize the forms of assessment or boost the scores of boys. Similarly, a natural reaction to the polarization of GM and LEA schools might be to merge the two systems, or abolish one of them. In some senses, then, while the former inequalities (by nation, poverty and occupational class) are more properly the realm of politics, the latter inequalities (by ethnicity, gender and type of school) are more naturally the prerogative of educators. However, it is not clear that this 'natural' difference in response is always a useful one. Until the inequalities in society have been addressed more fully (and perhaps more expensively) we cannot begin to answer questions such as whether there should be no achievement gaps in education. Therefore, the next and final section considers the relationship between society and education more generally.

Society is to Blame

To a large extent, problems in British education can be alleviated simply by rejecting the crisis account of what Slee (1998, p. 261) calls 'a pathological discourse of derision of poor teachers and failing schools', and the related notion of investment in human capital. Children in Britain already spend more time on examinations than those in any other European country (Rafferty 1999), perhaps because education has been hijacked by a very simple view of 'relevance', skill and generic or key skills (Barrow 1999). By reducing education to examination results and gain scores, human capitalists have discouraged schools from releasing creativity, teaching 'really useful knowledge . . . calculated to make you free' (Johnson 1993, p. 23), encouraging criticism (not an area that any government is likely to push), getting it right, seeing falsity and preserving society from what Barrow calls the 'higher nonsense'. It is ironic that several of the countries previously held up as models of both economic and educational excellence (see Chapter 4), and which Britain was set to follow as models of good practice, have now suffered an economic recession that was unrelated to their human capital, and are now looking to Britain and elsewhere for models of schooling to overcome their failures in creating 'thinking skills'.

It is good that, at the start of the twenty-first century, we take stock and acknowledge all the things that are going right in terms of education and social justice. But inequality and poverty still exist, despite the apparent progress of educational solutions. In fact, as has been shown, much of this educational progress has not even been properly understood. The reason would seem to be that education is a very poor form of social engineering. Despite this, it has been described by the present government as its 'best economic policy'. The rhetoric of human capital theory is driving the agenda here, and allowing failures of social justice, as much as failures of economy, to be blamed on the education system. This is more than schools can bear. It is surely much more likely that a fair and successful educational system will be the product of an equitable and prosperous society than vice versa. It is, therefore, time that education was valued more for its own sake and less as a potential solution to socio-economic problems, but that those problems were tackled more directly.

The most telling evidence from school effectiveness studies is easily missed, sometimes by the researchers themselves but more often by policy-makers. School effects are defined as those differences in pupil outcomes (usually defined as examination results) which can be attributed to what happens in schools, and they consist of the parcels of variation left after socio-economic conditions and family background have been accounted for ('residuals'). Valuable though these school effects may be, they are dwarfed in scale by the impact of the background factors, which are of the order of five to ten times as important in predicting school outcomes. For example, GCSE scores at the school level can be predicted with over 80 per cent accuracy on the basis of pupil eligibility for free school meals alone. In general, those schools with 'good' results have a low proportion of poor families, which is why they are also generally found in desirable locations with expensive housing. One easy way for a school to attain better results might be to take fewer pupils from poor families. This is what some commentators feel the market may encourage them to do (Ball 1993), although this may not be what has generally happened in practice.

However, a better alternative might be a policy to reduce the incidence of poverty in society. The appeal of this lies not only in natural justice, but it could also lead to an overall improvement in school outcomes as all schools reduce their proportion of disadvantaged children. Unfortunately, this is not a policy that can be implemented by education alone (despite recent unsubstantiated claims about the importance of education to the economy, in Gorard et al. 1998b, pp. 5–7). Education is generally a very poor form of social engineering, which is why a policy of 'education, education, education' could be such a misguided one for Britain. It forces all of the effort to improve social conditions into a concentration on that 10 to 20 per cent of the variance in school outcomes attributable to education, in the belief that over the long term this will cash out into improvements in both the economy and social justice. Meanwhile, over the last ten years the number of families eligible for free school meals has continued to rise significantly. There are so many aspects of social policy where socio-economic background plays a key role in outcomes that it is surely inefficient for government to treat each separately: health programmes for poor families, school programmes for disaffected children and so on. It would be more efficient to treat any underlying phenomenon directly. Of course, this suggestion may not generally be popular with those working in health or education for example, since it might involve shifting expenditure away from service provision towards a more general programme of poverty reduction.

The need for such a new approach is confirmed by evidence that, despite the ongoing social desegregation in schools, society itself is actually becoming more polarized in Britain. 'In recent years differences in income between the least well off and those with higher incomes have widened . . . [income] increased by 23% for the middle fifth and 40% for the top fifth' (National Commission on Education 1993, p. 20). Although the National Commission does not present genuinely proportionate evidence in support of its claim (Table 10.1), it is clear that the net real income of the lowest earners has not

Table 10.1. Median net real income after housing costs

Year	Bottom 20%	Middle 20%	Top 20%
1979	81	143	254
1988/89	81	176	355

Source: National Commission on Education 1993, table 2.1.

increased over time, so that any increase in the income of other groups would lead to greater polarization.

The situation here is reminiscent of that described in Chapter 3, where it is shown that indicators of poverty such as FSM are increasing over time, while their distribution in schools is becoming more equal. One clear conclusion is that changes in school composition do not readily cash out into changes in social structure (and in retrospect it seems absurd to consider that they would). 'Over the long run the most powerful educational policy is arguably one which tackles child poverty, rather than any modest intervention in schooling' (Robinson 1997, p. 3). It is not even clear, contra human capital theory, that boosting attainment will affect the national economy, since there is no relationship between attainment and the growth of GNP in Britain.

> We must accept that education is an ineffective form of social engineering . . . if we want to distribute wealth and power in our society, we should distribute it by direct political means . . . we should see education, not as a means of redistributing the cake, but as *part* of the cake itself. (Crombie and Harries-Jenkins 1983, p. 84).

This conclusion, drawn chiefly from the findings for initial schooling, has been confirmed in a recent large-scale study of participation in adult learning as well (Gorard et al. 1998b, 1998c, 1998d, 1998e, 1999d, 1999c). The first phase of that study concludes that, while society may benefit from a well-trained workforce, there are currently tensions in relevant writing between an economic imperative and an inclusive definition of a learning society, which may be found to be in conflict. Some people want more money spent on initial or higher education, while others wish to put the money into compensatory literacy schemes, for example. Either way the pressure is to spend more and more money on education, but a more radical, some might say realistic, agenda requires more than educational change. It entails social and labour market reform as well. Unfortunately, this radical agenda is undermined by concentration on higher education, while increased participation is advertised as widened participation. Generally, education is accepted as what it is, even though standards may be decried, and its growth is generally encouraged. Non-participants are, therefore, seen merely as a pool of potential clients for the existing set-up who must be enticed into post-compulsory opportunities without eroding quality.

The findings of this recent study of adult participation and, more crucially, non-participation may have several implications for policy-makers looking towards the creation of a 'Learning Society'. Despite the variety in the plethora of remedies, there is a relative over-emphasis in current government policy on front-loaded forms of educational provision, to the detriment of adult education and training. The high level of predictability about patterns of adult participation suggests that barriers and obstacles to learning such as cost, time and lack of child-care, while genuine, will not be overcome in an ad hoc way. The fact that an individual's social and family background at birth has such an impact on their later life suggests that policy-makers may be advised to concentrate on reducing inequalities in society, rather than simply trying to increase the opportunities for everyone to learn. In summary, it is perhaps more likely, in trying to create a Learning Society, that a just society will lead to an increase in participation than that an increase in educational participation will lead to a just society.

A final piece of 'good news' may be that the role of society as a determinant of education is becoming weaker over time. As both examination scores (such as GCSEs) and indicators of poverty (such as FSM) are increasing over time, but high GCSE scores are related to low FSM, there must, therefore, be a change in their relationship over time. What is it? Some commentators would simply see this as a lowering of standards over time, but it is more likely to be a loosening of the link between social background and academic outcomes. It is already clear that sixteen- to nineteen-year-old participation, and possibly higher education, is less determined by class background than previously (Gorard et al. 1999a), meaning that at this level there has been a genuine widening of participation. Could we be actually breaking down the barriers in society to both participation and achievement?

One of the remaining problems, that is not apparently reducing over time, is inequality in participation in adult, continuing and vocational education or training. This is a complex issue worthy of much greater attention, but in summary it appears that social justice in later learning is actually decreasing over time (as assessed, for example, by class and gender). As with inequalities in schools, technical fixes are being offered for this, but based on little or no research. One such example is the virtual and digital college movement. Unfortunately, if physical barriers are not the main problem preventing access, and there is little evidence that they are, then technology will have little impact on social justice. In fact, differential access to technology simply replicates the existing differential access to institutions of learning (Gorard and Selwyn 1999). This area remains a significant challenge for the future.

If there is one really solid conclusion to be drawn from this reanalysis of the crisis account, it is that too much is expected of education in terms of economic impact and equality. The government approach of initiatives to improve educational standards is 'fundamentally flawed', by ignoring the condition of pupils in favour of mechanistic inputs to schools (Hoghughi 1999). The teacher unions, initially pleased by increased attention for schools, are beginning to feel that education is being given the responsibility to solve all society's ills. Unfortunately, it may be that 'One of the few strategic levers available to the New Labour government . . . is to police the education and training of the workforce in the economy and in the educational market-place' (Cole 1998, p. 315). Therefore, the way out of any mess is now the lazy solution of education, and poor old schools are being overburdened with the National Curriculum, SATs, basic skills and citizenship and the list of responsibilities grows (Alibhai-Brown 1999).

Education is almost certainly *not* our best economic policy. Nevertheless, it is important – too important to pretend and play the basic human capital game any longer. Lifelong learning is clearly not an investment for employers, since they do not want to pay for it and successive governments have apparently been too scared to make them do so. Nor is it an investment for society. There is no evidence of an economic return. However, such comments could also apply to health and safety legislation, the minimum wage, the National Health

Service and the abolition of slavery, for example. Each case has good reasons for implementation, but a simple return on the investment is not one of them. Education may be similar to each of these. An overemphasis on human capital leads to a lopsided education system where formal education is over-rated, qualifications are confused with skills and there is always a demand for more and longer, targets and standards and inspections until we are 'audited out of sight' (Chambers et al. 1998). Is there a better way?

Conclusion

The reanalyses of school processes and outcomes described in this book leads to a more positive picture than originally envisaged, but this should not be allowed to obscure the difficulties that remain. Differences in resources, opportunities and attainment may be decreasing over time but they still exist. It is important not simply to eradicate these differences, which could be most economically and cynically achieved by reducing educational resources, opportunities and attainment to the lowest existing level. For example, there is already a suggestion that the process of decreasing social segregation between schools relies overmuch on a coincident increase in indicators of poverty. The challenge is, therefore, to continue reducing the 'gaps' described here while increasing across the board the base figures on which they are calculated. Similarly, any policies to deal with the apparent underachievement of boys at school must also identify and remedy potential underachievement among girls. These are some of the current genuine challenges for social justice in education.

This book is a criticism of the crisis account of British education. Despite the use of examples for illustration, these examples are generally chosen from the most powerful, well-known or academically respected sources available to the author. The book is *not* intended as a criticism of any specific commentator, government or administration. The misunderstandings, miscalculations and misapplication of research findings described here are too common and too long-standing for this to be the fault of any individual or group. There is no doubt that all those who are working for social justice, regardless of political persuasion and whether or not they wish to emphasize the role of structure or agency in their explanations, are trying to do the best they can. What we often seem to lack, for a variety of reasons, is solid evidence from the past, to help us make decisions in the present, to improve both education and social justice for the future. I hope that this book represents a small step in that enormous undertaking.

~ Appendix A ~

Further Comments on the Smithfield Study

These comments on the Smithfield project appeared as part of Gorard and Fitz (1998a), and in response one of the researchers wrote and circulated a defence of the work which was also a critique of my own study described in Chapter 3. The response (Lauder 1999) has not been published, and therefore has not been refereed. Lauder isolates two major thrusts of my critique of the Smithfield conclusions. I stated that the variation in the intake cohort to the study schools as a whole was not taken into account when considering the variations in individual schools (see above). This could be significant, since in some cases there is more variation in the 'population' than in any school, yet the authors call the population distribution flat while the fluctuations in school distributions are considered to be evidence of changes in segregation. There is a technical issue here, of using the data that is available to make the conclusions as accurate as possible, and also a clear case of double standards. I repeat the relevant passages from the original draft of my paper.

> In fact, the Smithfield data as reported shows that parental unemployment varies from 7% to 5% and back again over the four years (increasing proportionately by 40% from 1991 to 1992 for example), SES moves from 3.12 to 3.66 and 'up' again (an increase of 17% from 1990 to 1991 for example), while the proportion of Maori families declines by 14% (from 14% in 1992 to 12% in 1993). These changes in the overall composition of the sample from year to year are proportionately much larger than the between-school changes later reported to be an outcome of dezoning. When two of the researchers were faced in person with this calculation showing that the basic assumption of the whole analysis was invalid, they claimed that the figures I used were not correct. When shown that my figures were those in the published tables in Waslander and Thrupp (1997) they replied that these tables were misprints (without providing the correct figures either then or subsequently). These two, Hughes and Lauder, are no strangers to critical comments on their statistical results and claims that

their figures may be in error (e.g. Cheng 1994, Harker and Nash 1996, Hughes et al. 1996b). In the last of these cases involving a totally different study, their explanation for at least some of the misunderstanding was that tables were 'set incorrectly in the copy we sent to NZES . . . which we did not pick up prior to publication' (p. 200). In the case of the typesetting errors in Waslander and Thrupp (1997) the errors had not been picked up even after publication until pointed out as a result of the Cardiff meeting. Interestingly the errors had also not been picked up either before or after the original publication of the tables two years earlier. *The tables in Waslander and Thrupp (1995) show the same figures as the 1997 chapter for annual changes in mean SES and parental unemployment.*

These paragraphs also make it clear that, despite Lauder's comment (1999, p. 8), I had not forgotten the 'misprint' errors in Waslander and Thrupp. When I published my critique in an international journal, I removed the misprint saga as being potentially embarrassing to those involved. Perhaps this was a mistake. The errors have *never* been corrected, despite a promise to do so in the Cardiff meeting. The correct figures could have been inserted in the response 'paper' by Lauder (1999) and, given the international prominence accorded the original paper (e.g. by Halsey et al. 1997), perhaps it would have been wise to do so. In this context, it may be significant that the offending table does not appear in the recent book of the Smithfield project, which, nevertheless, continues to claim that the school population in their study remained constant over time (Lauder et al. 1999). The authors back this claim up using ethnicity and SES scores from eleven schools rather than four (with a correspondingly flatter distribution). However, it is still the same four schools for which the *actual* changes over time are calculated, and on which their results in the book are predicated. The main impact of this change has, therefore, simply meant that the reader can no longer check their calculations, since there are no base figures for the four schools alone. What benefit the authors hope to gain by this alteration is open to speculation. It is also interesting that, despite the flatter distribution of the overall intake to the eleven schools, there are still changes in the school population which dwarf the variations in individual school intakes. For example, on p. 86 Lauder et al. (1999) describe the school population as 'generally consistent' and produce in evidence a table showing changes of 25 per cent in the proportion of Maoris (from 1993 to 1994), and changes of 5 per cent in the mean socio-economic status (from 1994 to 1995). Both of these changes in the school 'population' are proportionately larger than any changes in the pattern of individual school intakes.

Even allowing for the misprint, and thus ignoring any demographic variation in the four schools, it is clear from tables 3 and 4 in the original paper that it is primarily ethnic-minority and less-elevated-social-class families that are now using more non-local schools (Waslander and Thrupp 1995). As already explained, their table 3 shows that the proportion of Maori families not using their local school doubled from 12 to 24 per cent from 1990 to 1991, and the proportion of Pacific Islanders more than doubled from 10 to 22 per cent. Their table 4 shows that the mean SES of those using 'adjacent' schools declined by 11 per cent during 1990 to 1993. The authors, however, state that there has been an increase in the mean SES of those using schools for which they would have been ineligible before 1991, and, therefore, that dezoning leads to the reinforcement of privilege. Unfortunately for them, the tables are there in the paper and in the book. Put bluntly, the table contents are the *opposite* of the written conclusions (and it should be noted that these are not the tables with the uncorrected misprints). Readers can simply look these tables up.

The most effective evidence from the Smithfield project comes from their use of Coleman's dissimilarity index (similar in nature to the segregation index used in Chapter 2). This measure *does* take demographic changes into account, and the study is valuable in that it has data for 1990, clearly before abolition of zoning (therefore they have before and after figures). Examples of these data appear (in Waslander and Thrupp 1995, table 8) and they show that dissimilarity between schools declined after 1990 in terms of both parental unemployment and mean SES. The abstract to the 1995 paper states that 'choice intensified socio-economic segregation between schools', but table 8 shows quite clearly that the peak of segregation was in 1990, before the reforms, and lowest in 1991 when allocation to school was by ballot. Again the story of the text and the tables are contradictory, and again the tables are there in both paper and chapter form for anyone to check. It may be significant that, like the table showing intake characteristics, table 8 does not appear in the new book (Lauder et al. 1999). It is certainly interesting that, despite its removal, the same conclusions are 'drawn' by the authors. Again the only practical difference the removal makes is that the reader can no longer check the results. In these circumstances, despite the ingenuity of much of the original study, it is difficult to give much credence to the results of the Smithfield project in its conclusions concerning segregation over time.

In this context, it is interesting that the annual school census figures from the Ministry of Education in New Zealand show a very different pattern from that described in the Smithfield study. Using the entire secondary school population of New Zealand, the highest level of ethnic segregation in terms of both Maori and Pacific Island students was in 1990, before dezoning, and it reached its lowest point for ten years in 1993, before the introduction of 'enrolment schemes' (similar to the standard enrolment number in British schools), after which segregation has crept back up but without yet reaching the 1990 level (personal communication with Martin Connelly, Ministry of Education, Wellington). The Smithfield conclusions of increasing segregation since 1990 are simply incorrect.

~ Appendix B ~

Comparing Three Indices of Segregation

The segregation index used in this work is similar in many respects to the standardized segregation index (Coleman et al. 1982) and the dissimilarity index (e.g. as discussed by Lieberson 1981, and used by Waslander and Thrupp 1997). However, when applied to education, previous measures have not taken account of the size of each school, and have, therefore, been used to compare segregation between two subgroups of students rather than as a general measure of social stratification. If the two groups being compared are equally segregated then the dissimilarity index, for example, is unhelpful. Using the percentage stratification, on the other hand, allows both groups to be assessed in relation to the school population as a whole. It has the advantage of not relying on the assumption that the overall composition of schools is generally consistent from year to year.

The index of dissimilarity (ID) is perhaps the most widely used measure of residential segregation for urban geographers. It is easy to compute, has a clear meaning, falls between 0 and 100, and avoids the unwanted influence of population composition. It 'describes the percentage of one group or the other which would have to move if there was to be no segregation between the groups' (Lieberson 1981, p. 62). The 'index wars' fought in the 1950s and 1960s by social scientists are described further in Appendix C. For the present purpose, the interesting thing is to observe how closely the figures of all three methods match.

As an example, using the standardized segregation index (D) with the Caerphilly LEA data produces the results in Table B.1, which are clearly very closely linked to the segregation index used in this book (S). Similarly, using the index of dissimilarity (ID) with the Swansea LEA data produces the results in Table B.2, which correlate perfectly with the results from the segregation index (S).

In a sense then it does not matter for the purposes of this book which index is used, or how large the numeric results are. The important question is, how are the results changing over time?

Table B1. Comparison of Coleman's and Gorard's segregation index

Index	1988	1989	1990	1991	1992	1993	1994	1995	1996
D%	11	11	10	12	14	12	14	14	16
S%	9	9	8	9	10	8	10	10	12

Table B2. Comparison of dissimilarity and Gorard's segregation index

Index	1990	1991	1992	1993	1994	1995	1996	1997
ID%	81	78	74	74	71	68	69	68
S%	35	33	31	30	28	26	27	26

~ Appendix C ~

Examining the Paradox of Achievement Gaps

There are at least two methods of calculating achievement gaps (between groups of students in education) in common current usage, similar to those used to calculate social segregation and class mobility. Each method clearly seems valid to its proponents, yet their results in practice are radically different, and often contradictory. This appendix considers both of these methods and some related problems in the calculation of achievement gaps, in an attempt to resolve the contradiction. The issue is a simple one, but one with significant implications for social researchers, as well as commentators in many areas of public policy using similar indicators of performance.

The Paradox of Achievement Gaps

The calculation and discussion of achievement gaps between different subgroups of students ('differential attainment') has become common among policy-makers, the media and academics. An 'achievement gap' is an index of the difference in an educational indicator (such as an examination pass rate) between two groups (such as males and females). In addition to patterns of differential attainment by gender, recent concern has also been expressed over differences in examination performance by ethnicity, by social class and by the 'best' and 'worst' performing schools. The concerns expressed in each case derive primarily from growth in these gaps over time.

Accounts generally use one of two substantially different methods of calculating differential attainment over time. The first and most common method uses percentage points as a form of 'common currency'. Thus, if 30 per cent of boys and 40 per cent of girls gain a C grade in maths GCSE in one year, and 35 per cent of boys and 46 per cent of girls gain the equivalent a year later, the improvement among girls is said to be greater, in the way that six

(46–40) is greater than five (35–30). This is justified by its advocates since percentages are, in themselves, proportionate figures. If true, it would mean that girls were now even further 'ahead' of boys than in the previous years. Thus, the gender gap has grown.

The second general method calculates the change over time in proportion to the figures that are changing. This approach is advocated by Newbould and Gray in a study of gendered attainment (Arnot et al. 1996; see also Gorard et al. 1999b). For them, an achievement gap is the difference in attainment between boys and girls, divided by the number of boys and girls at that level of attainment. More formally, the *entry gap* for an assessment is defined as the difference between the entries for girls and boys relative to the total entries.

$$\text{Entry Gap} = (GE{-}BE)/(GE{+}BE).100$$

where GE = number of girls entered; and BE = number of boys entered (or in the age cohort). The *achievement gap* for each outcome is defined as the difference between the performances of boys and girls, relative to the performance of all entries, minus the entry gap.

$$\text{Achievement Gap} = (GP{-}BP)/(GP{+}BP).100 - \text{Entry Gap}$$

where GP = the number of girls achieving that grade or better; and BP = the number of boys achieving that grade or better.

Now, the interesting thing about these two common methods is that they give different results from the same raw data. For example, Gibson and Asthana (1999) claim that the gap in terms of GCSE performance between the top 10 per cent and the bottom 10 per cent of English schools has grown significantly from 1994 to 1998. Their figures are reproduced in Table C1, which shows the proportion of students attaining five or more GCSEs at grade C or above (the official benchmark), for both the best and worst attaining schools in England. It is clear that the top 10 per cent of schools has increased its benchmark by a larger number of percentage points than the bottom 10 per cent. The authors conclude that schools are becoming more socially segregated over time, since 'within local markets, the evidence is clear that high-performing schools both improve their GCSE performance fastest and draw to themselves the most socially-advantaged pupils' (in Budge 1999, p. 3).

Table C1 Changes in GCSE benchmark by decile

Decile	1994 %	1998 %	Gain '94–98
Top	65.0	71.0	6.0
Bottom	10.6	13.1	2.5

This conclusion would be supported by a host of other commentators using the same method (including Robinson and Oppenheim 1998, and Woodhead in *TES* (12 June 1998), p. 5). Similar conclusions using the same method have been drawn about widening gaps between social classes (Bentley 1998), between the attainment of boys and girls (Stephen Byers in Carvel 1998a; Bright 1998; *Independent* 1998), between the performance of ethnic groups (Gillborn and Gipps 1996), and between the results of children from professional and unemployed families (Drew et al. in Slater et al. 1999).

The second method, using the same figures, might produce a result like Table C2. Although the difference between the deciles grows larger in percentage points over time, this difference grows less quickly than the scores of the deciles themselves. On this analysis, the achievement gaps are getting smaller over time. This finding is confirmed by the figures in the last column showing the relative improvement of the two groups. The rate of improvement for the lowest ranked group is clearly the largest. The bottom decile would, in theory at least, eventually catch up with the top decile (Gorard 1999a). The same reanalysis can be done in each of the examples above to show that the gaps between schools, sectors, genders, ethnic groups, and classes are getting smaller over time. This would be the exact opposite in each case to the published conclusions.

To summarize the position so far: using the most popular method of comparing groups over time there appears to be a crisis in British education. Differences between social groups, in terms of examination results expressed in percentage points, are increasing over time and so education is becoming increasingly polarized by

Table C2. Changes in GCSE achievement gaps by decile

Decile	1994 %	1998 %	Ratio 1998:1994
Top 10%	65.0	71.0	1.09
Bottom 10%	10.6	13.1	1.24
Achievement gap	72.0	68.8	

gender, class, ethnicity and income. Using the second method, when these differences are considered in proportion to the figures on which they are based, the opposite trend emerges. Achievement gaps between groups of students defined by gender, ethnicity, class and income actually appear to be declining. Education is becoming less polarized over time. This is the 'paradox of achievement gaps'. Both methods are used in different studies. Both have been extensively published and peer-reviewed. Some writers have even used the equivalent of both methods in the same study (e.g. Levačić et al. 1998; Lauder et al. 1999). Surely someone has to decide once and for all which method to use, as they are not simple variants of one another?

The 'Index Wars'

Very similar analyses also occur in social science more generally, and similar problems have arisen in health research (Everitt and Smith 1979), in studies of socio-economic stratification and urban geography (Lieberson 1981), in occupational gender segregation (Blackburn et al. 1995), in social mobility work (Erikson and Goldthorpe 1991) and in predictions of educational pathways (Gorard et al. 1999a). Results are disputed when an alternative method of analysis produces contradictory findings. Some of these debates are still unresolved, dating back to what Lieberson (1981) calls the 'index wars' of the 1940s and 1950s, perhaps even to the work of Wright (1937). In each case the major dispute is between findings obtained using absolute rates ('additive' models) and those using relative rates ('multiplicative' models).

Absolute rates are expressed in simple percentage terms, while relative rates (odds ratios) are margin-insensitive in that they remain unaltered by scaling of the rows or columns (as might happen over time for example). This difference is visible in changes to the class structure and changes in social mobility. In Table C3, 25 per cent of those in the middle class are of working-class origin, whereas in Table C4 the equivalent figure is 40 per cent (from Marshall et al. 1997, pp. 199–200). However, this cannot be interpreted as evidence that Society B is more open than Society A, as the percentages do not take into account the differences in class structure between Societies A and B, nor their changes over time ('structural differences').

Table C3. Social mobility in Society A

	Destination middle class	Destination working class
Origin middle class	750	250
Origin working class	250	750

Table C4. Social mobility in Society B

	Destination middle class	Destination working class
Origin middle class	750	250
Origin working class	500	1500

Relative rates are calculated as odds ratios ((a/c)/(b/d)), cross-product ratios (ad/bc) or disparity ratios (a/(a+c)/b/(b+d)). Disparity ratios are identical to the segregation ratios used by Gorard and Fitz (1998b, 2000a). Odds ratios estimate comparative mobility changes regardless of changes in the relative size of classes, and have the practical advantage of being easier to use with loglinear analysis (Gilbert 1981; Goldthorpe et al. 1987; Gorard et al. 1999a).

> From the point of view of social justice . . . this is of course both crucial and convenient, since our interest lies precisely in determining the comparative chances of mobility and immobility of those born into different social classes – rather than documenting mobility chances as such. (Marshall et al. 1997, p. 193)

The cross-product ratio for Table C3 is 9, and for Table C4 it is also 9. This finding suggests that social mobility is at the same level in each society, despite the differences in class structure between them. In many ways this crucial difference in approach and findings is being repeated in the more recent dispute over changes in segregation between schools (see Chapter 3).

Some previous work has confounded changes in social fluidity with changes in the class structure. Nevertheless, disagreement about the significance of absolute and relative mobility rates continues (e.g. Clark et al. 1990, pp. 277–302). Gilbert concluded that 'one difficulty with having these two alternative methods of analysis is that they can give very different, and sometimes contradictory results' (1981, p. 119). The similarities to the issue of achievement gaps are fairly obvious. In each case, different commentators use the same figures to arrive at different conclusions. One group is using additive and the other is using multiplicative models.

Comparing Indices

Four alternative methods have been mentioned for assessing relationships in a simple two-by-two contingency table. The cross-product (or odds) ratio is commonly used to estimate social mobility, and the segregation (or disparity) ratio (or dissimilarity index) can be used for the same purpose, but is perhaps more generally applicable to the analysis of changes in stratification over time. The achievement gap is used to analyse differential attainment by subgroups, but is also useful for defining differential access to public services. These three methods are all multiplicative. Percentage points differences have also been used in all of these areas as a rough-and-ready guide which is easy to calculate. This method is additive in nature.

Despite the differences, there are many similarities between all of the methods and their variants (Darroch 1974). At the limiting case of no relationship (no interaction, or no change over time), and also for its complete opposite, the methods are identical. Given a two-by-two table of the form:

$$
\begin{array}{cc}
a & b \\
c & d
\end{array}
$$

For the cross-product ratio, no change is defined as: ad/bc = 1, equivalent to *ad = bc*.

For the segregation ratio, no difference is defined as:
a/(a+c) / ((a+b)/(a+b+c+d)) = 1, equivalent to a/(a+c) = (a+b)/(a+b+c+d), equivalent to *ad = bc*.

For the achievement gap, no gap is defined as:
(a–b)/(a+b) – ((a+c)–(b+d)) / ((a+c)+(b+d)) = 0, equivalent to (a–b).((a+b)+(c+d)) = (a+b).((a+b)–(c+d)), equivalent to *ad = bc*.

For the percentage point method, no difference is defined as:
100a/(a+c) – 100b/(b+d) = 0, equivalent to 100a/(a+c) = 100b/(b+d), equivalent to *ad = bc*.

For other values, although each method gives varying results, all can be used to gauge a pattern or estimate the strength of a relationship. For example, if 100 girls and 100 boys sit an examination, and thirty girls and twenty boys achieve a particular grade, the results produced are as in Table C5 (that is, the cross-product ratio is 1.7). If in a later test sixty of 100 girls and forty of 100 boys achieve the same grade, the figures from the first and last methods change, while the others remain the same.

Table C5. Comparing indices across two related tables

Method	Test 1 (30%, 20%)	Test 2 (60%, 40%)
Cross-product	1.7	2.3
Segregation girls	1.2	1.2
Segregation boys	0.8	0.8
Achievement gap	0.2	0.2
Percentage points	10	20

The method of percentage points suggests that the gap between girls and boys has doubled from Test 1 to Test 2, whereas the cross-product ratio suggests that the gap has increased less dramatically. Both other methods suggest no difference in the differences over time. There are, of course, other indices of segregation and inequality: Yule's Q, the Variance ratio, Information theory index, Atkinson index and the Gini coefficient. All are multiplicative, but can give slightly different pictures using the same dataset. Some of these indices can be considered defective, for example by not being composition invariant or registering the principle of transfer

(James and Taeuber 1985), while others lead to similar conclusions to those used here and in Appendix B.

Resolving the Paradox of Achievement Gaps?

Although arguments can and have been made for using either multiplicative or additive methods as measures of association in *one* table, the chief problem lies in their different results when comparing the patterns in two or more tables. Alone among the methods, using percentage points does not take into account the proportion $(a+b)/(c+d)$, which accounts for rises and falls in the frequency of the phenomenon being observed. Using this method, a commentator can have no genuine idea of the significance of the resulting points difference. This can be emphasized in two ways. First, if 1 per cent of men were MPs but 0 per cent of women were, this would be an enormous difference and one that social science commentators would be right to draw attention to. On the other hand, if 75 per cent of men and 76 per cent of women were in paid employment, the difference may be of little account. However, both examples yield a score of 1 point in the additive method, suggesting that this method is fine for a rough guide to the presence or absence of a pattern, but of little value as a scaled measure of achievement gaps. Second, if the example of differential attainment by boys and girls is constructed differently, then a two-by-two table of time of test versus gender (30, 20, 60, 40) can be created which shows no change over time using *any* of the methods. In addition, it is surely no coincidence that, when changes in percentage points are calculated proportionately to the base frequencies from which they derive, changes over time between subgroups are almost constant even in cases where the percentage point method suggests a dramatic widening of differential attainment (e.g. for the top nine deciles presented by Gibson and Asthana 1999).

Of course, it can be argued that none of these methods is appropriate if scores such as the GCSE benchmark are not at least of interval level measurement. Since the number of GCSEs per student in any sizeable group may be approximately normally distributed, it can be argued that changes in the percentage gaining five (or any other arbitrary number) would be less significant near the 50 per cent mark. In fact, it is almost certain that, if the

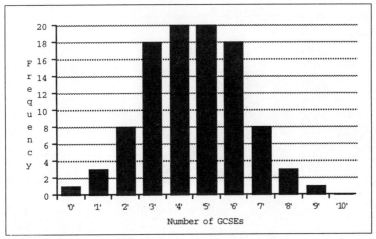

Figure C1. Distribution of GCSEs among candidates (high score)

distribution of qualifications is not uniform in the population, then changes over time will not be linear. At the 50 per cent mark, where the distribution is taller, a small movement along the x axis (representing a change in the number of GCSEs per student) would produce a disproportionately large change in the percentage attaining the benchmark. At either end (near 0 and 100 per cent), a much larger change on the x axis would be needed to produce the same effect. This may be illustrated by the imaginary data presented in Figures C1 and C2, which represent the frequency in one school of students gaining none to ten GCSEs (at grade C, for example). In Figure C1, exactly fifty of 100 students gain five or more GCSEs. If all students gained one more GCSE, the benchmark figure for the school would rise to 70 per cent.

In Figure C2, only four of 100 students gain five or more GCSEs (the actual pattern of frequencies for Figure C2 is the same as Figure C1 but moved three places towards the origin of the x axis). In this case, if all students gained one more GCSE, the benchmark figure for the school would rise to 12 per cent. Increases in terms of absolute percentage scores are much more difficult for low-attaining schools. In this context it is interesting to note that the supposedly advantaged group in Table C1 is much nearer the sensitive 50 per cent mark than their supposedly weaker comparator (that is, if followed through to its logical conclusion,

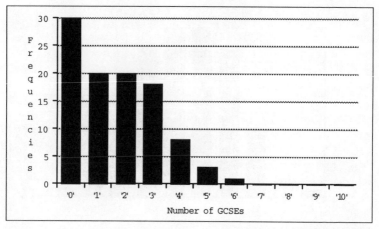

Figure C2. Distribution of GCSEs among candidates (low score)

this line of reasoning would agree with the multiplicative method in concluding that the improvement in the lower attaining groups was the greater). There are problems with this line of reasoning, however, especially when applied to a non-continuous variable such as number of GCSEs per student, but discussion of these will have to remain a subject for the future. If benchmarks are *not* interval in nature then the crisis account of widening gaps in British education probably cannot be sustained anyway.

Conclusion

At present, the situation is that the specific method of calculation used to assess changes in relative performance over time determines the result obtained. A consensus about the two general methods must be reached quickly by the research community. In terms of social mobility research the preference of most commentators on methodology is clear. Darroch (1974, p. 213) says 'on balance, the author believes that Hm [the multiplicative definition] is preferable to Ha [the additive definition]'. Gilbert (1981, p. 119) suggests that the percentage point difference method can be used 'to assess the association in a percentage table quickly and roughly', but states an overall preference for the relative ratio methods for the kind of practical reasons described above. Ironically, Marshall et al. are more dogmatic in their preference for the relative approach for social mobility studies, but include in their own work a percentage point difference approach to relative changes in educational qualifications over time (1997, p. 113).

It is not always clear (from literature review and personal experience) that the commentators using the percentage point difference approach are aware that other, and better, methods are available. Without restarting the index wars, it would be wise for this issue to be at least *debated* in relation to the paradox of achievement gaps. If the multiplicative model is preferred (as I believe it should be), the consequences would be momentous for much existing research, for the cumulated conclusions of some entire fields of endeavour, the validity of many 'qualitative' studies in related areas, for public research funding priorities and above all for educational policy. As with the earlier debates about class and stratification, other fields of social science investigation would be affected as well. Some of the more immediate consequences can be seen in the substantive findings presented in this book.

~ Appendix D ~

Subject Groupings

The subjects taken by students are defined as those in the SCAA/ACAC results leaflets, such as home economics and history. Some of these subjects have very few entries, so for clarity in some analyses the subjects are grouped together. In the first instance all entries of whatever subject are summed to give the overall picture. In general, subjects are subsequently analysed as English, mathematics, Welsh, sciences, humanities, languages, design-related and other subjects as defined below.

1. Mathematics	
2. English	English
	English literature
3. Welsh	Welsh first language
	Welsh second language
	Welsh literature
4. Sciences	Physics
	Chemistry
	Biology
	Single-award
	Double-award
	Other sciences
5. Humanities	History
	Geography
6. Languages	French
	German
	Spanish
	Other languages
7. Design-related	Design and technology
	Technology
	Craft, design and technology
	Information systems, computing
	Home economics
	Art and design

8. Other subjects   Social sciences
Economics
Music
Classics
Religious studies
Physical education, dance
Business studies
All other subjects

~ Appendix E ~

Alternative Versions of the Achievement Gap

To make this clearer, the argument is rehearsed in a slightly different form. In English, for example, more girls appear in each high grade at GCSE or level at Key Stages 1–3, and more boys appear in each low grade (see, for example, Table E1). One can deduce little from this

Table E1. KS3 English 1997

	'fail'	level 1	level 2	level 3	level 4	level 5	level 6	level 7	level 8	total
Girls	143	65	353	1121	3541	5802	4110	1776	176	17089
Boys	212	168	935	2328	5058	5395	2550	889	76	17612

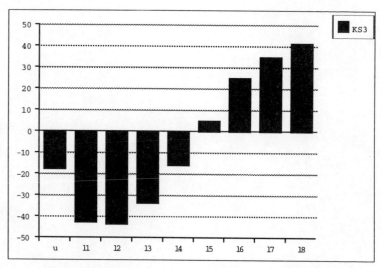

Figure E1. Proportions at each grade KS3 English 1997

since the difference in number of boys and girls at each grade must first be related to the number attaining that grade, and to the numbers in the respective gender cohorts for that assessment. To calculate the gaps for each grade in isolation (that is, not at grade C and above, and so on) from the point of view of boys' underachievement, one can apply the 'gap' method from this study to the data at each grade, but *without* cumulating (see Figure E1).

The graphs for other subjects with gaps look similar. In all years and subjects (where there is a gap) the difference in favour of girls is largest at the highest grade, and in favour of boys it is largest at a mid to low grade. The difference at the level of fail in any assessment is always one of the lowest. Of course the bars in Figure E1 are not gaps in themselves, except at level 8, since one cannot deduce from one bar in isolation which gender is doing better (for example, more boys getting level 3 could be a sign of an advantage over girls, but in the whole picture it looks more like a sign of disadvantage). This is why the cumulated version used in Chapter 9 is preferred, but it should be noted that the same story could be told using either version consistently.

~ Bibliography ~

Achen, C. (1982). *Interpreting and Using Regression*, London: Sage.

Alibhai-Brown, Y. (1999). Will education lead society out of racism?, *Times Educational Supplement,* 18 June, 16.

Ambler, J. (1997). Who benefits from educational choice? Some evidence from Europe, in E. Cohn (ed.), *Market Approaches to Education*, Oxford: Elsevier Science.

Archbald, D. (1996). Measuring school choice using indicators, *Education Policy*, 10/1, 88–101.

Arnot, M., David, M., and Weiner, G. (1996). *Educational Reform and Gender Equality in Schools*, Manchester: Equal Opportunities Commission.

Bagley, C., and Woods, P. (1998). Rejecting Schools: Towards a Fuller Understanding of the Process of Parental Choice, presentation at the BERA Annual Conference, Belfast.

Baker, D., and Jones, D. (1993). Creating gender equality: cross national gender stratification and mathematical achievement, *Sociology of Education*, 66, 91–103.

Ball, S. (1993). Education markets, choice and social class: the market as a class strategy in the UK and the USA, *British Journal of Sociology of Education*, 14/1, 3–19.

Ball, S. (1999). Labour, learning and the economy: a 'policy sociology' perspective, *Cambridge Journal of Education*, 29/2, 195–206.

Ball, S., and Gewirtz, S. (1997). Is research possible? A rejoinder to Tooley's 'On school choice and social class', *British Journal of Sociology of Education*, 18/4.

Ball, S., Bowe, R., and Gewirtz, S. (1996). School choice, social class and distinction: the realization of advantage in education, *Journal of Education Policy*, 11, 89–112.

Barber, M. (1996). *The Learning Game*, London: Indigo.

Barber, M., and Sebba, J. (1999). Reflections on progress towards a world class education system, *Cambridge Journal of Education*, 29/2, 183–93.

Barrow, R. (1999). The higher nonsense: some persistent errors in educational thinking, *Journal of Curriculum Studies*, 31/2, 131–42.

Bauch, P. (1989). Can poor parents make wise educational choices?, in W. Boyd and J. Cibulka (eds.), *Private Schools and Public Policy: International Perspective*, London: Falmer Press.

Beaton, A., Mullis, I., Martin, M., Gonzalez, E., Kelly, D., and Smith, T. (1996). *Mathematics Achievement in the Middle School Years: IEA's Third Mathematics and Science Study*, Chestnut Hill, MA: Boston College.

Bellin, W., Farrell, S., Higgs, G., and White, S. (1996). A strategy for using census information in comparison of school performance, *Welsh Journal of Education*, 5/2, 3–25.

Bellin, W., Farrell, S., Higgs, G., and White, S. (1999). The social context of Welsh-medium bilingual education in anglicised areas, *Journal of Sociolinguistics*, 3/2, 183–93.

Bellin, W., Osmond, J., and Reynolds, D. (1994). *Towards an Educational Policy for Wales*, Cardiff: Institute of Welsh Affairs.

Bentley, T. (1998). *Learning beyond the Classroom*, London: Routledge.

Berki, B. (1999). Parental choice in danger, *Times Educational Supplement*, 23 April, 2.

Berry, W., and Feldman, S. (1985). *Multiple Regression in Practice*, London: Sage.

Black, P. (1992). *Education: Putting the Record Straight*, Stafford: Network Educational Press.

Blackburn, R., Siltanen, J., and Jarman, J. (1995). The measurement of occupational gender segregation: current problems and a new approach, *Journal of the Royal Statistical Society*, 158/2, 319–31.

Blair, M. (1994). Black teachers, Black students and education markets, *Cambridge Journal of Education*, 24/2, 277–91.

Bolton, E. (1993). Imaginary gardens with real toads, in C. Chitty and B. Simon (eds.), *Education Answers Back*, London: Lawrence & Wishart.

Bourdieu, P., and Passeron, C. (1992). *Reproduction in Education, Society and Culture*, London: Sage.

Bowe, R., Gerwirtz, S., and Ball, S. (1994). Captured by the discourse? Issues and concerns in researching 'parental choice', *British Journal of Sociology of Education*, 15/1, 63–78.

Bowen, W. (1972). Assessing the economic contribution of education, in B. Cosin (ed.), *Education: Structure and Society*, Harmondsworth: Penguin.

Boyson, R. (1975). *The Crisis in Education*, London: Woburn Press.

Bradley, S., Johnes, G., and Millington, J. (1999). 'School choice, competition and the efficiency of secondary schools in England', Lancaster: Management School, Lancaster University (mimeo).

Bright, M. (1998). The trouble with boys, *Observer*, 4 Jan., 13.

Brown, M. (1998a). The tyranny of the international horse race, in R. Slee, G. Weiner, and S. Tomlinson (eds.), *School Effectiveness for Whom? Challenges to the School Effectiveness and School Improvement Movements*, London: Falmer Press, 33–47.

Brown, M. (1998b). BERA President's letter to Secretary of State, *Research Intelligence*, 65, 14–15.

Budge, D. (1999). Gulf separating weak and strong increases, *Times Educational Supplement,* 30 April, 3.

Bunting, C., Constantine, A., and McTaggart, M. (1999). Boys take up books to narrow the gender gap, *Times Educational Supplement*, 29 Sept., 3.

Carvel, J. (1998a). Tory market theory 'widened schools performance gap', *Guardian*, 11 June, 5.

Carvel, J. (1998b). Help for boys lagging behind girls at school, *Guardian,* 7 Jan., 19.

Cassidy, S. (1999a). Pass mark 'fiddle' is strenuously denied, *Times Educational Supplement*, 28 May, 2.

Cassidy, S. (1999b). Test scores did not add up, *Times Educational Supplement*, 16 July, 5.

Cassidy, S. (1999c). English papers at 14 were 'too hard', *Times Educational Supplement*, 4 June, 6.

Cassidy, S. (1999d). Wealth wins top marks, *Times Educational Supplement*, 21 May, 7.

Cassidy, S. (1999e). Girls now beat boys at A-level, *Times Educational Supplement*, 6 Aug., 7.

Cassidy, S. (1999f). Gender gap widens to a gulf, *Times Educational Supplement*, 29 Jan., 6.

Cassidy, S. (1999g). Boys spell alot better infact, *Times Educational Supplement*, 9 July, 5.

Cassidy, S. (1999h). Popular exams get revision bonus, *Times Educational Supplement*, 13 Aug., 1.

Cassidy, S. (1999i). Number is up for homework, *Times Educational Supplement*, 25 June, 2.

Cassidy, S. (1999j). Science sacrificed on the altar of literacy, *Times Educational Supplement*, 25 June, 1.

Census (1991). Data available from National On-line Manpower Information System, Durham.

CERI (1997). *Education Policy Analysis 1997*, Paris: OECD.

CERI (1998). *Education at a Glance: OECD Indicators*, Paris: OECD.

Chambers, P., Gorard, S., Fevre, R., Rees, G., and Furlong, J. (1998). *Changes in Training Opportunities in South Wales 1945–1998: The Views of Key Informants*, Cardiff: School of Education.

Chaudhary, V. (1998). Problems that arise when boys will be lads, *Guardian*, 6 Jan., 8.

Cheng, W. (1994). Do schools matter? A critique of 'Social inequalities and differences in school outcomes', *New Zealand Journal of Educational Studies*, 29/1, 201.

Chubb, J., and Moe, T. (1990). *Politics, Markets and America's Schools*, Washington, DC: Brookings Institute.

Clark, J., Modgil, C., and Modgil, S. (1990). *John Goldthorpe: Consensus and Controversy*, London: Falmer.

Cole, M. (1998). Globalisation, modernisation and competitiveness: a critique of the New Labour project in education, *International Studies in Sociology of Education*, 8/3, 315–34.

Coleman, J., Campbell, E., Hobson, C., McPartland, J., Mood, A., Weinfield, F., and York, R. (1966). *Equality of Educational Opportunity*, Washington, DC: US Government Printing Office.

Coleman, J., Hoffer, T., and Kilgore, S. (1982). *High School Achievement: Public, Private and Catholic Schools Compared*, New York: Basic Books.

Comrey, A. (1973). *A First Course on Factor Analysis*, London: Academic Press.

Conway, S. (1997). The reproduction of exclusion and disadvantage: symbolic violence and social class inequalities in 'parental choice' of secondary education, *Sociological Research On-line*, 2/4.

Cookson, P. (1994). *School Choice*, London: Yale University.

Coons, J., and Sugarman, S. (1978). *Education by Choice: The Case for Family Control*, Berkeley, CA: University of California Press.

Corbett, A. (1993). The peculiarity of the English, in C. Chitty and B. Simon (eds.), *Education Answers Back*, London: Lawrence & Wishart.

Costley, M. (1999). Hain calls for school curb on calculators, *Western Mail*, 11 Jan., 1.

Cox, C., and Dyson, A. (1990). An open letter to Members of Parliament, in B. Moon, J. Isaac, and J. Powney (eds.), *Judging Standards and Effectiveness in Education*, London: Hodder & Stoughton.

Creemers, B. (1994). The history, value and purpose of school effectiveness studies, in D. Reynolds, B. Creemers, P. Nesselradt, E. Shaffer, S. Stringfield and C. Teddlie (eds.), *Advances in School Effectiveness Research and Practice*, Oxford: Pergamon.

Cresswell, M., and Gubb, J. (1990). The Second International Maths Study in England and Wales: comparisons between 1981 and 1964, in B. Moon, J. Isaac, and J. Powney (eds.), *Judging Standards and Effectiveness in Education*, London: Hodder & Stoughton.

Crombie, A., and Harries-Jenkins, G. (1983). *The Demise of the Liberal Tradition*, Leeds: University of Leeds, Department of Adult and Continuing Education.

Daly, P. (1991). How large are secondary school effects in Northern Ireland?, *School Effectiveness and School Improvement*, 2/4, 305–23.

Darroch, J. (1974). Multiplicative and additive interactions in contingency tables, *Biometrika*, 61/2, 207–14.

Daugherty, R. (1995). *National Curriculum Assessment: A Review of Policy 1987–1994*, London: Falmer Press.

David, M., West, A., and Ribbens, J. (1994). *Mother's Intuition? Choosing Secondary Schools*, Lewes: Falmer Press.

Dean, C. (1998). Failing boys public burden number one, *Times Educational Supplement*, 27 Nov., 1.

Dean, C., and Rafferty, F. (1999). Watchdog acts against selection, *Times Educational Supplement*, 6 Aug., 3.

Delamont, S., and Rees, G. (1997). *Understanding the Welsh Education System: Does Wales need a Separate 'Policy Sociology'? Working Paper 23*, Cardiff: School of Education.

DENI (1997). *A Review of Research Evidence on the Apparent Underachievement of Boys*, Belfast: Department of Education Northern Ireland Research Briefing RB5/97.

DES (1990). *Statistics of Education: Schools 1989*, London: Department of Education and Science.

DES (1991). *Statistics of Education: Schools 1990*, London: Department of Education and Science.

DES (1992). *Statistics of Education: Schools 1991*, London: Department of Education and Science.

DfE (1993). *Statistics of Education: Schools 1992*, London: Department for Education.

DfE (1994). *Statistics of Education: Schools 1993*, London: Department for Education.

DfE (1995a). *Statistics of Education: Schools in England 1994*, London: HMSO.

DfE (1995b). *Statistics of Education: Public Examinations GCSE and GCE in England 1994*, London: HMSO.

DfEE (1996). *Statistics of Education: Schools in England 1995*, London: HMSO.

DfEE (1997). *Statistics of Education: Schools in England 1996*, London: HMSO.

DfEE (1998a). *Statistics of Education: Schools in England 1997*, London: HMSO.

DfEE (1998b). *Statistics of Education: Schools in England 1998*, London: HMSO.

DfEE (1998c). *Statistics of Education: Public Examinations GCSE/GNVQ and GCE in England 1997*, London: HMSO.

DfEE (1999a). *A Fresh Start: Improving Literacy and Numeracy*, Nottingham: DfEE Publications.

DfEE (1999b). *Statistics of Education: Schools in England 1998*, London: HMSO.

Echols, F., McPherson, A. and Willms, J. (1990). Parental choice in Scotland, *Journal of Educational Policy*, 5/3, 207–22.

Edwards, T., Fitz, J., and Whitty, G. (1989). *The State and Private Education: An Evaluation of the Assisted Places Scheme*, London: Falmer Press.

Elmore, R., and Fuller, B. (1996). Empirical research on educational choice: what are the implications for policy-makers?, in B. Fuller and R. Elmore (eds.), *Who Chooses? Who Loses?*, New York: Teachers College Press.

Erikson, R., and Goldthorpe, J. (1991). The constant flux: a study of class mobility in industrial societies, Oxford: Clarendon Press.

ESIS (1998). *Welsh and English LEAs: Results Contextualised by % Eligible for Free School Meals*, report by Education Support and Inspection Service of Bridgend, Caerphilly, Merthyr and Rhondda Cynon Taff.

ETAG (1998). *An Education and Training Plan for Wales*, Cardiff: Education and Training Action Group.

Eurostat (1995). *Education across the European Union: Statistics and Indicators*, Brussels: Statistical Office of the European Communities.

Eurostat (1998). *Social Portrait of Europe September 1998*, Brussels: Statistical Office of the European Communities.

Everitt, B., and Smith, A. (1979). Interactions in contingency tables: a brief discussion of alternative definitions, *Psychological Medicine*, 9, 581–3.

Farrow, S., Tymms, P., and Henderson, B. (1999). Homework and attainment in primary schools, *British Educational Research Journal*, 25/3, 323–42.

Fitz, J., Halpin, D., and Power, S. (1993). *Education in the Market Place: Grant Maintained Schools*, London: Kogan Page.

Fitz-Gibbon, C. (1996). *Monitoring Education: Indicators, Quality and Effectiveness*, London: Cassell.

Foster, P., and Hammersley, M. (1998). A review of reviews: structure and function in reviews of educational research, *British Educational Research Journal*, 24/5, 609–28.

Fuller, B., Elmore, R., and Orfield, G. (1996). Policy-making in the dark, in B. Fuller and R. Elmore (eds.), *Who Chooses? Who Loses?*, New York: Teachers College Press.

Gazial, H., and Blass, N. (1999). The extended school day in Israel: do research findings really matter?, *Educational Policy*, 13/1, 166–79.

Gewirtz, S., Ball, S., and Bowe, R. (1995). *Markets, Choice and Equity in Education*, Buckingham: Open University Press.

Ghouri, N. (1999a). Football approach risks an own goal, *Times Educational Supplement*, 4 June, 9.

Ghouri, N. (1999b). Desperate to talk to a teacher, *Times Educational Supplement*, 4 June, 14.

Gibson, A., and Asthana, S. (1998a). Schools, pupils and examination results: contextualising school 'performance', *British Educational Research Journal*, 24/3, 269–82.

Gibson, A., and Asthana, S. (1998b). School performance, school effectiveness and the 1997 White Paper, *Oxford Review of Education*, 24/2, 195–210.

Gibson, A., and Asthana, S. (1999). Schools, markets and equity: access to secondary education in England and Wales, presentation at AERA Annual Conference, Montreal.

Giggs, J., and Pattie, C. (1994). Wales as a plural society, *Contemporary Wales*, 5, 25–43.

Gilbert, N. (1981). *Modelling Society: An Introduction to Loglinear Analysis for Social Researchers*, London: George Allen & Unwin.

Gillborn, D., and Drew, D. (1993). The politics of research: some observations on 'methodological purity', *New Community*, 19/2, 354–60.

Gillborn, D., and Gipps, C. (1996). *Recent Research on the Achievements of Ethnic Minority Pupils*, London: OFSTED.

Gillborn, D., and Gipps, C. (1998). Watching the watchers: research, methods, politics and equity. A response to Foster and Hammersley, *British Educational Research Journal*, 24/5, 629–34.

Gipps, C. (1993). Policy-making and the use and misuse of evidence, in C. Chitty and B. Simon (eds.), *Education Answers Back*, London: Lawrence and Wishart, 31–44.

Glatter, R., Woods, P., and Bagley, C. (1997). Diversity, differentiation and hierarchy. School choice and parental preferences, in R. Glatter, P. Woods and C. Bagley (eds.), *Choice and Diversity in Schooling. Perspectives and Prospects*, London: Routledge.

Goldring, E. (1995). Communal opportunities to learn, parental involvement and school choice: Israel and the United States, paper presented at ESRC/CEPAM Invitation Seminar, Milton Keynes.

Goldthorpe, J., Llewellyn, C., and Payne, C. (1987). *Social Mobility and Class Structure in Modern Britain*, Oxford: Clarendon Press.

Gomm, R. (1995). Strong claims, weak evidence: a response to Troyna's 'Ethnicity and the organization of learning groups', *Educational Research*, 37/1, 79–86.

Gorard, S. (1996). Fee-paying schools in Britain: a peculiarly English phenomenon, *Educational Review*, 48/1, 89–93.

Gorard, S. (1997a). *School Choice in an Established Market*, Aldershot: Ashgate.

Gorard, S. (1997b). A choice of methods: the methodology of choice, *Research in Education*, 57, 45–56.

Gorard, S. (1997c). Paying for a Little England: school choice and the Welsh language, *Welsh Journal of Education*, 6/1, 19–32.

Gorard, S. (1998a). In defence of local comprehensive schools in south Wales, *Forum,* 40/2, 58–9.

Gorard, S. (1998b). Four errors . . . and a conspiracy? The effectiveness of schools in Wales, *Oxford Review of Education,* 24/4, 459–72.

Gorard, S. (1998c). Social movement in undeveloped markets: an apparent contradiction, *Educational Review,* 50/3, 249–58.

Gorard, S. (1998d). Schooled to fail? Revisiting the Welsh school effect, *Journal of Education Policy,* 13/1, 115–24.

Gorard, S. (1998e). The middle way, BERA Internet Conference, *www.scre.ac.uk/bera/debate/index.html.*

Gorard, S. (1999a). Keeping a sense of proportion: the 'politician's error' in analysing school outcomes, *British Journal of Educational Studies,* 47/3, 235–46.

Gorard, S. (1999b). 'Well. That about wraps it up for school choice research': a state of the art review, *School Leadership and Management,* 19/1, 25–47.

Gorard, S. (1999c). Divisions are not getting any deeper, *Times Educational Supplement,* 18 June, 26.

Gorard, S. (2000). For England see Wales: the distinctiveness and similarities of education in England and Wales, in D. Phillips (ed.), *The Education Systems of the United Kingdom,* Oxford: Oxford University Press.

Gorard, S., and Fitz, J. (1998a). Under starter's orders: the established market, the Cardiff study and the Smithfield project, *International Studies in Sociology of Education,* 8/3, 299–314.

Gorard, S., and Fitz, J. (1998b). The more things change . . . the missing impact of marketisation, *British Journal of Sociology of Education,* 19/3, 365–76.

Gorard, S., and Fitz, J. (2000a). Investigating the determinants of segregation between schools, *Research Papers in Education,* 15/2, 115–32.

Gorard, S., and Fitz, J. (2000b). Do markets lead to stratification? The experience of schools in England and Wales, *Educational Policy,* 14, 3.

Gorard, S., and Selwyn, N. (1999). Switching on the Learning Society? Questioning the role of technology in widening participation in lifelong learning, *Journal of Education Policy,* 14/5, 523–34.

Gorard, S., Rees, G., Furlong, J., and Fevre, R. (1997a). *Outline Methodology of the Study: Patterns of Participation in Adult Education and Training,* Cardiff: School of Education.

Gorard, S., Fevre, R., Rees, G., and Furlong, J. (1997b). *Space, Mobility and the Education of Minority Groups in Wales: The Survey Results, Patterns of Participation in Adult Education and Training,* Cardiff: School of Education.

Gorard, S., Rees, G., and Jephcote, M. (1998a). The role of contour lines in school improvement, *Research Intelligence*, 66, 30–1.

Gorard, S., Rees, G., Fevre, R., and Furlong, J. (1998b). The two components of a new Learning Society, *Journal of Vocational Education and Training*, 50/1, 5–19.

Gorard, S., Rees, G., Furlong, J., and Fevre, R. (1998c). Progress towards a Learning Society? Patterns of lifelong learning, *Innovations in Education and Training International*, 35/4, 275–81.

Gorard, S., Rees, G., Fevre, R., and Furlong, J. (1998d). Learning trajectories: travelling towards a learning society?, *International Journal of Lifelong Education*, 17/6, 400–10.

Gorard, S., Rees, G., Fevre, R., and Furlong, J. (1998e). Society is not built by education alone: alternative routes to a Learning Society, *Research in Post-Compulsory Education*, 3/1, 25–37.

Gorard, S., Rees, G., and Fevre, R. (1999a). Two dimensions of time: the changing social context of lifelong learning, *Studies in the Education of Adults*, 31/1, 35–48.

Gorard, S., Salisbury, J., and Rees, G. (1999b). Reappraising the apparent underachievement of boys at school, *Gender and Education*, 11/4, 441–54.

Gorard, S., Rees, G., and Fevre, R. (1999c). Families and their participation in learning over time, *British Educational Research Journal*, 25/4, 517–32.

Gordon, I. (1996). Family structure, educational achievement and the inner city, *Urban Studies*, 33/3, 407–23.

Gray, J., and Jones, B. (1986). Towards a framework for interpreting examination results, in R. Rogers (ed.), *Education and Social Class*, Lewes: Falmer Press.

Gray, J., and Wilcox, B. (1995). *'Good School, Bad School': Evaluating Performance and Encouraging Improvement*, Buckingham: Open University Press.

Griffiths, M. (1998). *Educational Research and Social Justice: Getting off the Fence*, Buckingham: Open University Press.

Guardian (1998). Grim reading for males, *Guardian*, 6 Jan., 12.

Gubb, J. (1999). Everything you need to know about anything, *Times Educational Supplement*, 4 June, 30.

Hackett, G. (1999). Flagship council flagging, *Times Educational Supplement*, 29 Jan., 6.

Halpin, D., Power, S., and Fitz, J. (1997). Opting into the past? Grant maintained schools and the reinvention of tradition, in R. Glatter, P. Woods and C. Bagley (eds.), *Choice and Diversity in Schooling: Perspectives and Prospects*, London: Routledge.

Halsey, A., Lauder, H., Brown, P., and Wells, A. (1997). *Education Culture, Economy, and Society*, Oxford: Oxford University Press.

Halsey, A., Heath, A., and Ridge, J. (1980). *Origins and Destinations: Family, Class and Education in Modern Britain*, Oxford: Clarendon Press.

Hamilton, D. (1997). Peddling feel-good fictions, in J. White and M. Barber (eds.), *Perspectives on School Effectiveness and School Improvement*, London: Institute of Education.

Hamilton, D. (1998). The idols of the market place, in R. Slee, G. Weiner and S. Tomlinson (eds.), *School Effectiveness for Whom? Challenges to the School Effectiveness and School Improvement Movements*, London: Falmer Press, 13–20.

Hammersley, M., and Gomm, R. (1993). A response to Gillborn and Drew on 'race', class and school effects, *New Community*, 19/2, 348–53.

Hargreaves, D. (1996). Diversity and choice in school education: a modified libertarian approach, *Oxford Review of Education*, 22/2, 131–47.

Hargreaves, D. (1999). Revitalising educational research: lessons from the past and proposals for the future, *Cambridge Journal of Education*, 29/2, 239–49.

Hargreaves, L., and Comber, C. (1998). Gender issues in primary classroom processes: what difference does twenty years make?, presentation to ECER Annual Conference, Ljubljana.

Harker, R., and Nash, R. (1996). Academic outcomes and school effectiveness: Type 'A' and Type 'B' effects, *New Zealand Journal of Educational Studies*, 32/2, 143–70.

Hatcher, R. (1998a). Class differentiation in education: rational choices?, *British Journal of Sociology of Education*, 19, 1.

Hatcher, R. (1998b). Labour, official school improvement and equality, *Journal of Education Policy*, 13/4, 485–99.

Higgs, G., Bellin, W., Farrell, S., and White S. (1997). Educational attainment and social disadvantage: contextualising school league tables, *Regional Studies*, 31/8, 779–93.

Hillage, J., Pearson, R., Anderson, A., and Tamkin, P. (1998). *Excellence in Research on Schools*, Sudbury: DfEE Publications.

Hillman, J., and Pearce, N. (1998). *Wasted Youth*, London: Institute of Public Policy Research.

Hirsch, D. (1997). What can Britain learn from abroad?, in R. Glatter, P. Woods and C. Bagley (eds.), *Choice and Diversity in Schooling: Perspectives and Prospects*, London: Routledge.

Hirschman, A. (1970). *Exit, Voice, and Loyalty: Responses to Decline in Firms, Organizations, and States*, Cambridge, MA: Harvard University Press.

Hoghughi, M. (1999). Families hold the key, *Times Educational Supplement*, 12 Feb., 15.

Holt, M. (1981). *Evaluating the Evaluators*, London: Hodder & Stoughton.

Hook, S. (1999). Failing schools and dying cities, *Times Educational Supplement*, 7 May, 5.

Huff, D. (1991). *How to Lie with Statistics*, Harmondsworth: Penguin.

Hughes, D., Lauder, H., Watson, S., Hamlin, J., and Simiyu, I. (1996a). *Markets in Education: Testing the Polarisation Thesis*, The Smithfield Project Phase Two: Fourth Report to the Ministry of Education (New Zealand).

Hughes, D., Lauder, H., and Strathdee, R. (1996b). The short term limits to school effectiveness studies, a reply to Harker, *New Zealand Journal of Educational Studies*, 31/2, 199–201.

IEA (1988). *Science Achievement in Seventeen Countries: A Preliminary Report*, Oxford: Pergamon.

Independent (1998). Classroom rescue for Britain's lost boys, *Independent*, 5 Jan., 8.

Istance, D., and Rees G (1994). Education and training in Wales: problems and paradoxes revisited, *Contemporary Wales*, 7, 7–27.

James, C., and Phillips, P. (1995). The practice of educational marketing in schools, *Educational Management and Administration*, 23/2, 75–88.

James, D., and Taeuber, K. (1985). Measures of segregation, in N. Tuma (ed.), *Sociological Methodology*, San Francisco: Jossey-Bass.

Jencks, C., Smith, M., Ackland, H., Bane, M., Cohen, D., Gintis, H., Heyns, B., and Nicholson, S. (1972). *Inequality: Assessment of the Effect of Family and Schooling in America*, New York: Basic Books.

Johnson, R. (1993). Really useful knowledge, 1790–1850, in M. Thorpe, R. Edwards, and A. Hanson (eds.), *Culture and Processes of Adult Learning*, London: Routledge.

Jones, B., and Lewis, I. (1995). A Curriculum Cymreig, *Welsh Journal of Education*, 4/2, 22–35.

Jones, D. (1997). Bilingual mathematics: development and practice in Wales, *The Curriculum Journal*, 8/3, 393.

Jones, E., and Reynolds, D. (1998). *Education Policy: An Agenda for the National Assembly*, Cardiff: Institute of Welsh Affairs.

Jones, G. (1990). From intermediate to comprehensive education, in W. Evans (ed.), *Perspectives on a Century of Secondary Education in Wales*, Aberystwyth: Centre for Educational Studies.

Jones, G. (1996). *Wales 2010 Three Years On*, Cardiff: Institute of Welsh Affairs.

Kacapyr, E. (1996). Are you middle-class?, *American Demographics*, www.demographics.com.

Kelley, P. (1999). Do teachers make any difference?, *Times Educational Supplement*, 19 March, 22.

Kelly, A. (1996). Comparing like with like, *Education*, 187, 1.

Kelsall, R., and Kelsall, H. (1974). *Stratification*, London: Longman.

Keys, W., Harris, S., and Fernandes, C. (1996a). *Third International Mathematics and Science Study: National Report Appendices*, Slough: NFER.

Keys, W., Harris, S., and Fernandes, C. (1996b). *Third International Mathematics and Science Study: First National Report Part 1*, Slough: NFER.

Kitchen, A. (1999). The changing profile of entrants to mathematics at A level and to mathematical subjects in higher education, *British Educational Research Journal*, 25/1, 57–74.

Kluge, G. (1998). Wealth and people: inequality measures, *Entropy and Inequality Measures, ourworld.compuserve.com*.

Lake, M. (1992). Under the influence, *Managing Schools Today*, 1/9, 12–14.

Lauder, H. (1999). Misconceiving the market: a note on research into the impact of educational markets in England and Wales, presentation to Kings College Market Forces, Seminar June (mimeo).

Lauder, H., Hughes, D., Watson, S., Waslander, S., Thrupp, M., Strathdee, R., Simiyu, I., Dupuis, A., McGlinn, J., and Hamlin, J. (1999). *Trading in Futures: Why Markets in Education Don't Work*, Buckingham: Open University Press.

Le Grand, J., and Bartlett, W. (1993). *Quasi-Markets and Social Policy*, Basingstoke: Macmillan.

Lee, V., Croninger, R., and Smith, J. (1994). Parental choice of schools and social stratification in education: the paradox of Detroit, *Educational Evaluation and Policy Analysis*, 16/4, 434–57.

Lestor, J. (1979). Was there a golden age?, in H. Pluckrose and P. Wilby (eds.), *The Condition of English Schooling*, Harmondsworth: Penguin.

Levačić, R., and Hardman, J. (1998). Competing for resources: the impact of social disadvantage and other factors on English secondary schools' financial performance, *Oxford Review of Education*, 24/3, 303–28.

Levačić, R., and Hardman, J. (1999). The performance of grant-maintained schools in England: an experiment in autonomy, *Journal of Education Policy*, 14/2, 185–212.

Levačić, R., Hardman, J., and Woods, P. (1998). Competition as a spur to improvement? Differential improvement in GCSE examination results, presented to International Congress for School Effectiveness and Improvement, Manchester.

Levin, B., and Riffel, J. (1997). School system responses to external change: implications for school choice, in R. Glatter, P. Woods, and C. Bagley (eds.), *Choice and Diversity in Schooling: Perspectives and Prospects*, London: Routledge.

Levin, H. (1992). Market approaches to education: vouchers and school choice, *Economics of Education Review*, 11/4, 279–85.

Lieberson, S. (1981). An asymmetrical approach to segregation, in C. Peach, V. Robinson and S. Smith (eds.), *Ethnic Segregation in Cities*, London: Croom Helm.

MacGregor, K. (1999). Market forces dictating, *Times Higher Educational Supplement*, 16 April, 9.

MacKay, T. (1999). Education and the disadvantaged: is there any justice?, *The Psychologist*, 12/7, 344–9.

McPherson, A., and Willms, J. (1987). Equalisation and improvement: some effects of comprehensive reorganisation in Scotland, *Sociology*, 21/4, 509–39.

Marshall, G., Swift, A., and Roberts, S. (1997). *Against the Odds? Social Class and Social Justice in Industrial Societies*, Oxford: Clarendon Press.

Maxwell, A. (1977). *Multivariate Analysis in Behavioural Research*, New York: Chapman and Hall.

Maynard, A. (1975). *Experiments with Choice in Education*, London: Institute of Economic Affairs.

Menard, S. (1995). *Applied Logistic Regression Analysis*, London: Sage.

Mooney, T. (1999). Welcome to the poverty gap, *Guardian Education*, 6 July, 2–3.

Mortimore, P., and Mortimore, J. (1986). Education and social class, in R. Rogers (ed.), *Education and Social Class*, Lewes: Falmer Press.

Mortimore, P., and Sammons, P. (1997). Endpiece: a welcome and a riposte to the critics, in J. White and M. Barber (eds.), *Perspectives on School Effectiveness and School Improvement*, London: Institute of Education, 175–87.

Nash, R. (1998). A realist approach to school composition effects: a response to 'How school mix shapes school processes', *New Zealand Journal of Educational Studies*, 33/2, 223–30.

National Commission on Education (1993). *Learning to Succeed*, London: Heinemann.

Noah, H., and Eckstein, M. (1992). Comparing secondary school leaving examinations, in M. Eckstein and H. Noah (eds.), *Examinations: Comparative and International Studies*, Oxford: Pergamon Press.

Norusis, M. (1994). *SPSS 6.1 Base System Users' Manual*, Chicago: SPSS.

Nuttall, D. (1979). The myth of comparability, *Journal of the National Association of Inspectors and Advisers*, 11, 16–18.

Nuttall, D. (1987). The validity of assessments, *European Journal of the Psychology of Education*, 2/2, 109–18.

Nuttall, D., Goldstein, H., Presser, R., and Rasbash, H. (1988). Differential school effectiveness, *International Journal of Educational Research*, 13/7, 769–76.

O'Malley, B. (1998). Measuring a moving target, *Times Educational Supplement*, 18 Sept., 22.

OECD (1993). *OECD Education Statistics 1985–1992*, Paris: OECD.

OECD (1995). *Schools under Scrutiny*, Paris: OECD.

OECD (1996). *Evaluating and Reforming Education Systems*, Paris: OECD.

OFSTED (1998). *Standards and Quality in Education 1996/97*, *http://www.official-documents.co.uk/document/ofsted/ciar/second.html*.

OHMCI (1993). *Achievement and Under-achievement in Secondary Schools in Wales 1991–92*, Cardiff: OHMCI, occasional paper 1.

OHMCI (1996). *Success in Secondary Schools*, Cardiff: OHMCI.

OHMCI (1997). *The Relative Performance of Boys and Girls*, Cardiff: OHMCI.

Osborne, D., and Gaebler, T. (1993). *Reinvention of Government: How the Entrepreneurial Spirit is Transforming the Public Sector*, New York: Plume.

Ouston, J. (1998). The school effectiveness and improvement movement: a reflection on its contribution to the development of good schools, presented at ESRC Redefining Education Management seminar, Open University, 4 June.

Packer, A., and Campbell, C. (1993). The reasons for parental choice of Welsh-medium education, paper presented at Minority Languages Conference, Cardiff.

Paechter, C. (1998). *Educating the Other: Gender, Power and Schooling*, London: Falmer Press.

Parsons, E. (1998). Parental choice and the social mix of secondary schools, presentation at BERA Annual Conference, Belfast.

Passmore, B. (1998). Cardiff responds to call for Welsh, *Times Educational Supplement*, 4 Dec., 6.

Pedhazur, E. (1982). *Multiple Regression in Behavioural Research*, London: Holt, Rhinehart & Winston.

Petre, J. (1998). Boys lose gender race in the nursery, *Sunday Telegraph*, 25 Jan., 21.

Petre, J. (1999). Education standards in decline, says survey, *Sunday Telegraph*, 25 July, 13.

Phillips, M. (1996). *All Must Have Prizes,* London: Little, Brown & Co.

Plewis, I., and Goldstein, H. (1997). Excellence in schools – a failure of standards, *British Journal of Curriculum and Assessment*, 8/1.

Porter, M. (1990). *The Competitive Advantage of Nations*, London: Macmillan.

Postlethwaite, T. (1985). The bottom half in secondary schooling, in G. Worswick (ed.), *Education and Economic Performance*, London: NIESR.

Powers, J., and Cookson, P. (1999). The politics of school choice research: fact fiction and statistics, *Educational Policy*, 13/1, 104–22.

Prais, S. (1990). Mathematical attainments: comparisons of Japanese and English schooling, in B. Moon, J. Isaac and J. Powney (eds.), *Judging Standards and Effectiveness in Education*, London: Hodder & Stoughton.

Raffe, D., Brannen, K., Croxford, L., and Martin, C. (1997). The case for 'home internationals' in comparative research, presented to European Research Network on Transitions in Youth, Dublin, Sept.

Rafferty, F. (1995). UK score in Europe called into question, *Times Educational Supplement*, 24 Nov., 1.

Rafferty, F. (1999). UK teenagers through exam mill, *Times Educational Supplement*, 30 July, 1.

Reay, D. (1998). Engendering social reproduction: mothers in the educational marketplace, *British Journal of Sociology of Education*, 19/2, 195–209.

Redpath, R., and Harvey, B. (1987). *Young People's Intention to Enter Higher Education*, London: HMSO.

Rees, G., Fevre, R., Furlong, J., and Gorard, S. (1997). History, place and the learning society: towards a sociology of lifetime learning, *Journal of Education Policy*, 12/6, 485–97.

Reynolds, D. (1990a). The great Welsh education debate, *History of Education*, 19/3, 251–7.

Reynolds, D. (1990b). School effectiveness and school improvement: a review of the British literature, in B. Moon, J. Isaac and J. Powney (eds.), *Judging Standards and Effectiveness in Education*, London: Hodder & Stoughton.

Reynolds, D. (1995). Creating an educational system for Wales, *Welsh Journal of Education*, 4/2, 4–21.

Reynolds, D., and Bellin, W. (1996). Welsh-medium schools: why they are better, *Agenda*, Cardiff: Institute of Welsh Affairs, Summer.

Reynolds, D., and Farrell, S. (1996). *Worlds Apart? A Review of International Surveys of Educational Achievement Involving England*, London: HMSO.

Reynolds, D., Creemers, B., Nesselrodt, P., Schaffer, E., Stringfield, S., and Teddlie, C. (1994). *Advances in School Effectiveness Research and Practice*, London: Pergamon Press.

Riddell, S. (1992). Gender and education: progressive and conservative forces in balance, in S. Brown and S. Riddell (eds.), *Class, Race and Gender in Schools*, Glasgow: SCRE, 44.

Robinson, P. (1997). *Literacy, Numeracy and Economic Performance*, London: London School of Economics: Centre for Economic Performance.

Robinson, P., and Oppenheim, C. (1998). *Social Exclusion Indicators*, London: Institute of Public Policy Research.

Russell H. (1999). Gulf widens in school exam results, *Independent*, 11 March, 4.

Rutter, M., and Madge, N. (1976). *Cycles of Disadvantage: A Review of Research*, London: Heinemann.

Salisbury, J., Rees, G., and Gorard, S. (1999). Accounting for the differential attainment of boys and girls: a state of the art review, *School Leadership and Management*, 19/4.

Sammons, P., Mortimore, P., and Thomas, S. (1996). Do schools perform consistently across outcomes and areas?, in J. Gray, D. Reynolds, C. Fitz-Gibbon and D. Jesson (eds.), *Merging Traditions: The Future of Research on School Effectiveness and School Improvement*, London: Cassell.

Sammons, P., Thomas, S., Mortimore, P., Owen, C., Pennell, H., and Hillman, J. (1994). *Assessing School Effectiveness: Developing Measures to Put School Performance in Context*, London: OFSTED.

Schagen, I., and Morrison, J. (1998). *QUASE Quantitative Analysis for Self-Evaluation: Overview Report 1997: Analysis of GCSE Cohorts 1994 to 1996*, Slough: NFER.

Sharp, C. (1999). *Strategies to Raise Achievement at Key Stage 2: A Process of Educational Change*, www.nfer.ac.uk.

Shipman, M. (1997). *The Limitations of Social Research*, Harlow: Longman.

Siegel, S. (1956). *Nonparametric Statistics*, Tokyo: McGraw-Hill.

Skills and Enterprise Briefing (1999). *Skills and Enterprise Briefing Issue 5/99*, Sudbury: DfEE Publications.

Skills and Enterprise Network (1999). *Skills and Enterprise Network Annual Conference Report*, Sudbury: DfEE Publications.

Slater, J., Dean, C., and Brown, R. (1999). Learning gulf divides rich and poor pupils, *Times Educational Supplement*, 2 April, 1.

Slee, R. (1998). Higher education work in the reductionist age, *International Studies in Sociology of Education*, 8/3, 255–70.

Smith, T., and Noble, M. (1995). *Education Divides*, London: Child Poverty Action Group.

Smyth, E. (1998). School effectiveness in the Republic of Ireland: a multidimensional analysis, presentation to BERA Annual Conference, Belfast.

Speed, E. (1998). *Gender Issues and Differential Achievement in Education and Vocational Training: A Research Review*, Manchester: Equal Opportunities Commission.

Spring, J. (1982). Dare educators build a new school system?, in M. Manley-Casimir (ed.), *Family Choice in Schooling*, Toronto: Lexington.

Stevens, J. (1992). *Applied Multivariate Statistics for the Social Sciences*, London: Lawrence Erlbaum.

Stobart, G., Elwood, J., and Quinlan, M. (1992). Gender bias in examinations: how equal are the opportunities?, *British Educational Research Journal*, 18/3, 261–76.

Stoll, L., and Fink, L. (1996). *Changing our Schools: Linking School Effectiveness and School Improvement*, Buckingham: Open University Press.

Sutcliffe, J. (1999). Schools 'improved' by Tory market, *Times Educational Supplement*, 25 June, 1–2.

Taeuber, K., Wilson, F., James, D., and Taeuber, A. (1981). A demographic perspective on school desegregation in the USA, in C. Peach, V. Robinson and S. Smith (eds.), *Ethnic Segregation in Cities*, London: Croom Helm.

TES (1993). *Times Educational Supplement School Performance Tables 1993.*

TES (1994). *Times Educational Supplement School Performance Tables 1994.*

TES (1995). *Times Educational Supplement School and College Performance Tables 1995.*

TES (1996). *Times Educational Supplement School and College Performance Tables 1996.*

TES (1997a). Success as Welsh close on England, *Times Educational Supplement*, 12 Dec., 10.

TES (1997b). Parents opt for medium way, *Times Educational Supplement*, 12 Dec., 11.

TES (1999a). Equality 2000?, *Times Educational Supplement*, 4 June, 14.

TES (1999b). GM could not fix class, *Times Educational Supplement*, 24 April, 16.

TES (1999c). Watchdog fails to link spending to results, *Times Educational Supplement*, 12 March, 4.

Thomas, S., Sammons, P., Mortimore, P., and Smees, R. (1997). Differential secondary school effectiveness: comparing the performance of different pupil groups, *British Educational Research Journal*, 23/4, 451–70.

Thomson, R. (1998). Schools in valleys better than rivals in England, *Western Mail*, 7 May, 7.

Thrupp, M. (1997). How school mix shapes school processes: a comprehensive study of New Zealand schools, *New Zealand Journal of Educational Studies*, 32/1, 53–82.

Thrupp, M. (1998). Reply to Nash, *New Zealand Journal of Educational Studies*, 33/2, 231–235.

Tooley, J. (1994). In defence of markets in education, in D. Bridges and T. McLaughlin (eds.), *Education and the Market Place*, London: Falmer.

Tooley, J. (1997). On school choice and social class, *British Journal of Sociology of Education*, 18/2.

Tooley, J., and Darby, D. (1998). *Educational Research: A Critique*, London: OFSTED.

Troyna, B. (1993). Underachiever or misunderstood? A reply to Roger Gomm, *British Educational Research Journal*, 19/2, 167–74.

Tuckett, A., and Sargant, N. (1999). *Marking Time: The NIACE Survey on Adult Participation in Learning 1999*, Leicester: NIACE.

Vance Randall, E., Cooper, B., and Hite, S. (1999). Understanding the politics of research in education, *Educational Policy*, 13/1, 7–22.

Waslander, S., and Thrupp, M. (1995). Choice, competition, and segregation: an empirical analysis of a New Zealand secondary school market, 1990–93, *Journal of Education Policy*, 10/1, 1–26.

Waslander, S., and Thrupp, M. (1997). Choice, competition, and segregation: an empirical analysis of a New Zealand secondary school market, 1990–93, in A. Halsey, H. Lauder, P. Brown and A. Wells (eds.), *Education Culture, Economy, and Society*, Oxford: Oxford University Press.

Weiss, C. (1996). Foreword, in B. Fuller and R. Elmore (eds.), *Who Chooses? Who Loses?*, New York: Teachers College Press.

Wells, A. (1996). African-American students' view of school choice, in B. Fuller and R. Elmore (eds.), *Who Chooses? Who Loses?*, New York: Teachers College Press.

Welsh Office (1995a). *A Bright Future: Getting the Best for Every Pupil at School in Wales*, Cardiff: HMSO.

Welsh Office (1995b). *A Bright Future: The Way Forward*, Cardiff: HMSO.

Welsh Office (1995c). *Statistics of Education and Training in Wales: Schools No. 3*, Cardiff: HMSO.

Welsh Office (1996a). *A Bright Future: Statistical Update*, Cardiff: HMSO.

Welsh Office (1996b). *Digest of Welsh Local Area Statistics 1996*, Cardiff: Welsh Office.

Welsh Office (1997a). *A Bright Future: Beating the Previous Best*, Cardiff: Welsh Office.

Welsh Office (1997b). *Building Excellent Schools Together*, Cardiff: HMSO.

Welsh Office (1998). *Statistics of Education and Training in Wales*, Cardiff: HMSO.

Welsh Office (1999). *Preparation of Education Strategic Plans: Welsh Office Circular 14/99*, Cardiff: Welsh Office.

Western Mail (1997a). England–Wales gap does not exist, 11 April, 8.

Western Mail (1997b). Schools closing gap with England, 10 Dec., 1.

Western Mail (1997c). Even English parents back Welsh taught in classroom, 28 Nov., 2.

Western Mail (1998). Welsh medium – a message for all teaching, 3 June, 10.

Whitehead, J. (1998). *BERA Internet Conference*, *www.scre.ac.uk/bera/debate/index.html*.

Whitty, G., Power, S., and Halpin, D. (1998). *Devolution and Choice in Education*, Buckingham: Open University Press.

Willms, J., and Echols, F. (1992). Alert and inert clients: the Scottish experience of parental choice of schools, *Economics of Education Review*, 11/4, 339–50.

Witte, J. (1990). Introduction, in W. Clune and J. Witte (eds.), *Choice and Control in American Education*, Vol. 1, *TheTheory of Choice and Control in Education*, London: Falmer Press.

Witte, J. (1998). The Milwaukee voucher experiment, *Educational Evaluation and Policy* Analysis, 20/4, 229–51.

Woodhead, C. (1998). Academia gone to seed, *New Statesman*, 20 March, 51–2.

Woodhead, C. (1999). Education was a lottery . . ., *News of the World*, 25 July, 16.

Woods, P., Bagley, C., and Glatter, R. (1997). *The Public Market in England: School Responsiveness in a Competitive Climate. Occasional Research Paper 1*, Buckingham: School of Education, Open University.

Woolford, H., and McDougall, S. (1998). The teacher as role model, presentation to British Psychological Society Conference, Department of Psychology, Swansea University (mimeo).

Worpole, K. (1999). Driving forces, *Guardian*, 8 June, 17.

Wright, J. (1937). Some measures of distribution, *Annals of the Association of American Geographers*, 27, 177–211.

WSSA/OHMCI (1996). *Tackling the Underachievement of Boys*, Cardiff: OHMCI.

Younger, M., and Warrington, M. (1996). Differential achievements of girls and boys at GCSE: some observations from the perspective of one school, *British Journal of Sociology of Education*, 17/3, 299–313.

Zhou, X., Moen, P., and Tuma, N. (1998). Educational stratification in urban China, *Sociology of Education*, 71, 199–222.

~ Index ~

CHESTER COLLEGE LIBRARY